# THE LETTERS AND TIMES

*of the*

# TYLERS

## VOLUME III

# THE LETTERS AND TIMES

*of the*

# TYLERS

## BY LYON G. TYLER

## VOLUME III

DA CAPO PRESS • NEW YORK • 1970

A Da Capo Press Reprint Edition

This Da Capo Press edition of *The Letters and Times of the Tylers* is an unabridged republication of the first edition published in Richmond, Virginia, and Williamsburg, Virginia, between 1884 and 1896.

*Library of Congress Catalog Card Number 71-75267*

SBN 306-71316-0

Published by Da Capo Press
A Division of Plenum Publishing Corporation
227 West 17th Street, New York, N. Y. 10011
All Rights Reserved

Manufactured in the United States of America

# THE LETTERS AND TIMES

*of the*

# TYLERS

## VOLUME III

SHERWOOD FOREST.
Residence of President Tyler from 1845 to 1862.

THE

# LETTERS AND TIMES

OF

# THE TYLERS.

BY

## LYON GARDINER TYLER, M. A., LL. D.,

President of William and Mary College, Author of " Parties and Patronage in the United States," Editor of William
and Mary College Quarterly Historical Magazine, Member
of the Executive committee of the Virginia Historical Society, Member of American Philosophical Society, etc.

———◇———

JOHN TYLER —" He became his station as President singularly
well."—*Charles Dickens*.
" The most felicitous among the orators I
have known."—*Jefferson Davis*.
" His own state papers compare favorably in
point of ability with those of any of his predecessors."—*Alexander H. Stephens*.
" One of the most fascinating men I had ever
known—brilliant, eloquent, even more charming
than Mr. Calhoun in conversation."—*Hon. Henry W. Hilliard, Author of " Pen Pictures,"
U. S. Minister to Brazil*.

IN THREE VOLUMES

## VOL. III.

WILLIAMSBURG, VIRGINIA :
1896.

# PREFACE.

————:o:————

IN 1884, I published the first volume of a work entitled "Letters and Times of the Tylers." In 1885, a second volume was published. In the eleven years which have intervened, many original letters, and copies of letters in responsible hands, have come to light. As some of these have important connection with the events related in the volumes mentioned, I have deemed it proper to add a third volume to an already extensive work. In the present publication, important public questions are more fully illustrated by letters of distinguished statesmen, assisted by foot notes and cross references. Short personal sketches and summaries of great historical subjects, like the Annapolis Resolutions, The Bank, The Whig Party, the Annexation of Texas, Appointments to Office, are given. The letters were, in the main, derived from the collections of Virginius Newton, of Richmond, Dr. J. S, H. Fogg, of Boston, Gen. Duncan S. Walker, of Washington, the Lenox Library of New York, Judge C. W. Tyler, of Clarksville, Tenn., and John N. Cushing, of Newburyport, Mass. These collections represent respectively the correspondences of Hon. Thomas Newton, of Henry A. Wise, of Robert J. Walker, of James K. Polk, of Cave Johnson, and of Caleb Cushing. Thomas H. Clay, of Boston, grandson of Henry Clay, furnished the two letters of John Tyler addressed to Mr. Clay, published on pages 75 and 92 respectively.

My object has been to get at the truth, and to furnish authentic replies to some few of the current misrepresentations of historical writers. The three volumes thus presented to the public have this at least to recommend them, that they appear to be the only work which exhibits, by a continuous series of letters, the views of representative southern men on important public questions from the Revolution to the War of 1861. The comments and narratives of the editor may pass for what they are worth.

The present volume is limited to two hundred and fifty copies; and of the first and second volumes, a sufficient number remains to supply such persons as may desire to have a complete set. Address, Henley T. Jones, Bookseller in Williamsburg, Va. Price of three volumes complete $7 ; vol. III., $3.00.

LYON G. TYLER,

William and Mary College, Williamsburg, Va , 1896.

# CONTENTS OF VOLUME III.

# John Tyler, Sr.

FROM A MANUSCRIPT FURNISHED THE NATIONAL ENCYCLOPEDIA
OF AMERICAN BIOGRAPHY.

TYLER, JOHN, twelfth governor of the state of
Virginia, born Feb. 28, 1747, in James City
county, the son of John Tyler, marshal[1] of the colonial vice-admiralty court, and of Anne Contesse,
daughter of Dr. Louis Contesse, a French Huguenot physician of Williamsburg. Mr. Tyler attended
the College of William and Mary as a student, with
Mr. Jefferson, and, reared in the environment of the
old vice-admiralty court, early chose the law as his
vocation. Mr. Jefferson studied law under George
Wythe, and Mr. Tyler under that equally distinguished patriot, Robert Carter Nicholas. In company with Mr. Jefferson, he listened to Henry's
speech on the stamp act and caught fire at the sound
of Henry's voice. He became so bitter an opponent
of the British government that his father often predicted he would be hanged as a rebel. About 1770,
he moved into the county of Charles City, and, in
1774, was appointed on the committee of safety for
the county. When the powder was abstracted
from the magazine at Williamsburg in 1775, by Lord
Dunmore, John Tyler, then captain of a militia
company in Charles City, hastened to join his troops
with those already on the march under Patrick Henry.[2] By the convention which assembled, in 1776, he
was made judge of admiralty, but, in 1778, took his seat

---

(1) He died in 1773, but it is an error that he was the last marshal
of the Colonial vice-admiralty court, as stated in Vol. I, p. 52.

(2) President John Tyler's MS. letter to the New Eng. Hist. and
Gen. Society.

in the legislature, where his bold, uncompromising patriotism put him at once among the leaders of the revolution. He held successively all the responsible offices of the house of delegates, was chairman of the committee of justice, of the committee of the whole, and eventually, in 1781, speaker, succeeding Richard Henry Lee whom he defeated, in 1783, for the chair· During the whole revolution his courage was unfaltering. Schools for the people, funds for the army, and taxes for the just creditors of the state, were the themes of his oratory on every occasion. In February, 1781, the rapid depreciation of the paper money forced congress to request of the states a power to levy an impost of 5 per cent. Mr. Tyler was one of the committee of the house of delegates who drafted the bill, and acted as the messenger of the house to the senate to convey the request for its concurrence. The law was, however, reversed the next year by the activity of the party of Dr. Arthur and Richard Henry Lee, who opposed the increase of federal power. Congress, however, under the lead of James Madison, urgently repeated, in 1783, the former request.

Peace ensued, and there was a general relaxation of the invigorative policy. Despite the opposition of Mr. Tyler, the legislature voted to take off the restrictions imposed on British trade, and to invite the Tories back. But when they found their calculations of a liberal, definitive treaty defeated, the legislature voted to allow congress the 5 per cent impost, and to retaliate by decisive measures on British trade. Edmund Randolph explained that at this time, 1784, there were three parties in the legislature. Mr. Henry had one corps, R. H. Lee a second, and the speaker (Tyler) a third, " founded on a riveted opposition to our late enemies, and everything that concerned them." Mr. Henry and Mr. Tyler had

generally acted together in opposition to the Lees;
but Henry's advocacy of the return of the Tories
and his policy of postponing taxation led to his temporary separation from Mr. Tyler, though it pacified
the old antagonism with the Lees and procured, Mr.
Tyler says, Henry's unanimous re-election to the gov-
norship in 1784.

Mr. Tyler and Mr. Henry agreed, however,
on the construction of the treaty of peace, which,
they maintained, had been violated by the British in two particulars, viz: by the retention of the
western posts, and the failure to return the slaves and
records carried off during the war. They, therefore,
unlike Mr. Madison and other eminent statesmen, were opposed to permitting the operation of
the provision of the treaty forbidding any impedi-
ment in the way of the collection of debts due British subjects before the war. In this they had the
support of the Virginia people. The feeling of hostility dominated the masses, who felt the severe effects
of the new British duties on American exports; and
the impulse now given to the question of revenue and
trade was due to this. In the house, in the fall of
1784, Mr. Tyler moved that congress should be allowed to collect the 5 per cent duty, without waiting
for the consent of Rhode Island, which obstinately
held out against the measure, Mr Madison opposed
the proposition, and it was defeated. In 1785, being
narrowly defeated by Benjamin Harrison for the
speakership, after having beaten him for the house in
Charles City county, Mr. Tyler was, with Mr. Madison,
a member of the committee in the house of delegates to whom the question about revenue and commerce was referred. In the last moment of the session, January, 1786, he forced through the house a
measure for a convention of all the states to be
called at Annapolis, which should have full power to

amend the articles of confederation, by a provision authorizing congress to regulate the trade of the union. The Annapolis convention led the next year, 1787, to the celebrated convention at Philadelphia, which formed the present federal constitution.

Many years after the deaths of Mr. Madison and Mr. Tyler, Mr. George Tucker said that Mr. Madison told him that he was the writer of the "Annapolis resolutions," and that it was owing to the jealousy felt in Virginia against the Federal government that Mr. Madison, who had been a member of Congress, did not offer them.

As this statement to Mr. Tucker does not pretend to be other than one on memory, it is not at all certain that Mr. Madison might not have had in mind some of the other propositions before the committee.[1] At any rate any question on this subject is silenced by the express language of Mr. Madison himself at the time. He refers to the resolutions in a private letter as the 'resolutions of Mr. Tyler."[2] Certain it is that Mr. Madison was not known in connection with the resolutions in the house of delegates during his life time, and the success of the measure was due to influences not connected, as Mr. Tucker alleges, with the federal government. The restrictive policy of the British was what induced the legislature to adopt it. Mr. Tyler headed the party in favor of retaliating upon Great Britain for her restrictive policy and in introducing the resolution, his

---

(1) Thus Elliot ascribes to Mr. Madison the general resolution offered in the house of delegates, 30 Nov., 1785, for empowering congress to regulate trade. But he does not give him the resolution to convoke the assembly at Annapolis. Elliot's Debates, i, p. 115.

(2) Writings of Madison i., p. 222.

main object was to create a stronger government for
this purpose.  Mr. Madison was not in sympathy with
the retaliatory policy and was, therefore, without
much influence[1] in the Virginia legislature, as he
states himself.

Mr. Tyler, who, by virtue of a re-election to the
court of admiralty in 1786, was also judge of
the state supreme court, was vice-president of the
Virginia convention of 1788, called to accept or reject
the constitution proposed.  But he vehemently denounced the article in it which permitted the slave
trade, and with most of the lawyers of Virginia he feared
the opportunity for construction which its ambiguous
provisions afforded, and was in favor of a new convention to correct its defects.  He was baffled in this
hope, though the amendments which were offered in
the state convention and afterwards in part adopted
by congress removed many of his objections.  Mr.

(1) Erroneous conclusions are readily drawn.  Thus, Mr. George
Tucker, confounding Mr. Tyler who had been speaker with Mr. Harrison, the speaker at this assembly and who had been opposed to the
increase of federal power, speaks of Mr. Madison *persuading* Mr.
Tyler to offer the resolution.  In the same way Mr. Grigsby ("Va.
Convention of 1788,") learning that the resolutions in question, as preserved in the state archives, were in the hand writing of Mr. Beckley,
the clerk of the house of delegates, got the idea that Mr. Madison
caused him to copy it, in order the better to conceal his agency in
the matter.  But, according to my own examination, nearly all the
resolutions of this session and other sessions, as preserved, stand in
Beckley's writing—it being evidently his duty to copy and engross
all the bills.  ( See also Vol. I. pp. 132 34.)

When Mr. Bancroft issued the first edition of his work on the
constitution of the United States, he adopted the view that Mr. Tyler
was a "states-rights zealot," who had been persuaded into action by
Madison.  But when I undertook to show him that Mr. Tyler, until
the federal convention of 1787, had always supported the federal
government, and was in fact the leader of the party who passed the
Annapolis resolutions with the hope of more effective retaliation on
Great Britain, he admitted his error and corrected his statement in
the subsequent edition.

Tyler, on the abolition of the state admiralty court by the operation of the new constitution, was elected, in 1788, a judge of the general court of Virginia, in which office he remained for twenty years.

He celebrated his stay on the bench by an opinion in the case of Kamper vs Hawkins, on the authority of the constitution over mere legislative enactment, and contributed to making the overruling power of the judiciary an accepted principle of American jurisprudence. Numerous offices were tendered to him. In 1781, Mr. Jefferson, then governor of the state, had invited him into his council, but he had preferred service in the legislature. In 1803, he was appointed by the council to succeed Mann Page as chancellor of the Williamsburg district, but declined the appointment.[1] In 1808, he was elected chief magistrate of the commonwealth, and in that office, which he filled for three years, he urgently pressed the importance of schools, and became the founder of the literary fund devoted to the purpose of education. In 1811, he was appointed by Madison judge of the district court of the United States for the state of Virginia, to fill the vacancy caused by the death of Judge Cyrus Griffin. Mr. Jefferson did him the honor to make his nomination the single exception to the rule that he had laid down for his government, "never to solicit an appointment from the President." As federal judge, Mr. Tyler, in the circuit court of the United States, sat with John Marshall, the chief justice, to whom he was politically opposed, and contended successfully against the principle of a universal common law jurisdiction for the Federal courts, favored by his colleague. He supported the war with Great Britain in 1812, and decided the first

---

(1) This fact was overlooked in Vol. I.

prize case that came up for adjudication in that war.
He died January 6th, 1813, and his only regret was
"that he could not live long enough to see that proud
British nation once more humbled by American arms."
Mr. Tyler's eminent contemporaries expressed the
highest opinion of him. It was Judge Tyler who reported to William Wirt the speeches of Henry on
the stamp act and on the war, mingling his own fiery
eloquence with the bare outline of Henry's language
as remembered by him.[1] He was invited by Governor Monroe in 1799 to deliver a public oration on
Washington and Henry, who died that year, but he
declined from press of duty. As speaker of the
house of delegates, he voiced the resolutions which,
in 1781, complimented Jefferson on his administration of the state. Judge Roane, of the Virginia supreme court, declared that "his mind was of
the highest order," and that "his great soul" was
manifested in its contempt of dress, ornament and of
everything but "principle." And Henry Clay, who
knew him as a young man, said[2] in congress, in
1841, that "a purer patriot or a more honest man never
breathed the breath of life." He had the singular experience of presiding in the highest branches of each
of the departments of the state government; as speaker of the house of delegates, judge of the supreme
court, and governor of Virginia. In politics Mr. Tyler
was a member of the Republican party.

He married Mary, only daughter of Robert Booth
Armistead, of York county, Va., a descendant of
William Armistead, who came to Virginia about 1636.
Judge Tyler lies buried at " Greenway," Charles City
co., Va.

---

(1) See Tyler's "Life of P. Henry" p. 133; Wirt's " Henry"—preface:
Judge Tyler's MSS. furnished William Wirt.

(2) Cong. Globe, 1st session 27th congress, appendix, p. 345.

# Letters.

———

Trenton, Oct. 30, 1784.

SIR:

I have the honor to inform your Excellency that I arrived here last night, and can with pleasure add we have the prospect of a representation of the states in a few days. As yet neither of my colleagues have joined me; but I understand Mr. Lee is in Phil$^a$, and of course expect him to-day. In a visit I lately made by the North river to the lakes, in the necessity I was under of returning thro' Canada to the States, I was informed of some of the measures adopted by the British Government in that province, which I conceived highly interesting to us; that the commanding officer had received orders to retain the possession of the posts which fell within our lines by the treaty, and which sho$^d$ have been evacuated sometime since, and that many of the vessels on the lakes, laid aside under the provisional treaty for a peace establishment, were again put in commission. This information I had from authority so respecuable as to gain my entire assent, which further added that this procedure was founded on the conduct of the States of New York and Virginia, which they accuse of having violated the treaty. From every information I could obtain I have reason to believe that the temper of that court is very unfriendly to us and that they require only the most flimsy pretext to create a rupture; their councils are, it is true, in a divided state, but, in the talents and superior popularity of Mr. Pitt, this may not long be the case. I have thought it my duty to give to y Excellency this information and have the honor to be with great respect and esteem

Your most humble servant,

JAS MONROE. [1]

————

(1)   A letter similar to this was written by Mr. Monroe to Mr. Tyler, then speaker of the house of delegates, but it cannot be found. The above will serve well as a companion letter to the one which follows.

[TO JAMES MONROE.]

Richmond, Nov. 26, 1784.

DEAR SIR:

I received your favor of the 14th of this month, and am happy to find you have escaped the Indians and British in your late route through Canada.

I suppose your Hon'ble Body will take the business of the Treaty up as soon as you make a number sufficient for the purpose, and communicate to us your determination.

It is evident to me that the Intention of Britain was never to surrender the Posts, thereby giving up the trade of the Lakes; and their policy is now to negociate for this object by ceding the points of confiscation and sterling debts. As to any hostile measures further I am persuaded to the contrary. They feel the consequences of trade and commerce with America too sensibly to pursue such mistaken policy as that which lost not only this commerce but the subjection of the States. A nation determined to draw the sword never wants a pretext. Now, to say that we have broke the Treaty is monstrous when all mankind know that they broke it in two Instances, from the very beginning to this hour. However, whatever your Body shall determine will be my rule on this head, although, I confess, my heart wou'd bleed to be compel'd to yield to any Nation under Heaven unjustly, and I know not what is Liberty or independence, if neither can be asserted with fortitude. We have bled for these, let us bleed again if they shall be violated, and be finally determined whether we are a nation free or Tributaries to a Tyrant. I can't say enough in this Letter, so will drop the Subject and proceed to inform you that Henry is Governor, our worthy and upright Jones one of the Council, Roan [1] and Selden [2]

I am sorry from my heart that my Friend Mercer [3] did not make his Intentions known sooner, as I am well assured he wou'd have been appointed to a Seat in the Executive.

----

(1) Spencer Roane, afterwards Judge of the state supreme court. He married a daughter of Patrick Henry.

(2) Miles Selden.

(3) John Fenton Mercer.

We are doing nothing yet, a great waste of time much to
our disgrace, but nothing is left on my hands, as I took up
everything laid before us by the Gov^t long since, and Bills
of safety and defense order'd, besides many others for internal policy.  I wrote to Hardy (1) telling him to pay my respects
to you and Mr. Mercer, which, I beg, you will do to them.
The next letter shall be to Col^o Mercer.  I am now closely
engaged.  I can say no more at present, but that I am with
great regard your very humble servant,

JNO. TYLER.

_____

TO JUDGE ST. GEORGE TUCKER.(2)

Greenway, July 10^th, 1795.
Dear Sir:

"I received a Pamphlet written by a Citizen of Williamsburg, by the hands of Mr. Semple, from you, in answer to
Mr. Jedediah Morse, whose silly and prejudiced opinion of
the People of Williamsburg and everything belonging to it is
truly and sensibly refuted and brought into contempt.

The name of this Geographer evinces his locality of sentiment and the place of his Birth, where I will undertake to
say there is scarcely such a thing as a fellow-feeling prevailing, although we are consolidated and made one—no Philan-
thropy—nothing like that liberty of Sentiment which per-
vades and animates our Southern world.

To be sure, how many dirty efforts are made by these
Northern cattle to reduce the consequence of Virginia.

Every circumstance of human Life (both civil and politi-

(1)  Sam Hardy, member of the Continental Congress.

(2)  Judge St. George Tucker was the son of Henry Tucker of
Bermuda and a descendant of Daniel Tucker, who came to Virginia
in the year 1608, and was subsequently governor of the Bermuda
Islands.  See Appleton's Cyclopedia for a sketch of him.  At this
time Judge Tucker was a judge of the general court of Virginia, and
professor of law in William and Mary College.

His pamphlet in reply to Morse has been republished in the
" William and Mary Quarterly Historical Papers " for January, 1894.

cal) proves how unfit the States were for such an Union as
ours. How many Males and Females are there, who might
live tolerably happy merely as Friends and Neighbors who
would not be happy if married together! Tempers, customs,
manners, Education and a thousand things more should be
well weighed and consider'd before an Union should take
place. But God help us! we are allied too closely and strong
to be divorced, easily, although our Husbands and Wives
shou'd be ever so tyrannical.

But enough of this for the present, and if this is not
enough, the Treaty (1) will make up the deficiency, and of this
I am not in a temper to speak either with temper or in words
of respect for the great Agent who has been so kind as to
legislate in conclave with Granville our best Rights away; and
moreover to establish a court of Judieature within the States
to grant Judgements on British debts vs. the American People—O People, where is thy spirit?

To return to the Pamphlet. I hope Mr. J$^a$ Morse will be
convinced that there is yet at poor old Will: Mary one professor whose abilities and Virtue are fully equal to the Task
of retrieving that station to which she is justly entitled in
y$^e$ eyes of the learn'd and rescuing her from the hands of
ignorance, the parent of prejudice and violence, and that this
professor is St. George Tucker, a Judge of the Gen$^1$ Court of
Virginia and Professor of Law in W$^m$ & Mary College, who, I
am sure, professes also humanity, liberality of sentiment and
Geographical knowledge enough to deteck a falsehood utter'd by whom it may.

I think my Friend you have all the wit and Satire of the
old Dean of St. Patrick. And I do sincerely wish you would
be as industrious in lashing the iniquities of the Times; it
would have a good effect. If I had your literary advantages,
I wou'd never cease to scourge until I had in some degree
worked a reformation. Dam the Treaty, Jay and Morse,
how they perplex me—one by his universal Geography confined to a spot, the other by his universal and everlasting peace

---

(1) The reference here is to the commercial treaty negotiated
by John Jay in 1794, which to the mind of Southern statesmen was
an entire surrender of Southern interests,

which his Britanick Majesty invokes God to forbid should ever be interrupted, which can last but a moment if on the faith of him or his Creatures our peace is to depend. I wonder what Idea these gen$^n$ have of universal and everlasting and particularly what Jay understands by reciprocity.

I am sure if George is to be damn'd forever, if his peace with America is interrupted in a very short time, I wou'd not feel the Weight of that paltry crown for his chance. But he has the comfort which Pitt may minister to him, that it would take away from those attributes which we all ascribe to the divinity, to suppose an ass the object of his vengeance for ever. Jay's reciprocity is to exchange the Substance for the shadow, for let the Words of the Treaty be ever so plausible yet we can not be benefitted in the same manner, as we do not nor ever will stand in the same situation with England. We have no funds in England to be sequestered in case of War, but they have in America, and here he has given up the best security for a lasting peace. It wou'd be novel indeed to see Englishmen drawing from our Treasury the sinews of War, while we were really in that state which we all shou'd prevent, if too great a sacrifice was not to be made for it. What is the difference between 500 Tunn Burthen and 90? Such are the mutual advantages resulting from Jay's Idea of mutuality. But Jedediah's universality is like his mental Faculties confined within a very narrow circle indeed. Such also his moral obligations, or he wou'd not have departed from the Truth so grossly.

Have you made any more attacks on the Bishop [1] either in the political or scientific Line? Ah Tucker, you have as much mischief as I, though with a better face you can do it, because, while I rely on Parent nature, you bring to her aid the mighty Phalanx of the schools. And by Heavens! Madamd *Dacier* [2] inspires you too, as if she was determined that no Brother Judge should vie with you nor Judge's Wife with

[1]    Bishop James Madison, President of William and Mary College, from 1777 to 1812.

[2]    Anne Dacier, daughter of Tanaquil Faber, or Le Fevre, and wife of Andrew Dacier. She was born at Saumer in 1651, and was a prodigy of learning. The allusion here is to the second wife of Judge Tucker, who was a very learned woman.

JOANNA TYLER,
Died in 1767.
Aunt of John Tyler, Sr., and wife of Dr.
Kenneth McKenzie, of Williamsburg.

her. By the great God, I am too much a republican to bear such inequality, therefore I will make it up in raising at least one Henry and McCawley in my Family, to be on a footing with you.[1]

Remember, when I speak of the Bishop, I feel the highest veneration for his character as a man, but I like him not the better for his canonicals, they will not let men be enough of Republicans; besides he went to *Great Britain* for the exalted station.[2] Now who wou'd ever be sent to Heaven by such a People? Even if it were possible they wou'd in the hight of human depravity work such a wonder, I am well assured that God will never make choice of such an agent.

This must have tired you, therefore I must come and see you and take more time to communicate by mouth what the pen wou'd be tedious in uttering.

I am y<sup>r</sup> most ob<sup>t</sup> Ser<sup>t</sup><br>and Friend,<br>Jno: Tyler.

----

[TO GOV. JAMES MONROE]

Greenway, Dec<sup>r</sup> 27, '99.

Dear Sir:

After the bustle is a li :le over, I set down to congratulate you on the signal vic ory you have obtain'd over your Enemies; and also for th t which is gain'd by Truth over

----

St. George Tucker married, 23 Sept., 1778, Frances Randolph, widow of John Randolph and daughter of Theodorick and Frances (Bolling) Bland, of Cawson's.

St. George Tucker married, second, 8 Oct., 1791, Lelia Carter, widow of George Carter, of Corotoman, and daughter of Sir Peyton and Anne (Miller) Skipwith.

(1) Judge Tyler named his eldest son, Wat Henry Tyler," after the two greatest British rebels" (as his wife told Mr. Henry, who was present at the baptism)—Wat Tyler and Patrick Henry.

(2) James Madison was ordained first Bishop of the Episcopal Church of Virginia by the Bishops of England. See Sprague's "Annals of the American Church" for sketch and the National Cyclopedia of Biography, by James T. White & Co.

falsehood, and Democracy over Tyranny all over the World, "Vive la Republique."

I hope you are well and your good Lady and Children, and I hope also to see you all with a few of the chosen at Greenway in the course of the year Such as Randolph, [1] Foushee, [2] etc., etc.

I have not time to compare the characters of Washington and Henry, or I wou'd clearly show that fewer blunders fell to the share of the latter than the former, and yet I have no objection to paying a tribute to the past services and virues of either.[3]

Your friend and Ser<sub>t</sub>

JNO. TYLER.

---

TO GOV. JAMES MONROE.

Thursday Evening, Feb'y 9<sup>th</sup>, 1801.

Dear Sir:

In conformity with my promise I avail myself of the first opportunity which has occur'd since my arrival here to give you those impressions which my mind has received from an assiduous attention bestowed to-day to the debates in Congress, and also from communications with the most influential characters who think with us on the important Election. I enclose to you a copy of resolutions, and upon every question growing out of them it appeared that the Feds had a majority of about six votes—they have passed all the resolutions without amendment except the last, and to that they have made an amendment, which is that all elections shall be condsidered as *incidental* to the main power of voting by States, that each State shall have a vote: this was opposed by Mess<sup>rs</sup> Gallitin, Randolph, Nicholas and Macon. As in

(1)    Edmund Randolph, under whose father-in-law, Robert Carer Nicholas, Judge Tyler had studied law.

(2)    Dr. William Foushee, of Richmond.

(3)    Washington and Henry both died this year—the one in June and the other in December. Gov. Monroe invited Judge Tyler to make an address.

GREENWAY.

Home of John Tyler. Sr.    Birth-place of President Tyler.

part it was made a question between the larger and smaller states, and as few of our foremost Republicans upon this principle voted with the Feds, it cannot be considered as a vote entirely upon principle as bearing wholly upon the presidential election, but still it gave rise to very uneasy sensations not only with myself but those with whom I associate. In a word, the opinion as far as it can be formed by the most intelligent is—that they will unquestionably pursue precisely the same system of policy that the Senate of Pensy did, and that, in a caucus, which they held last night, it was resolved to put everything to the hazard.

Be assured that the Election depends on one of three persons—Bayard from Del. and Craik and Baer from Maryland. The former there are reasonable hopes from (Mr. Randolph says there are not the smallest from either); the 2$^d$ full as good. Mr. Fitzhugh is decidedly in favour of Mr. J. (Mr. C's Lady, it is said, will renounce her husband if he does not vote for Mr. J; this is the expression of *her* opinion, a fact), and you can judge, combining [*torn*] circumstances with the interests Maryland has, how far they ought to be relied on. Baer, it is said by Mr. Christie, has declared he shall vote for Mr. J. This has to-day been denied. Mr. Nicholson is very sick. Upon the whole it is believed things do not bear as favorable an aspect as they did three days ago.

I delivered with my own hands your Letter to Mr. Irvin. you shall hear from me to-morrow.

Yrs. sincerely,

S. TYLER. [1]

There object is apparently confined to electing Mr. Bur, or rather the other. He is the instrument by which they mean to effect any worse purpose. Mr. Jn⁰ Nicholas I am inclined to think, is sanguine in favor of Mr. [*torn*] but there appears to be little or no *concert*

[1] Samuel Tyler was a nephew of Judge John Tyler, and was educated at William and Mary College, was a member of the house of delegates in 1798-99, and one of the council of James Monroe, who sent him to New York to watch the progress of the difficulty regarding the election of Jefferson. He was elected by the general assembly to succeed Mann Page as chancellor of the Williamsburg district, an office which had been tendered to his uncle. He married Elizabeth Bray Johnson, and died in 1812.

TO JAMES MONROE.

11TH, 5 O'CK.

In very great haste I scrawled to you on the subject of the pre. Election; at 5 o'ck. there have been seven Ballots, they stand 8 for Jefferson, 6 Burr, two divided. On the first vote, Virginia gave 16 for J., and the State of N. Carolina gave 9 for J., one Burr. On the second Virg$^a$ gave 14 for J., 5 Burr; N. C., 6-4. Vermon tand Maryland divided. An effort was made to set aside the vote of Georgia on the ground of some informality: rejected. It is believed that the Repubs will remain firm and never relinquish one inch of ground, and that they will put everything to the hazard; the fact is this opp'n cannot elect Mr. Burr. But if they had passed appropriation Laws &c., my opinion is the opposite party would hold out to the last. Yet, I am still of opinion that Maryland will yield. I dine out, and therefore can give you only my own weak opinion, which is that Jef. will be the pres. Pens$^y$ has her courier here, and the report is that she had 22 thousand prepared to take up arms in the event of extremities; that the Ass: of Virginia should be convened if things remain in S: quo for this week I should decide as prudent, and that Pens$^y$ and Virg. should clasp hands, N. York would join, and that a Congress composed of these States and all South of the Poto: ought to be recommended; yet I would be understood to mean that this should be adopted only in last extremities: as I am clear the Foeds will yield.

I am to bring you a letter from Mr. Irvin on my return. I am very sincerely yr. friend &c.,

S. TYLER.

———

TO GOV. WILLIAM H. CABELL.

Greenway, May 22nd, 1803.

Dear Sir:

I received by express an appointment to the Court of Chancery in Williamsburg, which I shall always consider as the highest testimony of my Country's Esteem, and I most sincerely wish there were not so many objections to my acceptance of it. For some time I have thought it desirable, as it would place me in a situation where my sons could be educated under my own eyes, and where I might be more convenient to my married daughters, and by that means get discharged from the terrible business of riding my Life away, expending half the salery attached to my office; but since I saw my Nephew I have heard of the continuation of my oldest Daughter's [1] dangerous situation as to her health, who lies in the old city which may terminate unfortunately. If so melancholy an Event should take place, my absence from the Scene would be most advisable. Besides the reflection of relinquishing an agreeable seat in many respects, but more especially as to health, I own I am afraid of the experiment and am almost ashamed, that I should for once in my Life want decision.

You will be pleased, therefore, to receive this Letter as a full resignation of all pretensions to the office, not doubting but that you may yet find some person better qualified to discharge the duties of it than I am.

Accept my thanks for so honorable a mark of approbation confer'd, and assure the members that advised it that I feel very sensibly the obligation.

I am, with sentiments of the highest esteem,

Yr. very ob't H'ble serv't,

JNO. TYLER.

---

DEFENCE OF MR JEFFERSON.

CERTIFICATE of "the venerable John Tyler," published in the *Richmond Enquirer* of Sept. 10, 1805.

"Mr. Jefferson finding at the end of the second year of his administration in 1781, that some people were discontented with his conduct with respect to Arnold's and Cornwallis' invasions declined offering for the office of Chief Magistrate, but neither resigned nor refused the acceptance of it. His particular friends, however, expressed a wish to appoint him again, but on its having been moved that an enquiry should take place at the succeeding session into the conduct of the executive, nothing more was said on the subject, but Gen. Nelson, who was then at the head of the militia was elected

---

(1) Anne Contesse Tyler, who married Judge James Semple professor of law at William and Mary College.

governor. Mr. Jefferson was sent to the Assembly in the Fall
or Spring following, and there called on the house for the
threatened examination in a very handsome address, but by
this time even those who thought him culpable began to
think otherwise on a real reflection and better information,
and the house by a general vote directed their thanks to be
delivered to him from the chair by John Tyler, then their
speaker, who did it accordingly in a warm and affectionate
manner.

The appointment of G. Nelson was at Staunton where
the Assembly sat. Mr. Jefferson, I believe, was immediately
sent to Congress and from thence to France where he continued seven years discharging his important affairs, highly
to the interest of his country, and greatly to the satifaction
of the government of France.

JOHN TYLER."

Richmond, Sept. 9th, 1805.

---

TO THOMAS NEWTON [1]

Greenway, Jan<sup>y</sup> 20<sup>th</sup>, 1808.

Dear Sir,

I receiv'd your short, but very friendly communication in closing your report on the Subject of the Merchants'
Memorial, which I think highly commendable. It was strange
indeed that those people shou'd suppose a general policy was
to be laid aside to accommodate them. This is the class that
always will throw a clog about the Wheels of our gov$^t$, whenever their interest is a little concern'd. Why, my Wheat and
Corn are now unsold, but ready clean'd for delivery. What

---

(1). In 1706, George Newton m. Aphi.. Wilson, issue: nine children. Thomas Newton, one of these, m, Amy dau. of John Hutch-
ings, issue: five children—all of whom died in infarcy except a son,
named Thomas who m. Martha Tucker and was father of the correspondent of Gov. Tyler, as well as of George Newton, in his day a most
reputable citizen of Norfolk, Thomas Newton, the last named, was
a lawyer, and in 1801 was elected to congress. He was regularly returned for thirty years. He died Aug. 5th 1847, aged 79.

The first mentioned George Newton was son of George Newton,
who was in Virginia in 1670, and who m. Frances, dau. of Lemuel
Mason.

preference have they? not from the superior Love of Country, I am sure.

I suppose you have much conflict in the present state of affairs, and I am told much Intrigue on the subject of the next Election for President: take care you divide not; the still'd mouth'd Feds may break forth like an Electrical Spark and Set you all on Fire. Although I cou'd not help wishg Mr Jefferson to continue four years longer until the Tyranny was entirely trodden under foot, yet his letter contains in plain language, but yet sublime, such cogent reasons that I am almost willing to part with him. You know Cicero said, when Cæsar was destroyed by Brutus, "that it was not enough that the Tyrant was destroy'd, if the Tyranny still continued"—which prov'd a just saying, for it soon rear'd· its three-faced Head.

Why have you not written me how matters go with Rose. I am untaught through any channel or by any certain means.

Numa Pompilius preserved a peace for 40 years, but I much doubt whethei Mr Jefferson in right had not more to conflict with from the Federal Party and public prints, which were not known in the days of Rome. To the shade of retirement my Wishes for his quiet will follow him. I have known him 44 years and a more uniform Character the World never gave existence to, I believe. Write to me when you have leisure.

Y'r sincere friend and servt ,

Jno. Tyler,

TO GOV. WILLIAM H. CABELL.

Feb'y. 10th, 1808.

Dear Sir:

I find the Assembly has made a considerable alteration in the District Law which I think a good one as far as it goes, but surely equity ought to follow the law, and had another law gone hand in hand with it for the diffusion of knowledge on easy terms throughout the State, in a short time the morals and manners of the people would be considerably improved. The first mentioned subject was half done because of some influential members having a monopoly in three Chancery Courts. The second is done nothing in, because of the eternal war declared against the Arts and Sciences, and a determination to pay nothing by way of Taxes to yᵉ support and encouragement of Education, the true and solid foundation of free government.

This new system will derange me, I expect, in my old days, unless I am allow'd to have pretensions not inferior to my Brothers.

I have been four years longer in the Judiciary than any Judge of the Gen. Court, and 32 years in public service, so that, when the allotment is made, I may reasonably be allowed to expect a convenient Circuit. I am willing to go into the Norfolk or Williamsburg Circuit, which from every consideration I may reasonably enough expect. I beg you will be pleased to lay my pretensions before your Honorable Board, when it is proper to do so.

I am with sincere respect your most ob't. servant,

JNO. TYLER.

P. S. I am in the center of the Williamsburg rout and convenient to the Norfolk.                J. T.

———

TO THOMAS NEWTON.

Greenway, March 13ᵗʰ, 1808.

Dear Sir,

I find that Congress is about establishing an Army for the defence of the United States, which is more like a peace than a war establishment, but, be it as it may, my present application to you is in behalf of my Son-in-Law, Mʳ Thoˢ E. Waggaman,[1] who I can safely undertake to recommend as an able and proper person to entrust the paymaster's office with in the state of Tennessee. He is a Merchant of considerable note in that Country, is from the Maryland Family who are of high respectability in the State. His dwelling is at Nashville. As I dislike troubling the President (who I have known from my Infancy almost) on any subject,

———

(1). Thomas E. Waggaman, m. Martha Jefferson Tyler. He was a brother of George A. Waggaman of Louisiana, U. S. senator from 1832 to 35. See Waggaman genealogy, "William and Mary College Quarterly Historical Pap.," ii. No. 2.

but more particularly when any of my family are concern'd, I thought this made through you might come better to him. If you will do me the favor to mention the subject to him, I will be answerable for the faithful performance of the duties of the office.

I think your negotiatian makes but a poor progress, and yet two questions and categorical answers wou'd settle the matter. All the world are now contending for Neutral rights, and we, no less interested than all the powers, are lying back. Suppose England and France shou'd come to a settlement of their affairs, we should have all the power of England to contend agst, for nothing but that combination vs. her will bring her to a sense of Justice—Let me hear from you as to y$^e$ private part of this Letter, the balance do as you please about.

Yr friend and serv$^t$ ,<br>Jno. Tyler.

P. S. Two ministers cou'd do nothing while in England. One is sent here, but not with full powers. Is not this policy too flimsy to deceive? I am sorry so much altercation has taken place in our State about the next president, for my own part I am content with either of the candidates. They all stand high in my esteem and I am well satisfied our country will be ably and virtuously serv'd by either. I began to write only a few lines, but some blind Impetus will push me on.

Adieu, J. T.

----

TO THOMAS NEWTON.

Richmond,, Va., Dec$^r$ 16$^{th}$ 1808.

Dear Sir;

You promised to write to me when we last saw each other at Suffolk, but I suppose you have been too much engaged to dip your pen in ink on private Subjects. I congratulate you and my country on the Madisonian Victory, and the decision with which Congress is act$^g$. One step more and everything will come right; and that is to exchange Ministers and have no more intrigue and corruption, and never to send a resident Minister to any court nor receive one here. I never did hold with the policy of suffering authorized Spies among us, they always create mischief.

You have heard of my call to the office of Chief Magistrate by a strong vote unsolicited and undesired, which I cou'd not get over accept'g; my friends were so zealous. I receiv'd the message in bed at Mid–Night last Saturday--at my own House by express. The vote would have been much greater but for some mean insinuations of my being opposed to the administration and a friend to the Monroe Party; the most bearfaced lye that ever was utter'd, when it was well known by a certain set who countenanced the thing, that no man was more decided in the State; but I wou'd not descend to the abominable meanness of expressing myself improperly of Mr. Monroe, who I have long been in the strictest bonds of friendship with--I greatly hope that Mr. Jefferson will never believe I can be oppos'd to my Country's true interest, to gratify any wish for a friend's promotion. Nor can I ever be brought to believe he cou'd ever pursue One single measure designedly to injure a Country which gave him birth and made him so much the admiration of his friends and $y^e$ Envy of his Enemies. Little as he need to care about my Opinions, Yet I cannot bear that a good man shou'd believe I am capable of disapproving good measures and virtuous actions--not in my whole Life was ever a hint drop'd of my want of Patriotism before, and this to serve a particular purpose. Pray, when a safe opportunity offers, let him know I still love and revere his Virtues as I always have done,and my only regret is that I cou'd not be near enough to him always to light my Taper by his Fire. Don't call this adulation, it is not so. I always revered him.

God bless you.

$Y^r$ friend, etc.

JNO. TYLER.

_____

TO THOMAS NEWTON.

Feb$^y$ 4, 1809.

Dear Sir,

I enclose you two Copies of a Resolution passed the Legislature, which I hope will meet your approbation. You will therefore make the proper use of them, and I hope you will find no difficulty in obtaining for the lower part of our

ceive one here. I never did hold
with the policy of suffering authorized Spies among us they always
create mischief.

You have heard of my
call to the office of Chief Magistrate
by a strong vote unsolicited and
undesired which I could not get over
now; my friends were so zealous
I received the message in bed at
Mid Night last Saturday at my
own House by express — The Vote
wou'd have been much greater
but for some mean insinuations,
of my being opposed to the Administration and a friend to the
Monroe Party, the most barefaced
lye that ever was utter'd when it

State that defence[1] which is so necessary in the present Crisis.

I am with great respect
Your friend and Serv^t ,
J NO. TYLER.

---

Richmond, Aug. 15th, 1809.

Dear Sir:

I beg leave to recommend young Mr. Claiborne to your notice, who will apply for an examination in the Law.

I suppose you have seen the proclamation of the President, which brings into operation the non-intercourse Scheme again, and down went our wheat one shilling in the bushel and that perfidious Nation G. B., quite glutted with our produce—Nothing saves us from a War now but the Success of Napoleon. Indeed, we had better have gone to War two years ago and catched the spirit of the people, so that they could not have had time to calculate on the price of our produce, to which the Nation has sacrificed its honor and true Interest. O times! how changed.

I am sincerely your friend and servant,
J NO. TYLER.

---

(1). Refers to the fortifications at Norfolk.

# John Tyler.

FROM A MANUSCRIPT FURNISHED THE NATIONAL CYCLOPEDIA
OF AMERICAN BIOGRAPHY.(1)

TYLER, JOHN, tenth President of the United
States, was born at "Greenway," Charles City Co.,
Virginia, on the 29<sup>th</sup> of March, 1790, and died in Richmond, Va., January 18, 1862. He was the second son of
Judge John Tyler and Mary Armistead, his wife,
only child of Robert Booth Armistead of York Co.,
Va. In early boyhood he attended an "old-field
school," kept by a learned Scotchman, named Mc-
Murdo. Mr. McMurdo was a great tyrant, but greatly admired the little boy. At the age of eleven years
young Tyler was one of the ringleaders in a rebellion
against the schoolmaster, which had its humorous
features. The scholars attempted to tie McMurdo
to the floor. He resisted stoutly till he saw John
Tyler active in the matter. Then, in imitation of
the great Roman, he exclaimed, "Et tu Brute!" and
ceased to resist.

On complaining afterwards to Judge Tyler, the
indignant schoolmaster was met with the reply, "Sic
semper tyrannis."

The future President was graduated at William and
Mary college, in July, 1807. James Madison, the president of the college, and Judge Tyler had been college-
mates of Thomas Jefferson, and the political principles
of the rising statesman became naturally "states-
rights." At college he showed a strong interest in
ancient history. He was also fond of poetry and
music, and, like Thomas Jefferson, was a skillful
performer on the violin. In 1809, before attaining

---

(1) Published by James T. White & Co., New York. In preparing this sketch, I have made free use of the sketch in Appleton's
" Cyclopedia of Biography."

his majority, he was admitted to the bar, and had already begun to obtain a good practice, when he was elected to the legislature, and took his seat in that body in December, 1811. He was here a firm supporter of Mr. Madison's election; and the war with Great Britain, which soon followed, afforded him an opportunity to become conspicuous as a forcible and persuasive orator. The bank had always been unpopular in Virginia, but the Virginia senators at Washington, Mess. William B. Giles and Richard Brent, ignored the instructions of the legislature and favored its recharter in 1811. On 14 Jan., 1812, Mr. Tyler, in the Virginia legislature, introduced resolutions in which the senators were taken to task, while the Virginia doctrines as to the unconstitutional character of the bank, and the binding force of instructions, were formally asserted.

Mr. Tyler married, 20 March, 1813, Letitia, daughter of Robert Christian, and a few weeks afterward was called into the field at the head of a company of militia, to take part in defence of Richmond and its neighborhood, now threatened by the British. His military service lasted but a month, during which Mr. Tyler's company was not called into action. He was re-elected to the legislature annually until, in November, 1816, he was chosen to fill a vacancy in the house of representatives, caused by the death of Hon. John Clopton.

As a member of the house, during the 14th and 15th congresses, he soon made himself conspicuous as a strict-constructionist. He voted against the bill introduced by Mr. Calhoun in favor of internal improvements on the ground of its unconstitutionality and its lack of a principle of uniform application among the states. He voted against the bill chang-

ing the *per diem* allowance of $6 a day to members
of congress for an annual salary of $1500. He also
opposed the passage of the national bankrupt law,
and condemned, as arbitrary and insubordinate, the
course of Gen. Jackson in Florida. He was a member of the committee for inquiring into the affairs of
the national bank, and his most elaborate speech was
in favor of Mr. Trimble's motion to issue a *scire
facias* against it. In the next canvass he rested
his election on his speech against the bank, which he
distributed among his constituents; and was re-
elected to congress without opposition.

The most important question that came before
the 16th congress related to the admission of Missouri into the Union. Mr. Tyler's views on slavery
were like those of his father, Judge Tyler, who, in
the convention of 1788, had justified his opposition
to the adoption of the constitution greatly on the
ground that it permitted the continuance of the slave
trade, which had been engrafted on that instrument
by a bargain between the states of New England
and the states of South Carolina and Georgia. In
the debates over the admission of Missouri, Mr.
Tyler took the ground that slavery was an evil, but
that congress had no constitutional power to permit
slavery in the states and prohibit it in the territories,
when, by the express language of the constitution, the
territories had all the rights of the old states on their
admission into the Union. Nor did he deem the restriction on Missouri expedient. He held with Jefferson and Madison, that as the Northern states had
secured emancipation by the sale and diffusion of
their slaves, it was unfair, under pretext of saving
Missouri from the establishment of slaves, to darken
the cloud over Virginia by hemming the negro popu-

lation in, and confirming its existence there. The deepening of slavery in the old Southern states would make the laws concerning the slaves all the more rigorous, and the abolition itself under such circumstances would still leave Virginia a negro-ridden community. Mr. Tyler was convinced that no argument was more absurd than the objection that the increase of the "slave states" would keep pace with the progress of the North, constantly accelerated by the heavy emigration from Europe.

The adoption of the "compromise bill" admitting Missouri without restriction, but prohibiting slavery in all the territory north of the line 36° 30', seemed to Mr. Tyler a surrender of the whole question at issue ; and against the opinion of Calhoun, of Clay, and nearly the whole Southern representation, Mr. Tyler voted in the negative. Mr. Tyler was unquestionably foremost among members of congress in occupying the position that congress had no power to legislate for or against slavery in any territory. Nevertheless, he never denied his original judgment on the evils of a negro population, slave or free. In this he was quite a contrast to some who were foremost now in 1820, in sacrificing the South, but who not only afterwards reversed their opinion as to the compromise of that year, but went so far as to maintain that slavery was "a domestic, social and political blessing." At this congress the attack was made for the first time upon the tariff, which had been passed in the interest of protecting Northern manufactures, and Mr. Tyler made the opening objections. Such power did the young orator exhibit in this speech that Judge Baldwin, then chairman of the committee on manufactures, and afterwards Judge of the U. S. supreme court, went to his seat and prophesied, on the strength of what he had heard, great political advancement in the future. And Mr. Tyler afterwards obtained no political preferment, but he was certain to receive from his generous adversary a letter reminding him of his prediction.

In 1821, Mr. Tyler declined a re-election to congress on account of impaired health, and returned to private life. But in 1823, he was again elected to the house of delegates of Virginia. The next year he was nominated to fill the vacancy created in the United States senate by the death of John Taylor, but his friend, Littleton W. Tazewell, a much older man in politics, was elected.

In the Legislature in 1824, he opposed the attempt to remove William and Mary college to Richmond, and received his reward in being afterwards made successively rector and chancellor of the college, which prospered signally under his auspices. In December, 1825, he was chosen by the legislature to the governorship of Virginia, and in the following year he was re-elected by a unanimous vote.

A new division of parties was now begining to show itself in national politics. At the end of Monroe's administration, the Republican party held the field in solitary triumph. The Federal party, its ancient adversary, fatally shocked by the success of the war of 1812, had passed away. The administration of John Quincy Adams, which went into office in March, 1825, pronounced in favor of the American system of high tariffs, national bank and internal improvements. In plain terms, this meant to the Southern people, an unwarranted extension of the powers of the government and an appeal to the numerical majority of the North to grow rich at the expense of their section,

Before the presidental election in 1824, William H. Crawford was the only candidate of the Republican party whose opinions were unequivocal against the American system. He, accordingly, received the support of Mr. Jefferson and all the Virginia leaders, including John Tyler. When Mr. Crawford, by reason of a stroke of paralysis, was deemed out of the contest, Mr. Tyler and the rest of the strict-constructionists preferred John Quincy Adams to either Henry Clay or Andrew Jackson, both of whom had favored too much the new views.

When Adams came out in the same colors, the strict-constructionists, who had adhered to Crawford, remained neutral for a time, but were finally forced into co-operation with the followers of Andrew Jackson—the majority of whom were members of the old Federal party. Mr. Tyler went along with the rest of the Crawford men, but from the first his support of Jackson was conditioned on Jackson's sustaining the Republican doctrines as maintained in Virgir  Parties now assumed new names. The friends of Adams and Clay took that of National Repulicans, while the friends of Jackson and Crawford assumed that of Democrats  But each party claimed to be the true representatives of the old Republican party of Jefferson. Firmly devoted to his principles, Mr. Tyler would not be a partisan. He never attached any importance to the widely prevalent story of a corrupt bargain between Adams and Clay. When the Clay and Adams men in the legislature momentarily united in 1827 with a majority of the Crawford men and elected Mr. Tyler senator over John Randolph, some zealous friends of Jackson attempted to show that there must have been some secret and reprehensible understanding between Tyler and Clay. There was no truth in any

bargains, but the object was to drive Mr. Tyler into
avowals. The scheme failed. Mr. Tyler, unlike
Mr. Randolph, refused to become the partisan of
Jackson, and withheld his preference. He subsequently supported Jackson for president in the fall
of 1828, as a choice of evils only.

In February, 1830, sometime after taking part
in the Virginia Convention for revising the state
constitution, Mr. Tyler returned to his seat in the
senate and found himself first drawn to Jackson by
his veto of the Maysville Turnpike bill. But the confidence never cordially given was soon abruptly withheld. The new president continued with enthusiasm
the policy of his predecessor. High tariffs, large appropriations for internal improvements, speculation,
stock-jobbing, defalcations, partisan appointments
and unconstitutional assumptions of power, marked
the next twelve years. The followers of Crawford
were soon in open oppostion. Mr. Tyler, one of the
most prominent of these, strongly condemned Jackson's rewarding whole troops of editors with lucra-
tive offices, as also his appointing commissioners
to negotiate a treaty with Turkey without the
assent of the Senate, and approving numerous bills
for the improvement of rivers and harbors. Still, in
the presidential election of 1832, Mr. Tyler supported
Jackson as a less objectionable candidate than the
other two before the public, Clay and Wirt. Mr.
Tyler disapproved of nullification and condemned
the course of South Carolina, as both "impolitic and
unconstitutional." But he condemned the tariff measure of the adminisiration for the same reasons, and
for the additional one that they were the cause of
the errors of South Carolina. Jackson's famous
proclamation of December 10, 1832, was denounced

by him as "sweeping away all the barriers of the constitution," and as establishing in principle "a consolidated, military despotism." Under the influence of these feelings he undertook to play the part of mediator betwen Clay and Calhoun, and suggested to them the idea of the compromise tariff of 1833. On the so-called "force bill," clothing the President with extraordinary powers for the purpose of enforcing the tariff, which had caused all the trouble, Mr. Tyler showed the courage of his convictions. When the bill was put to the vote 20 Feb., 1833, some of its opponents happened to be absent; others got up and went out in order to avoid putting themselves on record.

The vote was then taken and stood : yeas 32, nay one (John Tyler).

The next four years witnessed a continuous disintegration of the Democratic party.

The Nullifiers led by Calhoun had left Jackson in 1832. In 1833, the majority of the Virginia Democrats, under the lead of Tazewell and Tyler of Virginia, abandoned him, pleading the danger of the doctrines avowed by the President in his proclamation against South Carolina. In 1834, the removal of the deposits drove off another element, headed by John Bell, Henry A. Wise and others. In 1835, the celebrated expunging resolution offered by Mr. Benton brought about a fourth defection, while in 1837, the proposal of the sub-treasury by Van Buren, who succeeded Jackson as President, brought about a new rupture. The tendency of these successive defections was to bring Mr. Tyler and his friends into closer and closer conditions with Clay and the National Republicans. Mr. Tyler opposed the removal of the deposits from the United States

bank, not because he favored the bank, but because
the President had no authority to become the custo-
dian of the public funds himself.  He voted in favor
of Mr. Clay's proposition to censure the President,
but his entire opposition was founded, of course, on
a theory of states-rights, which was really repugnant
in principle to all the views expressed by Clay and
the National Republicans in 1828.  The first difficulty towards a Union was overcome when the National Republicans dropped their old name, and in
1834, began to call themselves Whigs.  Yet there
was to the last mutual jealousy and distrust.  In
1836, no common candidate could be agreed upon.
The states-rights men nominated Hugh L. White,
of Tennessee, for president, and John Tyler for vice-
president.  The National Republicans, wishing to
gather votes from the other parties, nominated for
president Gen. William Henry Harrison, who, as a
soldier, was not indentified with any political faction.
The Democratic friends of Jackson nominated Van
Buren, who received many National Republican
votes in the election.[1]  There was a great deal of
bolting among the states.  Massachusetts threw its
votes for Webster for president, and South Carolina for Willie P. Mangum.  Virginia, which voted
for Van Buren, rejected his colleague, Richard M.
Johnson and cast its electoral vote for vice president on William Smith, of Alabama.  Mr. White
obtained the electoral votes of Tennessee and Georgia, twenty-six in all, but Mr. Tyler made a better
showing ; he carried, besides these two states, Maryland and South Carolina, making forty-seven in all.
No one of the candidates for the vice-presidency

---

(1) See " Parties and Patronage," p. 63.

having received a majority of the electoral college, the choice devolved on the Democratic senate, who chose R. M. Johnson. In the course of the year preceding the election, an incident occurred, which emphasized more than ever Mr. Tyler's hostility to the Jackson party. Benton had resolved to have "expunged" from the journal of the senate the resolution of censure passed by that body in 1834, upon Jackson, for removing the deposits from the United States bank, and his friends in the general assembly of Virginia passed through that body a resolution instructing the Virginia senators, Mess. B. W. Leigh and Tyler, to support Benton. This procedure placed both Mr. Tyler and his colleague in the senate, Mr. B. W. Leigh, in embarrassing positions; for both had been the champions in favor of the right of instructions. Mr. Leigh, however, would not obey the resolutions of the legislature, and made his disobedience unpardonable in the eyes of the Virginia people by holding to his seat; Mr. Tyler too would not obey, but he reconciled the people to him by resigning three unexpired years of his term. He maintained that an adhesion to the doctrine of instructions did not carry with it the obligation to violate the constitution.

About this time the followers of Calhoun were bringing forward what was characterized by some the "gag resolution" against all petitions and motions relating in any way to the abolition of slavery. Mr. Tyler's resignation occurred before this measure was adopted, but his opinion on the subject was pronounced in the senate. He condemned the measure as impolitic, because it yoked together two questions not necessarily connected, the right of petition and the right of slavery, and thus gave a distinct moral advantage to the abolitionists. On the 7th anniversary of the Virginia colonization society he was chosen its president. While maintaining the sovereignty of the states over the subject of slavery, he had been ever foremost in all projects to put a stop to the slave-trade and to ameliorate the condition of the slave. And, as early as 1832, he had, as chairman of the senate committee, proposed a code for the District of Columbia, one section of which prohibited the slave-trade in the District.

In the spring elections of 1838, Mr. Tyler was again returned to the Virginia legislature. Here he soon found himself in a strange conflict. After Mr. Tyler's resignation from the Senate in 1836, the Democrats had returned William C. Rives. But Mr. Rives had not fancied the subtreasury scheme of Mr. Van Buren, and in 1838, stood apart from the party which had elected him, and called himself a "conservative."

On the advice of Mr. Clay the majority of the Whigs determined to go for Mr. Rives in preference to Mr. Tyler—the hope being to fully identify Mr. Rives with the party by electing him over the professed Democratic opponent, John Y. Mason. Naturally indignant at this treatment, the personal friends of Mr. Tyler would not yield, and no election ensued at this legislature on account of the dead lock which resulted.

Meanwhile the disturbed condition of the monetary interest of the country had produced a decided effect upon the heterogenous elements of the Whig party. This condition had been, in part, caused by agencies reaching deeper than any administration, but in part also no doubt by some of the measures of Jackson—such as the removal of the deposits and

their lodgment in the so-called "pet banks," the distribution of the surplus followed by the sudden stop-
page of that distribution and the sharpness of the
remedy against speculation in the Western land sup-
plied by the specie circular, attended by the general
demoralization and corruption of the office holders.
The Whigs got together in their first national convention at Harrisburg in December, 1839. The
delegates there were nearly equally divided between
the two old parties—Democrats and National Republicans. By the defection of the Crawford ele
ment of the Democratic party more than half of
the Southern Democrats had fallen into the Whig
ranks, and the effect of this coalition of Northern
National Republicans with Southern Democrats (who
were Whigs because the Democratic party was not
Democratic enough) was to drive thousands of the
old National Republican party over to the party of
Jackson and Van Buren.[1] All the leading Whigs
of the South were original Democrats, and many of
them Nullifiers like Preston and Duff Green. In
the Whig Convention at Harrisburg no platform
of principles was adopted, though so far as public
utterances and private letters went, the old issues
of bank, tariff and internal improvements were distinctly surrendered by Clay, Webster, Adams and all
the leaders of the old National Republican party.[2]
Mr. Clay especially had gone so far in conciliating
Southern sentiment as to be considered the Southern candidate. The Northern representatives sought
to defeat his election by again putting up General
Harrison, to whom the South could not well object,
as he was a Southerner, but who was preferable to

(1)  "Parties and Patronage," 63.
(2)  Ibid 60.  See also Vol. I. 596-632 ;  II, 710-11.

Mr. Clay in the eyes of the manufacturers, since, although approving the compromise tariff of 1833, he had not been the mover of it. They succeeded in defeating Mr. Clay, and Gen. Harrison became the candidate of the Whig party for the presidency.[1] -

Something of the same game was attempted against Mr. Tyler, whose opinions were well known. Various overtures were made in secret to distinguished Whigs to allow their names to be used in nomination against him, but these movements to Mr. Tyler's injury were so far-fetched that, according to the statement of one of the conspirators themselves, the effort failed (in the case of William C. Preston for instance,) since "not a single Southern delegate approved the suggestion of his (Preston's) nomination for the vice-presidency."[2] Mr. Tyler was the choice of everybody but a few intriguers.

Borne upon a great wave of popular excitement "Tippecanoe and Tyler too" were carried to the White House. It is idle to suppose there were not causes for the great enthusiasm manifested, apart from the clap-trap of politics. There was not a department of the government which was not in confusion, not an office which was not the seat of peculation, and not a principle of the constitution which had not been scorned and insulted by the course of the men in authority, under Jackson and Van Buren. A deep seated conviction of the necessity of reform prevailed, and this conviction swept the Democrats from power.

The triumph of the Whigs was followed by startling results. A collision between their varying factions was perhaps unavoidable, but not necessari-

---

(1)   See Vol. I, 594.

(2)   Niles' Register, 61, p. 232; " Parties and Patronage," 112.

ly so at once. Mr. Clay hurried the quarrel. Without waiting for Harrison's inauguration he at once assumed the dictatorship of the Whig party and revived the old National Republican measures which
in his letters and public speeches he had declared
"obsolete." Matters had already come to a rupture
between Clay and Harrison when the latter died one
month after his inauguration. The presidency, thereupon, devolved upon the Vice-President, whose views
were even more fixed against the policy proposed
than Harrison's.

The national bank was announced by Clay as
the great cardinal object of the new Whig administration. But neither in his inaugural nor in his message, calling the congress in extra-session on the 31
of May, 1841, had Harrison indicated that the bank
would be agreeable to him. He had hopes, however, of getting the Whigs to compromise on a bank
of the District of Columbia, with branches in the
states established with consent of the states. (See
Rives' speech in Congressional Globe, 1841, Appendix, p. 367). And a similar hope animated
Mr. Tyler, his successor. He privately submitted
several financial projects to his cabinet, which,
while they avoided recognizing the power of
congress to create corporations in the states,
really in fact accomplished all that a national
bank could have effected respecting the finances
and business of the country. A measure similar
in all respects to the plan which Harrison favored
was finally adopted by the Whig cabinet and
recommended to congress by Mr. Ewing, the secretary of the treasury. Mr. Clay forced a fight on
the constitutional question by substituting a bill dif-
fering from the cabinet bill in allowing the bank to

establish its branches at will in the states. Despite the opposition of the Whig senators from Virginia, Messrs. Rives and Archer, and the Whig senators from Massachusetts, who were friends of Mr. Webster, the bill in this objectionable form passed both houses of Congress. But it did not become a law. The President was not only by all his past life committed against the principle of Clay's bill, but he had, in an interview with Mr. Clay at the beginning of the extra–session of Congress assembled in obedience to a proclamation of the late President, clearly forewarned him of the folly of his course. And in repeated conversations afterwards with Mr. Ewing and the other Whig leaders Mr. Tyler had "pertinaciously"[1] held to his expressed opinions on the subject. He therefore vetoed the bill, but by withholding the veto till the ten days allowed by the constitution had nearly expired, he afforded another signal proof of his wish to harmonize with the Whigs.

He could not yet fully believe that the Whigs would be so blind as to deliberately sacrifice the result of the recent election by an adherence to a course so stupid and absurd as a conflict with their own president. As Clay's objection was against requiring the assent of the states to the establishment of the bank, or its branches within them, the President thought that the Whigs might be satisfied with a proposition which by limiting the bank to dealings in exchanges would, under a recent decision[2] of the supreme court of the United States, avert the necessity of obtaining the expressed consent of the States for branches. In accepting this distinction Mr.

(1) Mr. Ewing's Statement, Niles 61, p. 33.
(2) Bank of Augusta vs Earle, decided in 1839—see Peters' U. S. Reports.

Tyler made no surrender of his consistency; for it was a distinction made by the law of nations, which was itself founded on the voluntary consent of states. But as the will of a free state or nation is not subject to a coercive code, Mr. Tyler made provision for the possible interdiction by a state of branches of the bank within it. He wrote a suitable reservation upon the margin of the paper made the basis of the bill, and the paper with this reservation was carried by A. H. H. Stuart to the Whig caucus.[1]

Now the bill, as adopted by Congress, did not contain the marginal words; and yet, both Stuart, who admitted the amendment, and three cabinet officers asserted that the bill conformed to the President's opinions ! A second veto follow.

The Whig leaders had already shown a disposition to entrap the President. Before the passage of Mr. Clay's first bill, John Minor Botts was sent to the White House with a private suggestion for a compromise. Mr. Tyler refused to listen to the suggestion, except with the understanding that should it meet with his disapproval, he should not hear from it again. The suggestion turned out to be a proposal that a limited time should be allowed a state to exercise its right of approval, and otherwise restricting its power. The president indignantly rejected the suggestion "as a contemptible subterfuge behind which he would not skulk." The device, nevtheless, became incorporated in Mr. Clay's bill, and despite the President's understanding with Botts, it was pretended it was put there in order to smooth the way for the President to adopt the measure. After his veto of Aug. 16, these tortuous methods were

---

(1) Benton, ii, 212, 241, "Parties and Patronage," 119; See Vol. 11, 98-103.

renewed. Some of the Whigs proposed to revive the original cabinet measure, which had received their bitter denunciation and which the President had tolerated with the single thought that it might meet the wishes of the Whigs. John Minor Botts gave expression to the intentions of the Whigs in a letter unexpectedly disclosed to the public view. He avowed that the purpose of the revival of the cabinet measure was "to head the President" by passing an unpopular measure which nobody wanted, and afterwards amending it till the contested power was obtained. When the President promptly announced himself against the revival, the same methods were pursued in respect to the new suggestions.

Mr. Crittenden, one of the cabinet and a particular friend of Henry Clay, wrote privately [1] that he did not see why, with proper tact, "a bank might not be constructed with a greater recognition of Federal authority than the one which the President had vetoed." By changes in the wording, all the restrictions even of the first vetoed bill on the running and renewal of paper were omitted. The new measure became known as the "Fiscal Corporation," but in spite of objections of the President, sent to those in charge of the bill before its introduction in congress, it was passed by both Houses and forced upon the executive without amendment. The "Fiscal Corporation," was, as Benton and Buchanan conclusively showed in the Senate, a bank of local discount and not one of exchanges, as the President had suggested. As a bank of local discount it was defective in not containing a provision for the previous consent of the states for

---

(1) See Vol. II, 116.

the establishment of branches. Had it been *bona fide* a bank dealing in exchanges, it would still have been defective in not providing for the actual inhibition of a state against branches, as insisted upon by the President in his interview with A. H. H. Stuart and in conversations with others held many weeks before that interview. Some of the Whigs seem really to have hoped that such a storm would be raised as would frighten the President into signing the bill, or resigning his office. Threats were fulminated against him on all sides; private letters warned him of plots to assassinate him, and Mr. Clay in the senate referred to his resignation in 1836, and asked why he should not follow that example now. The adjournment of congress was fixed for Monday, the 13 Sept., 1841. The second veto was sent to congress on Sept. 9th. On the 11th, saturday, all the cabinet, save Webster, resigned. The members were fully aware that according to the President's view all vacancies happening during the session had to be filled and sanctioned by the senate during the session. Yet, if the five cabinet officers who resigned could have been satisfied by a delay of their resignation till Tuesday morning, of two days only, a larger opportunity would have been afforded Mr. Tyler of performing the work of making an almost entire cabinet, which, on the part of his predecessor, had required months to adjust. A brief retrospect places the subject in a clearer light. The Whig caucus, at which the design of "heading" the President was openly advocated by Mr. Botts, occurred on the night of the 16th of August, and sometime next morning its proceedings were reported to Mr. Tyler. It was the reason of the indifference with which Mr. Tyler received the argument of Mr. Bell, which, it is said, he requested. At the cabinet meeting on the 18th of August, he advised a postponement of the question until the next congress, but when the members would not agree to this he demanded of them whether they intended "to stand by him" in resisting all efforts to engraft upon the bill by any future legislation the features of an old-fashioned bank. He received all proper assurances, and the principle of the proposed bill was considered at large by the President and cabinet. Ewing and Mr. Webster were authorized to confer with the bank committees of congress, but they were expressly told, according to the statement of the cabinet officers themselves, "not to commit" him (the President) to any measure, and that the bill must be submitted for correction. This last was not done, though Mr. Ewing in his letter of resignation said that he "heard" it had been done. It is shown by undoubted testimony that the President strained every nerve to have the bill corrected, and that he sent repeated messages to those in charge of the bill. But they not only paid no attention to these messages, but ignored the marginal note placed by the President on the paper carried to them by Mr. Stuart on August 16th, at the earliest possible occasion, and would allow no amendments in the house of representatives.

The President, at the last, tried, with the aid of Mr. Webster to have the vote postponed. This also was refused. The only condition on which they would consent to a postponement, as made by them through Mr. Cushing, was that the President should not turn out his cabinet.

The President, Mr. Spencer, Mr. Cushing and

Mr. Wise say [1] that this overture was made, and H. A. Wise in congress challenged[2] the Whigs to impeach the President, if they wanted full proof of the facts. Mr. Ewing admitted the attempt made to accomplish the postponement, and further said that the Whigs declined "because the President would give no assurances."

The President would make no bargain of any kind, but before sending in his veto message he submitted it to his cabinet, and professed his willingness to incorporate in the paper a declaration against a second term which the Whig papers were continually charging as the object of his conduct. The cabinet members opposed his insertion of such a paragraph, and yet he encountered shortly the attacks of some of the very men who gave him the advice and who were foremost in ascribing to him the absurd ambition of a re-election.

Some of the leading Whig members of congress now issued addresses to the people, declaring "all political connection between them and John Tyler at an end from that day." Mr. Webster, who warmly condemned the course of Mr. Clay, adhered to the President. During the next two years, while the Whigs controlled congress, Mr. Tyler received little support from that party, and the case was not changed much for the better when the Democrats, controlled by the Van Buren wing of the party, succeeded to the seats which the Whigs had vacated. Mr. Tyler's reliance was on the wing of either party, known as the "state-rights" men in contradistinction to the Clay Whigs and Van Buren Democrats. Af-

(1)   Tylers II, 100; Niles 63, p. 140; Cushing's speech at New-buryport 1842, and "Parties and Patronage 124."
(2)   Cong. Globe 1842-43, p. 98.

ter the resignation in 1841, he filled his cabinet with states–rights Whigs, who, like himself, had voted for Harrison; and in 1843, he added several states–rights Democrats who were opposed to Van Buren, whose principles he had always distrusted.

The domestic history of the balance of Mr. Tyler's administration must be briefly told. The leading facts were the exchequer system rejected by the Whigs, made afterwards by Lincoln the basis of the present system of finance, the tariff which Mr. Tyler procured after two vetoes, the adjustment of the Rhode Island difficulties, the settlement of the war with the Florida Indians, the renovation of all the departments of the government, and the purification of the civil service by the enforcement of the merit system and the supervision of subordinates. The success that marked the administration in these particulars was chiefly due to Mr. Tyler, who drafted with his own hand the exchequer bill,[1] wrote the correspondence with the Rhode Island authorities, [2] saved the treasury by his vetoes and excited the most rigid personal surveillance over every officer in the departments. And no less marked was his personality in this management of the foreign policy of the administration, whose negotiations resulted in securing peace by the settlement of questions of fifty years standing and enormously advancing the authority and power of the Union.

When Mr. Tyler assumed the duties of president, his attention was at once arrested by the far-reaching diplomacy of Great Britain, which threatened to absorb the western continent. Securely entrenched on our northern borders, she held the whole line from Maine to Oregon in dispute.

(1)   Vol. II, 133, 249.
(2)   Ibid, 194.

Longing eyes were cast by her over that boundless, unsettled country stretching almost from the Mississippi river to the Pacific Ocean and comprising Texas, Colorado, New Mexico, Arizona, Idaho, Montana, Wyoming, Nevada, California, Oregon and Washington—a country for the most claimed by Mexico, but which scarcely ever beheld the emblems of her authority. Mexico herself was deeply in debt to British capitalists, and at an early day English agents were busy at work composing the difficulties of Texas with Mexico, in order to secure by commercial arrangements with both, the sovereign protectorate of both. In 1842, the "opium war" gave England a footing in China facing California, and, while the British fleet scoured the Pacific Ocean ready to entrench the British authority on the Sandwich Islands, or other convenient place of operations, the Hudson Bay Fur Company pushed men and settlements into Oregon, and incendiary agents of the abolition societies of Great Britain stirred up strife between the North and South on the slavery question.

The situation was a grave one for the future of the United States, but the mind of the President grasped the length and breadth of the problem and triumphantly over-reached the shrewd diplomats of Great Britain. The first victory was achieved when the senate ratified the celebrated treaty of Washington, known popularly as "the Ashburton treaty." [1] Of this treaty Mr. Webster, the secretary of state, himself says, that "the negotiations proceeded from step to step and from day to day under the President's own immediate supervision." Mr. Tyler not only suggested to Webster the principles on which the trou-

----

(1)  Vol. II, 201-243.

blesome questions about the Caroline, the Creole, and the right of impressment were settled, but it was wholly due to him that Lord Ashburton did not break off the negotiations, and go home. He conducted the correspondence in person with William H. Seward, the Governor of New York, concerning the case of McLeod, and revised and corrected in detail[1] the papers submitted by Webster and Lord Ashburton. Finally it was he that caused all the questions in controversy to be submitted to the senate in a single treaty against the advice of Webster, who would have submitted them separately—a suggestion which if adopted would have certainly caused the rejection of one or more of the provisions, and left the countries still dangerously embroiled. Not less pronounced was his agency in dictating the recognition of the independence of the Sandwich Islands in December, 1842, or in protesting, through Hugh S. Legare, who succeeded Webster as secretary of state in June, 1843, against the occupation of those Islands by the British Admiral, Lord George Paulet, who consummated his threatened attack in February, 1843, but was soon obliged to withdraw.

Above all was his agency displayed in securing the western country for the Union. It was Mr. Tyler, that as early as 1841, pointed out [2] to Webster the importance to all our interests of the acquisition of Texas. In 1842, he suggested to him, with the concurrence of Lord Ashburton, the negotiation of a tripartite treaty by which to end the Texas war with Mexico, and to add California and the West to the Union in return for the concession to Great Britain of the line of the Columbia river, as her boundary

(1)   Vol. II, 242.
(2)   Ibid, 126.

on the northwest, and the release to Mexico of the spoliation claims. He it was that sent Fremont on his exploring expeditions to the West, despite the protest of Col. Abert and the higher grade officers of the engineer corps, thus enabling that competent officer to make known the passes of the Rocky Mountains. And to Mr. Tyler, and not Webster, belongs the credit of encouraging the missionary Whitman in his plan of transporting caravans of emigrants to the West to counteract the work of the Hudson Bay Fur Company.

After Upshur's death in 1844, it was Mr. Tyler, and not Calhoun that secured the mastery of the Texas question. Calhoun was in entire ignorance of the efforts of the President to get Texas until nominated secretary. Then he thought it was an "unpropitious time" to carry through so important a measure, and he declared that he had remonstrated with his friends against accepting office under Mr. Tyler. He suffered nearly three weeks to elapse before he reached Washington, after his nomination as secretary of state. And when the treaty of annexation by which the act was sought first to be accomplished was defeated in the senate, Mr. Calhoun advised Mr. Tyler to abandon the project.[1] And again there is no doubt that it was the bold action of Mr. Tyler in allowing himself to be nominated for the presidency on the Texas platform that compelled one of the great parties to throw aside its old leader, Mr. Van Buren, and put up a distinctive Texas advocate in the place of Van Buren as their candidate for the presidency. It is now known too, that before Mr. Tyler left the presidency, a proposition similar to the tripartite treaty already described had received the

_____

(1)   See vol. II, 330 ; Calhoun's Speeches IV. p. 333, 369.

approval of Gen. Herrera, President of Texas, and a
cautious policy would have carried it through. The
plan was made known to Mr. Polk, and thus consti-
tuted one of the reasons of the mission of John
Slidell to Mexico—a mission conducted with such
poor tact as to disgust the Mexicans and to overthrow
Herrera. The treaty of Gaudaloupe Hidalgo, and
the Oregon treaty of 1846, only secured what a superior statesmanship, in the hands of Mr. Tyler,
would have acquired without a war, destined in its
results to convulse the Union on the slavery question. And that Calhoun was altogether wrong in
supposing that Mr. Tyler acted prematurely in regard to Texas is shown by the fact that twice the
Texans were on the point of making a treaty with
Great Britain and Mexico, renouncing in return for
the recognition of their independence the privilege
of annexation to the United States.

Mr. Tyler left the government on the 4th of
March, 1845, but before he departed he had the happiness to announce to congress the successful negotiation of the first treaty with China by Caleb Cushing.
When his term expired, the condition of the government was the happiest possible. Instead of state and
individual credit stricken down, the treasury ex-
hausted, the annual income of the government deficient by millions, the currency depreciated and almost worthless, and defaulters everywhere, exactly
the reverse was the case. A balance was found in
the treasury of $8,000,000, and but one defaulter,
and he, for the small sum of $15, had come to light
during his four years of office.

Mr. Tyler, during his administration, was a
strong advocate of civil service reform, and the chief

missions were for years filled with persons politically opposed to him.[1]

He allowed himself to be nominated in 1844, without any expectation of an election, but solely with the hope of inducing the Democrats to give up. Van Buren, and forcing a recognition of his friends.[2] He succeeded in both these objects, through Mr. Polk afterwards violated his promises to Mr. Tyler's friends and turned all his appointees out of office. After leaving the White House, Mr. Tyler took up his residence on an estate three miles from "Greenway," where his father had lived, in the county of Charles City, Virginia. To this estate he gave the name of "Sherwood Forest," and there he dwelt during the remainder of his life He ceased to take an active part in politics, but even in his retirement he exerted a great influence upon public opinion in Virginia. He was always for peace and conciliation. He made a number of addresses, which rank high as literary productions. He had borne great and undeserved misrepresentation, which by his sensitive nature was keenly felt. He was, therefore, greatly gratified to find his popularity in Virginia and the South return in a few years.

When Lincoln was elected, and South Carolina seceded, the Virginia people relied much upon his approved sagacity and elected him to the state convention in January, 1861, as also to conduct the ov-

(1) See a full discussion in "Parties and Patronage" of Mr. Tyler's management of the public offices; also Vol. II, 310—315.

(2) Mordecai M. Noah knew all the facts, as he was a friend in the beginning; but, when Tyler refused to give him the consulate at Liverpool because he was an editor, he garbled a conversation with Tyler in 1843, but admitted that Tyler said that "he entertained no hopes of an election himself."—Niles 64, p. 394. See "Parties and Patronage," p. 82; II. 317,341.

ertures of compromise, which Virginia submitted to the angry sections by the call of the peace conference. This body met in the city of Washington, in February, 1861. It was due to the suggestion of Mr. Tyler, who, however, intended to limit the representation in the conference to the border states. The undue invitation to all the Northern states defeated its efficiency as a remedy, and, instead of a compromise in the nature of the Crittenden resolutions, an ambiguous proposition was adopted, which Mr. Tyler opposed as only leading to future trouble. But even this proposition was treated with the utmost contempt by the Republican majority in congress, who would not even give it the poor courtesy of entering it upon the journals of either House. Mr Tyler was elected a delegate to the provisional congress, and was member-elect of the Confederate house of representatives, but died before he took his seat in the latter body on January 18, 1862. A great public funeral witnessed the interment of his remains in Hollywood Cemetery, Richmond, Virginia.

The high character of his attainments is attested by some of the most eminent men of his times. Mr. Jefferson Davis says, that " as an extemporaneous speaker, " he regarded him as "the most felicitous among the orators he had known." [1] Henry S. Foote said [2] that Mr. Tyler was "without a particle of hauteur or assumption in his aspect or demeanor," was "eminently frank and unconstrained in his conversation, and evinced as much of good nature and high bred politeness, as of intellectual resources." Charles Dickens, who saw him at Washington in 1842, declared [3] that he be-

---

(1) " Parties and Patronage," p. 92. (2) Foote's "Casket of Reminiscences," p. 57. (3) American Notes.

came his station as President "singularly well." "His own state papers," writes [1] Alex. H. Stephens of Georgia, "compare favorably in point of ability with those of any of his predecessors." And John Quincy Adams declared [2] that his Texas move was characterized by "equal intrepidity and address."

He married in 1813, as we have seen, Letitia Christian, daughter of Hon. Robert Christian of Virginia, and in June 1844, he married 2dly, Julia Gardiner, daughter of Hon. David and Juliana Gardiner, of New York.

## THE WHIG PARTY.

Carl Schurz says, in his interesting "Life of Henry Clay," that Clay's assertion in the Senate in 1841, that the question of "bank or no bank" had been the main issue of the last presidential canvass was "an astounding assertion," ii p. 207. He says that " the verdict of impartial history will probably be that John Tyler, by preventing by his veto the incorporation of another United States Bank, rendered his country a valuable service," ii p. 209. Still, Mr. Schurz seems to hate to give the Whigs entirely up, and, as a consequence, runs into inconsistencies.

On page 182 he says that the Whig party in 1840 "was a coalition rather than a party, without common principles and definite aims beyond the mere overthrow of those in power." He also says, p. 184, that "the Whig National Convention had adopted no platform, passed no resolutions, issued no address, put forth no programme," and that "their standard bearer, Gen. Harrison, had a record which fitted him for a Democrat, as well as for a Whig." What then does he mean on page 201 by saying that Mr. Tyler's inaugural address was "Whiggish in sound, but open to different constructions"? From his own statement, Whig principles, if there were any distinctively such, were open to different constructions. Mr. Tyler, like Gen. Harrison and Lincoln, laid down general principles in his inaugural, but even Benton thought he was more definite than any other president had ever been (Thirty Years View II, p. 212). In his message at the extra session, while stating distinctly that the people had decided against the old National Bank, he did not take ground against all Banks, for

(1) Stephens' "Pictorial Hist. U. S.," p. 479.  (2) Adams' " Memoirs," XII, p. 22.

he was willing to concur in the measure which he understood the cabinet had shaped to conform to a District bank, and of this he had thoroughly informed Clay. See Vol. II. p. 54; " Parties and Patronage," p. 116.

The following figures, taken from Stanwood's "History of Presidential Elections," fully refute the claim often made that the Whig party was substantially the same as the old National Republican party. The latter expired in 1832, and most of its members, in the South at least, affiliated with the Democrats.

|  | 1828 | | 1832 | | 1836 | | 1840 | |
|---|---|---|---|---|---|---|---|---|
|  | Dem. | Nat. Rep. | Dem. | Nat. Rep. | Dem. | Whig. | Dem. | W ig |
| Virginia........ | 26,752 | 12,101 | 33,609 | 11,451 | 30,261 | 23,468 | 43,892 | 42,501 |
| North Carolina.. | 37,857 | 13,918 | 24,862 | 4,563 | 26,910 | 23,626 | 33,782 | 46,376 |
| Georgia........ .. | 19,363 | none | 20,750 | none | 22,104 | 24,876 | 31,921 | 40,261 |
| Alabama ........ | 17,138 | 1,938 |  |  | 20,506 | 15,012 | 33,991 | 28,471 |
| Mississippi........ | 6,772 | 1,581 | 5,919 | none | 9,979 | 9,688 | 16,995 | 19,518 |
| Louisiana........ | 4,603 | 4,076 | 4,049 | 2,528 | 3,653 | 3,383 | 7,616 | 11,296 |
| Tennessee....... | 44,293 | 2,240 | 28,740 | 1,436 | 26,129 | 36,168 | 48,289 | 60,396 |

It will be observed that in 1828 and 1832, there was no National Republican party in Georgia. "All in Georgia were Jackson men while Gen. Jackson was in office," says Gov. George R. Gilmer, in his "Georgians," p. 561. The state went Whig in 1836 and 1840, and all the Whigs were necessarily Democrats. Tennessee, which gave only 1,436 to the National Republicans in 1832, gave 36,168 to the Whigs in 1836.

A similar startling change ensued in the other Southern states, and the changes in the North were hardly less significant. In the South it was certainly true that the Whigs were Whigs, because the Democratic party under Van Buren was not Democratic enough—in fact was thoroughly Federalistic and national, causing the true Democrats of Jeffersonian views to revolt and form the Whig party. The Whig party was probably evenly divided between the two old parties, but the weight of Mr. Clay's popularity was sufficient to give the National Republican element the superiority. Most of the old state-rights men were bulldozed by Clay, but Mr. Tyler's estimate of, the number that supported him out of the Whig ranks—150,000—was conservative. (" Parties and Patronage," p. 83.)

The assertion often made that Mr. Tyler's accession to the presidency was unlooked-for is disproved as follows. Duff Green states that he tried to have Mr. Tyler nominated by the Whigs in 1839 as vice-president, since he knew from a personal visit that Harrison's health was gone, and Tyler if made vice-president would be president.

("Parties and Patronage,"65, note 2; Bellford's Magazine, ix, 379—article on "The Nomination of Harrison and Tyler," by Ben E. Green.) On the very day of the nomination ex-president Adams predicted Mr. Tyler's accession ("Recollections of an Old Stager"--Harper's Magazine, 1874). After the nomination, but before the election, the Henrico committee publicly addressed questions to Mr. Tyler as to his course, in the event of Harrison's death--a contingency "by no means extravagant" in case of his election as president "almost at the age of three score and ten years," (I. p. 622). About the same time Mr. L. W. Tazewell, at Mr. Tyler's own house in Williamburg, predicted Mr. Tyler's succession (II. 95, 127). After the election the certainty of the event was accepted by many (II. p. 9, note 2).

The similar assertion that Mr. Tyler took the Whigs by surprise in vetoing the Bank bills is equally absurd. His views before his election were well known, and he had had repeated conversations with Clay and the Whig leaders before the extra-session (II. 54 etc.). If he delayed in sending in his first veto, it was not because he vacillated as to his course, but he told Bell that he wanted "to give time for the excitement to subside," and that "his mind to veto was made up from the first" (Niles, 6: p. 54).

It was also a favorite idea with the Whigs that Mr. Tyler vetoed the Fiscal Corporation because of his pique at Botts' coffee-house letter. But Botts showed that Mr. Tyler had, sometime before his letter came to hand, taken ground against the Bill (Niles, 61, p. 79). The Whig caucus met every night, and Mr. Tyler was kept fully informed of their proceedings (Vol. II., p. 81, note 1; 113). Senator Archer admitted that the Bill violated the decision of the Supreme Court in *Bank of Augusta vs. Earle*, but said that the defect created an unconstitutionality *in futuro* (Cong Globe, 1841. Append. 339; "Parties and Patronage,"124). Schouler,who does not like Southern men,says(Hist. U. S. IV.) that Tyler's objections to the Fiscal Corporation were "cobwebs," but the Whigs deemed them so vital as to refuse to accept them as modifications of their bill, though repeated messages were sent to them before any action was taken on their bill, and Mr. Tyler's friends in the House freely tried to amend the bill on its passage (II., 86, 100). J. Q. Adams who voted against the first bill vetoed, because it had the squint of state assent (Cong Globe 1841, p. 300), voted for the Fiscal Corporation, because it was without it.

The details of the cabinet meeting of Aug. 18 have been continually misrepresented by Schouler. Bell states that he would not pretend to relate "all that Tyler said," and Ewing and Webster were told by the President to aid the Whigs in drafting a bill in conformity with the president's views, but the president cautioned them "not to commit him" and to bring the bill to him for his correction. (Bell's statement, etc.). That Webster did not consider for a moment that the president had parted with his final control over the proposed bill, either in law or conscience, is shown by his note of Aug. 20 (II, p, 86), in which he writes, "if any measure pass, you will be perfectly free to exercise your constitutional power wholly uncommitted, etc." Ewing says that "he heard" the president approved the draft of the bill which was prepared after the cabinet meeting (Niles, 61, p. 331;) in a subsequent letter (Niles, 63) he gave Webster as his informant. But Webster, who certainly was as much concerned as Ewing, declared to Gales and Seaton that he "had not seen sufficient reason for the dissolution of the late cabinet by the voluntary act of its own members" (II. p. 111). Ewing also said in his letter of resignation that the President had approved the cabinet measure (Ewing's bill), but in the next breath declares that the president "may not have read it throughout." The President, in fact, had merely suggested to the cabinet a principle, approved by John W. Eppes in 1814 and by Calhoun and Jackson since and made by Harrison the fundamental condition of his own action (See Rives' speeches, Cong. Globe 1841, Appendix 351, 367). He stood in no way committed to Ewing's draft, and when Clay pronounced it (Ibid, p. 354) "a sickly, imbecile, incompetent local bank," he was at liberty to consider some other proposition· His whole action had been predicated upon the idea that the measure adopted should be satisfactory to the Whigs, and to him personally the feature of local discounting in Ewing's bill was repugnant. He therefore promptly set down upon the proposed revival of a measure, whose purpose could only have been that assigned by Botts in his "coffee house" letter. In view, however, of Clay's opinion of the local character of Ewing's bill, it was far-fetched indeed in Ewing to insist as he did, that the powers of the Fiscal Corporation and his measure were the same. Clay voted for the Fiscal Corporation and voted against Ewing's proposal. In matter of exchanges, Ewing's bill proposed only to employ State banks to transact business in the state "other than local discount" (exchanges); whereas the Fiscal Corporation proposed to create national banks in the States for that purpose—independent of the consent of the states. According to the Whig witnesses, Mr. Tyler was more cautious, if possible, with regard to the Fiscal Corporation than with regard to the first bill vetoed— called the Fiscal Bank of the United States. He insisted that the measure ought not be called a bank in relation to the Union at large, as in its regular banking functions and status it was only a District bank. It was a mere Fiscal Institute with reference to the government. The congress ran counter to the very power the president denied in calling it the Fiscal Corporation of the United States. They attempted to belittle the president by representing him as showing much feeling in various interviews, but their exaggerated statements only served to afford the strongest evidence of the president's intense concern and sincerity.

The assertion that Mr. Tyler was induced by Mr. Wise and others to veto the Bank bills is disproved by Mr. Wise's own statement. He did not hear of Harrison's death till two weeks after it had occurred, and was then in the country canvassing for congress (Cong. Globe, 1842-43, 147). Gilmer was doing the same (II,610, note 1). Mr. Tyler says that "withdrawn from the council of his friends he had but to follow the dictates of his own judgment," (II, 32). When Wise arrived in May, he dispelled at once Wise's *hopes* in favor of the Bank (Cong. Globe 1842-43, 147; also his letter of Dec. 29, 1842 to T. F. Marshall, this volume). Mr. Wise errs as to time and facts regarding his interview, as stated in " Seven Decades," p. 181." But his book was written after a great lapse of time, and without documents. It would seem from the "Seven Decades" that Wise, in this conference, told the President a good deal about his (Wise's) views; but Mr. Gilmer in a letter of May 25, 1841, writes that the president in a conference with him "told him (Gilmer) a good deal about his (the President's) views"—II,705. Mr. Wise told the Whigs, when they taunted him with instigating the President, that they certainly "ought to know the untruth of the charge." "They (Clay and the Whigs) had endeavored to control the president and had been disappointed." (Cong. Globe 1842, p. 916.) The expediency of confining the government to operations in exchanges had long been a favorite one with President Tyler. In his speech in 1834, he dwelt on this feature as the best of the U. S. Bank's operations. The subject was under conversation when Bayard introduced his resolutions in the senate five weeks before the first veto (II. p. 74, 99). Botts intimates that the President early talked to him about just such a measure as he wanted afterwards to make the Fiscal corporation. (Cong. Globe 1841, Append., p. 387). Kennedy quotes Tyler as saying to a Whig delegation that his veto(first veto) would shadow forth a measure "which had *long* been endeared to him." (Statesman's Manual). Hence Wise is certainly wrong in assigning the importance that he does to the interview with Rives (Seven Decades, p. 187). It is also fairly inferable from Wise (ibid p. 188), that he was the first to inform Mr. Tyler of the nature of the draft submitted to Congress by the Whigs and the first to notify the Whig committee having the bill in charge. But the *authorized* statements of the Washington *Madisonian* of October 26 & 27, 1842, and the statement of the president himself show that Mess. Gregg and Williams were first sent to the Whig committee, and that Wise dropping in subsequently he, too, was sent and that this happened "on the evening of the day the bill was introduced into the House of Representatives."

Perhaps what irritated the cabinet more than anything else was Mr. Tyler's refusal to inaugurate the spoils system. Granger, the Postmaster General, finally stated this (Niles, 61, p. 231; "Parties and

Patronage," 68.) He said he indignantly resigned when Mr. Tyler stopped his proscription (Parties &c. p. 69.) Bell was similarly provoked, and Ewing was greatly insulted because Mr. Tyler restored certain officers he had removed (Ibid. 71.) And yet in a letter dated September 5, 1841(MS.) Ewing warmly recommends to the President the appointment of two Whigs to office!

Schouler says that Tyler, in offering to retire at the end of his term, only showed that "his mind attached an importance to the sacrifice," and " at all events the impulse to stand aside shifted more quickly than the desire to gain credit for it." But a letter of Mr. Clay in my possession, written to Waddy Thompson, dated 23 April, 1841, imputes this ambition of an election to Mr. Tyler and the charge was generally endorsed by the Whig press. It was because *they* attached an importance to it that Mr. Tyler made the proposal. He put "the darling idea " into the power of his enemies, and Schouler ought to have been generous enough to give him credit for it. Mr. Tyler, it is true, subsequently accepted a nomination from his friends, but the state of things had been entirely changed. Tyler had certainly as much sense as some (!) of his critics and knew that he had " no chance," and so told many; but he held the balance of power and used it successfully to prevent the election of Van Buren and to compel the recognition of his friends. (II.337-350; "Parties and Patronage;" letters in this volume.) Mr. Tyler did not withdraw, because he saw " no chance " of an election. That fact he had recognized from the first, but he withdrew because he had accomplished his objects. Birney, who had not as many friends as Tyler, continued in the field, but is it logical to infer that he did so because he had no chance? The Whig slander fizzled out, when they described Mr. Tyler as instigating certain letters to the *New York Herald.* But for these rumors there has never been adduced the slightest authority, and in fact the rumors were absolutely false.

Mr. Tyler had first suggested to his cabinet a scheme of Banking, originating with Judge Nathaniel Beverley Tucker of Williamsburg. When they rejected this, he suggested to them the scheme of a Bank of the District of Columbia. As he stated in his inaugural, he intended to leave the character of the measure to congress, but this did not prevent him in private from suggesting general constitutional principles. Congress called upon the secretary of the treasury, Mr. Ewing, and he reported a bill which was rejected by Mr. Clay. Mr. Tyler throughout sought to please the Whigs in the plans proposed; after the adjournment of the extra-session he embodied his own ideas of finance in the exchequer bill. (II,129, 133, 249), which Mr. Webster (II, 133), and Sir Horsley Palmer, late president of the Bank of England (Lippincott's Mag., March, 1888), enthusiastically approved. Lincoln and Chase afterwards took up the plan and adopted its leading ideas—the central board and agencies, but substituted private banks for government offices in the states—a change by no means desirable. In the management of the finances or of the post-office, the Government needs numerous local agencies; but there is no necessity that every country post-office should be run by a corporation, and there is likewise no need that the fiscal agencies should be other than government agencies.

Extract from the speech of William C. Rives in the senate Aug. 19, 1841, Cong: Globe, Append. 367.

"I am firmly impressed with the belief, Mr. President, that if Gen. Harrison was now living &c., he would never yield his sanction to the establishment of branches of such a corporation as this bill proposes within the limits of the states, without their free, unshackled assent. * * * I will state that I have been informed that the assent of the states to branches within their limits was a favorite and fundamental idea with him in the organization of such an institution. This information, at least, has been communicated to me by gentlemen who stood in relations of the most intimate confidence with General Harrison, one of whom was a member of the committee who came to this city to perform the melancholy duty of attending the remains of the deceased President to their final resting place at North Bend.'·

Hon. Henry W. Hilliard, a whig from Georgia, who served many years in Congress and filled various positions in the diplomatic service of the United States, says in his 'Politics and Pen Pictures:' "The name of John Tyler had a charm for the Southern people. His single vote stands recorded against 'The Force Bill,' other Southern senators having withdrawn from the serate chamber. Mr. Tyler's high name among the statesmen of Virginia gave him consideration before the meeting of the Harrisburg Convention, and after his nomination he advanced rapidly in public favor. His personal appearance was very attractive; six feet in height, spare and active, his movements displayed a natural grace, and his manner was cordial but dignified. His head was fine, the forehead high and well developed, the aquiline nose and brilliant eye giving to his expression the eagle aspect, which distinguished him at all times and especially in conversation. His frankness imparted an indescribable charm to his manners, and the rich treasure of his cultivated mind displayed itself without effort or ostentation in the senate chamber, and in conversation he surpassed even Mr. Calhoun. His loyalty to his friends was as true as that of General Jackson. * * Mr. Tyler was as bold as Mr. Clay in making his opinions known in regard to measures affecting the administration of the government. * * He was one of the most fascinating men I had ever known—brilliant, eloquent, even more charming than Mr. Calhoun in conversation."

# Letters, &c.

[The following preamble and resolutions were adopted, on the motion of Gov. Tyler, by the Executive Council in Richmond. The original paper in his handwriting, along with a note from Thomas W. Gilmer, is still in the State archives. Gilmer's note runs: "Charlottesville, July 4th, 3 o'clock p. m., To the Editor of the Enquirer, Richmond, Virginia. Thomas Jefferson died today 10 minutes before one o'clock P. M. Yours in great haste. Thomas W. Gilmer."]

*Council Book* "Thursday, 6th July, 1826.

Present: Governor Tyler,

| | |
|---|---|
| Mr. Daniel, | Mr. Campbell, |
| Mr. Pendleton, | Mr. Colton, |
| Mr. Scott, | and |
| Mr. Botts, | Mr. Le Grand. |

Whereas it is made known to the Executive Department that Thomas Jefferson, the distinguished benefactor to his Country, departed this life on the 4th inst.—and this Department being impressed with a deep sense of the great loss which Virginia, the Union and the world at large have sustained in the death of this Philosopher, Statesman, Patriot, and Philanthropist—and whereas a sense of what we owe to the present, and all future generations, and not merely a regard to our own feelings, which of themselves would prompt us to the measure, requires at the hands of this Department a manifestation by all means in its power of respect for the memory of one whose whole life has been passed in unceasing devotion to the advancement of human happiness, and the establishment of Liberty on a sure and lasting foundation.——

Inspired by these sentiments, and impressed with the regret which the occasion is so well calculated to produce, we, the Governor and Council of the State of Virginia, do resolve as follows:

1. That the Hall of the House of Delegates, the Senate Chamber, and the Executive Chamber be hung in mourning together with the main entrances to the Capitol.

2. That the Bell in the Guard house be tolled through-the day.

3. That minute guns be fired from one hour of the sun of this day until the going down of the same.

4. That we will wear badges of mourning for one month, and that we recommend the same to all the Officers of the Government.

5. That we will cheerfully unite with our Fellow Citizens in any other measure of respect and veneration for the memory of the deceased.

It is advised that the foregoing preamble and resolutions be entered on the Journal of the Council.

A. L. Botts,[1]  P. V. Daniel,
W. F. Pendleton,  Robert G. Scott,
Samuel Colton,  Nash Le Grand."

———

TO JOHN RUTHERFOORD.[2]

Washington, February 23, 1829.
Dear Sir;

I learn not only from the newspapers, but from various private sources, that I am thought of as one of the representatives of the Richmond District in the Convention, and I take the liberty of frankly, but at the same time *confidentially*, making known to you my wishes on the subject.

I am everything but desirous of being in it. You have already, in the mere effort to afford facilities to the people, witnessed a severe struggle for political power between the upper and lower country. How much more violent is that struggle destined to be in the Convention! Does it become me, representing as I here do the interest of the whole State[3] to become a party in this contest? And yet this seems to be inevitable if I go into the Convention, representing as I should a tide-water district, the feelings and sentiments of

———

(1). Son of Benjamin Botts and brother of John Minor Botts.

(2). John Rutherfoord was first captain of the Richmond Fayette Artillery and became colonel of the Regiment. He was a member of the house of delegates, and in 1840, was lieutenant governor of Virginia, and, upon the resignation of Gov. T.W.Gilmer, presided for a year as governor. He continued the constant friend of Mr. Tyler and died at Richmond in July, 1866, aged 74. His son, John, was a promising young statesman who died early. John Rutherfoord, the latter's son, practices law in Richmond.

(3). Mr. Tyler was U. S. senator when he wrote this letter Despite his objections he was elected to the convention (1829.-'30)

which are well known to me, and which probably is destined
under any new arrangement to lose more than any other district in the State.  Would it be becoming in me, having always reference to the station which I hold, to enter into local
contests or political warfare with any of my constituents?
My situation is *sui generis* and ought to shut me out from that
assembly.

I have also strong private considerations operating upon
me.  In the first place, my health has been very bad and has
confined me a prisoner to my room for the last four weeks;
and, although I shall resume my seat in the Senate on the
first favorable change in the weather, I have not yet been
able to do so.  In the second place, my domestic affairs require all the attention I can bestow upon them.  Now I shall
have to leave home the 1st of Dec$^r$ not to return for 5 or 6
months, and if to that time be· added 2 months in the Convention, I become literally a stranger to my own household.

What then can be done to keep me out?  It can only be
done, it appears to me, through the instrumentality of some
of my particular friends among whom I rank yourself. Might
not arguments be urged to the members from the district by
yourself and Christian calculated to satisfy them, without my
being seen in it?  Nay, might not a ticket be agreed on by
you from which my name should be excluded?  I rely
upon your friendship which has so repeatedly been manifested ts me  Converse with Christian[1] ,and write me shortly.

I have said that I did not desire my own wishes or views
to be made known.  The reasons are obvious.  I do not wish
to manifest an indifference or repugnance to the public will,
which if once *openly declared* I must and will obey.  This is
the principle which has always governed me, and to which I
have always submitted.  To manifest openly, however, a disinclination to be in the Convention might be tortured by my
enemies into a fear of responsibility, etc., etc.  If this thing
be not arrested before I reach home, I fear it will be too late

---

(1).  John B. Christian, brother-in-law of Mr. Tyler, was son of
Robert Christian, who served as United States presidential elector.
John B. was a member of the house of delegates, judge of the general court, and of the supreme court.  He is not mentioned in Appleton's "Cyclopedia of Biography."

to move in it. My friends must manage it in my absence, otherwise if there be a settled design to run me, I fear it will be too late to arrest it. Yourself and Christian are the only persons to whom I have communicated these views, and whatever you decide upon will be satisfactory to me.

The cabinet arrangements are confidently spoken of— Van Buren, Secretary of State—Ingham of the Treasury-- Branch of the Navy,—Eaton, P. M. General; and Berrien, Attorney General. Mr. Tazewell is spoken of as Minister to England, and Floyd has been offered the Gov$^t$ of Arkansas, but declines it.

> Very truly,
> Yr. Frd..
> JOHN TYLER.

———

TO JOHN RUTHERFOORD.

March 14, 1830.

My Dear Sir:

Your letter of the 4$^{th}$ Inst. has remained thus long unanswered in consequence of the long arrear of correspondence in which I found myself involved by reason of the late day at which I arrived here. You are certainly amongst those whose letters I would most promptly acknowledge.

In reply to your enquiries as to the course which Congress will pursue in relation to the U. States Bank during its present session, I have to say that I have not heard a single intimation so far thrown out of any intention to intermeddle with the subject, nor do I believe that it is intended by any one to introduce any such measure. A bill is before the Senate prescribing punishment for forging its notes and out of that may possibly arise some incidental discussion If introduced or whenever hereafter introduced, the fate of the Bank will be decided not so much upon its merits, as with the view to the political advancement of some aspiring politician. I shall enter into no such view, but it is lamentably certain that all measures do now partake, more or less, of that aspect. There remains no prospect of change in this respect save through the action of the people themselves, and I confess to you that I almost despair of even this. Sectional cupidity is so strongly appealed to, and avarice is so controlling a passion of the human heart that it will be difficult, almost in the extreme, to overcome its seductive influences.

There is nothing sound in the state of parties here, you may rely upon it; and never have I seen more distinctly displayed the want of some convenient cement to bind men together. We still hold together, it is true, in the expression of partiality for the President, but that is all. He cannot be considered as standing at the head of a *party*, for in truth he has none. A Kentuckian is ready to denounce him if he yields aught to our constitutional scruples, and so are the Pennsylvanians, etc. etc., while the South sustains him from the fear of greater ill under the auspices of another.

The opposition is united to a man and will carry on the most unsparing warfare. They produce the effect, which may be salutary, of holding our heterogeneous materials together. Grundy in his speech announced the President as a candidate for re-election. What think you of it? I want peace for the country if it can be procured, a short rest from politcal intrigues. Will his re-election be calculated to produce this? I *have* inclined to the opinion that the President should only hold on for one term, because his first term seemed to me to be devoted to a system of electioneering to secure his re-election. But the evils on the other hand are equally appalling. So many Richmonds take the field now-a-days, and so many schemes are put afloat, that the proper decision on this point is difficult to be made—At this time too the country is peculiarly excited by the alarmists and fanatics, anti-Sunday mail, anti–masonic, abolition societies, and last, tho' not least, the sympathy and mock sensibility attempted to be created on behalf of the Southern Indians, all conspiring to one end, viz.: the overthrow of Jackson and the elevation of Clay. My own decided opinion is that Clay never was so formidable as at this moment. Kentucky will go to him *en masse* and probably the whole West, while New England would give but one voice and that in his favor. Let me have your views freely, fully, and in the same spirit of confidence in which you have mine.

The rumors which have reached you relative to the etiquette observed amongst the *grandees* is unfortunately true to a great extent, but there is less of mock majesty and state at the President's house, than I have ever before seen in the same mansion. The President has none of it. My reception at his dinner party was kind and hospitable, and, would *you old fashioned Virginian believe it?* he even went so far as *to in-*

*troduce his guests to each other*, a thing without precedent here
and *most abominably unfashionable.* At dinner he seemed to
me to have laid aside the royal diadem, and to have fancied
himself at the Hermitage, such was his unrestrained freedom
his unaffected deportment. All satisfied me that I stood in
the presence of an old fashioned republican, who, whenever and
in whatever he could, laid aside the affectation of high life.
If his measures be not as popular as his manners, the fault
lies elsewhere than at his own door. This I most potently
believe; and if ruin awaits him, the true cause thereof will be
found to lie in the circumstance of his having leaned too
much on *favorites.* This will be my commentary, and history
furnishes me the lights by which to make it.

With the tender of my best respects to Mrs. Rutherfoord,

I am Dr Sr,

Truly and faithfully yrs,

JOHN TYLER.

———

TO W. F. PENDLETON [1]

Washington, Jan. 19, 1833.

My Dear Sir:

Your letter of the 16th enclosing Mayo's pamphlet reached me this morning—my thanks are due to you for
this manifestation of your kindness. Your conduct upon
the occasion and the opinions you express are such as I should
have expected of an high-minded Virginian. As to the author
of this miserable pamphlet I simply regard him as an instrument in the hands of others to consummate a design long since
formed of supplying my place here after the 4th of March by
one whose opinions will be made to bend to the policy of the
hour whatsoever that policy may be—I leave him and his
co-workers in the hands of my very worthy and approved
good masters, the members of the General Assembly.
This I will however say that shortly after the President came
into power and after Mr. Tazewell and myself had taken our
stand against the appointment of *Editors by the Score* to office,
this man repeatedly called upon me in order to eke out an

———

(1) W. F. Pendleton was one of Mr. Tyler's Council in 1826, and
an original Crawford man. With Botts, Upshur and many of the
leading Democrats in Virginia, he left the party in 1833.

intimation that, if he were nominated to office, I would sustain him. Having failed in his efforts and resting under the belief doubtless, that his chance of success would be increased by my eviction, he does all in his power to accomplish it,—whether he hopes to recommend himself to those in high station by pursuing this course, I have no means of determining. He is at this time a Clerk in one of the public offices.

With equal promptitude I respond to your enquiries as to my opinions of *the doctrines* of the proclamation. The answer may be found in the history of my past life. I have been reared in the belief that the Gov't was founded on compact to which sovereign States were the parties—in the strongest devotion to the great and enduring principles of the report and resolutions of 1798-9, and if I have in a single instance in a course of public service of more than 20 years departed from them, such instance is unknown to me. When therefore the President requires of me to admit that this is *a unit gov't.*—a *social* and not a *conventional* system—that the people of all the Union acting as *one community*, and not the *States* acting as *separate* communities, adopted the constitution—that I am not the representative of Virginia, but of Rhode Island &c. &c.—that all my allegiance is due to this gov't. and that to Virginia I owe none—whatever may be the consequences personally to myself I say nay to these doctrines, esteeming them as I honestly do when carried into practice, subversive of all that I have ever considered as dear and sacred. If I stand alone in opposition to them, I am ready to abide my fate, and if that fate be perpetual banishment I care but little on my own account.

I would sooner desire the character of him who was called "Ultimus Romanorum" than the oily and supple Anthony. I oppose in every form in which the question may arise, the consolidation of the empire. History furnishes no example of a republic stretching its power unrestrained and unshackled over such an extent of territory as the U. States and preserving liberty. Our fathers would never have ratified such a system as is sufficiently proven by the numerous limitations which they have imposed upon the Gov't, as it exists. As I have lived so will I die in the avowal of the opinion that this Gov't is *federal* not *national*, a Gov't of league *inter pares* and not a consolidated Gov't of one community.

These opinions are expressed without restraint upon the use you make of them. I would be willing to utter them in the full presence of the General Assembly, and shall, while I remain here, vindicate them in the best way that I may be able; for I feel a deep conviction that upon their maintenance depends the preservation of American liberty.

With sentiments of high respect,

I am D^r Sir,

Y^r most ob^t Serv^t,

JOHN TYLER.

---

TO GEN. WM. F. GORDON [1]

Gloucester, Nov. 6th, 1834,

My Dear General :

I am but a day ago from the North, where I left the advocates of Presidential power shouting their loudest huzzas at the result of the New York election. Will you believe me when I declare to you that I was half inclined to join them, and my object in writing you is to tell you the reason. My visit to the North and East fully satisfied me that, if New York declared against Van Buren, Webster would at once be proclaimed candidate for the Presidency.

The South would not have entertained him, and the consequence would have been great danger to the Union. With political designs, the tariff would have been revived, and the slave question would probably have been moved in relation to the District. At all events we should either (I mean the South) have been thrown into the arm of some other N. or W. man, or the contest which would have arisen would have excited a feeling of hostility between the sections. This election avoids these contingences. Webster is driven from the field, and the whole North is in a state of despair.

---

(1) Gen. Gordon was, at this time, a member of Congress—a position he held from 1829 to 1835. It was during this year that he suggested the Sub-treasury scheme, afterwards taken up by the Democrats. He was an original Crawford man, and agreed with Mr. Tyler in condemning Jackson for the principles of his proclamation against South Carolina. In 1837, when Calhoun returned from the Whigs to the Democrats, Gordon went with him. He died in Albemarle Co., July 2, 1858. Armistead C. Gordon, late Mayor of Staunton and James L. Gordon of New York are his grandsons.

What are the prospects from the West? Equally bad The great Middle States are for Van Buren—rely upon that. Ohio and Kentucky are with us, while Indiana and Illinois will either go to Van Buren or support R. M. Johnson. In one word *no Bank man* can be elected. Every day will go farther and farther to establish this.

What then is the prospect before us? Absolutely one of gloom, unless a Southern man can be found who will unite the whole South, and thereby ensure to himself the support of all the Anti–Van Buren States. I say all the opposition states—and I say it with full knowledge that these states every where will now rally on the strongest man. Who then can unite the whole South? I have brought myself to think that Gov. Tazewell is that very man. Maryland waits but a nomination—perhaps she may move in advance with one of her counties, and at an early day. N. C and S. C. will rally to him I have no doubt, Georgia will not forget the steady and able advocate of her rights, when she most required an advocate; while Alabama and Mississippi will recollect that he is the first public man who ever proposed a reduction in the public lands, while Virginia, if her people are wise, will and ought to unite upon him as affording the means of bringing toge ther the old States-rights party whichthe proclamation separated,

What say you, my dear Sir, to these speculations? I am sanguine a decided move is all that is required. The North and East are panic struck, and all men avow their readiness to unite on my "Gentleman." I mentioned Tazewell to a Pennsylvanian, Kentuckian, and Marylander. They snatched at the suggestion. I should not be surprised if he is named in some public journal of each of these states forthwith. No matter where his name may be first brought out, it will spread like lightning—that is my opinion. Is there then cause for despondency? What if recent events shall ultimate as I predict—shall I not be right in saying that I felt disposed to join in the huzza? I asked myself to whom shall I address my notions—and I sat down to address you. I felt that you would even indulge me in a delusion, if you should so consider it, so full of pleasing anticipations for the Country and the liberty of the human race. I know I need not ask you to meditate on these things, but I will request you to show this

MARTHA JEFFERSON TYLER,
(Sister of President Tyler and wife of
Thomas E. Waggaman.)

to Gilmer, should it fall in your way; and if you think it well,
cause to be thrown out some suggestions in the Charlottesville
paper. When we meet in Washington, we will talk more at
large.

Y<sup>rs</sup> Most Truly,

J. TYLER.

---

TO W. F. PENDLETON.

October 27, 1836

My Dear Sir:

Your letter of the 14<sup>th</sup> reached me by the last mail
and I delay not to acknowledge it. Upon retiring from the
Senate and looking into my private affairs, I found them in
such utter disorder as to require my unremitting and undi-
vided attention. Hence I have been closely at home all the
summer and fall. In this I have but shared the fate of all
others who like myself have made themselves a voluntary
sacrifice to public service for the entire period of their man-
hood. My political opponents( enemies I will not call them )
are therefore entitled to my thanks for having allowed me a
fit season to put my house in order. Do not believe for a
moment, however, that I have been a listless observer of passing events. On the contrary, when I have seen a President
descend from the lofty eminence of being the representative
of a great confederacy to enter the dirty arena of politics and
throw himself forward as the most prominent advocate of
one of the aspirants to the succession, and then have the
affrontery to *breathe* the name of Jefferson, I have asked myself if it were possible that the Virginia people could pocket
the insult thus offered to their understanding. When, too, the
secretary of the Treasury has dared to issue an order declaring in effect that the currency of Virginia should not be received in exchange for the very lands granted by Virginia
in her munificence to the Gen'l Gov't, and witnessed the perfect apathy with which the edict has been received, I confess to you my D<sup>r</sup> Sir, that feelings and thoughts have
come over me which I had never expected to experience. I
have not, therefore, been listless, altho' in some measure
buried at home. As to the V. P., I scarcely permit it to

trouble me.[1]    The late elections are all auspicious to me personally.   The loss of Pennsylvania to the Whigs augments my chance of success by rendering it probable that, if there be no election by the people, I may be one of *the two* returned to the Senate, in which event without chicanery, my chance is best.   Ohio has gone against the Baltimore nominees with a strong hand, and if the Virginia vote be cast for me and that vote be sustained by the South, then my individual cause is neither desperate or hopeless.   In this region of the state many Van Buren votes will be given me merely as a matter of preference.   They do not believe themselves warranted in throwing away their votes, which they w$^d$ do by voting for Smith.   But be assured that I am entirely prepar'd for any result which may transpire, and when it is all over, as it will be shortly, what then is to be my future course?   This comes up to your enquiries; and in reply I have to say, that I am in the hands of the States rights party; that to the end of my life I will war against the consolidationists, and that, whether I battle it as a common soldier in the ranks or as one of the officers, my only battle-cry will be "Virginia, a free and independent State, a voluntary member of a great confederacy."   Whether, therefore, I shall be run next winter for the Senate or not, I leave to the members of that party to determine.   Nothing should be done but on full advisement and consultation, and the rally once made must be persevered in, to the end.   We shall constitute next winter but a small nucleus, which the perpetuity of our institutions requires us to maintain and cherish.   I cannot say half that I would to you in a letter, but must see you in Richmond, if possible, before Legislative action shall occur.   I regret to learn from you that Patton[2] is not heartily with us.   We should have had no difficulty in the State, if he had gone with us on the Deposit question.   He is too honest a man to answer the purposes of the spoils men.

----

(1) Mr. Tyler was at this time the candidate of the Whigs south for vice-president.   The statement made in my biography of him, that "the Democratic party was not Democratic enough," for the State-rights men is shown by this letter to be true.

(2) John M. Patton, in congress from 1830 to 1838, acting governor in 1840, subsequently judge of the court of appeals.   He died in 1858.

The only effect of his course has been to put down his friends and build up his enemies, and yet I am sure he would have had it otherwise. For him I entertain the warmest regard and love, as one of our most promising men.

I write you in haste,

Truly Y<sup>rs</sup>,

JOHN TYLER,

----

TO HENRY A. WISE.

Gloucester Place, January 23, 1837.

My D<sup>r</sup> Sir :

I have watch'd with no small interest the pro_ceedings of "the party" on the subject of the Tariff, and I have felt the deepest anxiety that the *Southerners* should fall into Cambreling's move, and loudly demand the reduction of the duties. When I voted for the Compromise Act, I did so in the best faith. I was firmly convinced that the reduct-ion was rapid enough, for altho' the manufacturing interest had greatly violated the rights of the South, and had brought us near to civil war, yet I felt as an American, and was there-fore well dispos'd to let down the system by slow degrees. Seven years were ask'd for, and with others I readily granted it. I well remember the opposition then made. It came precise-ly from the quarter which now proposes a most rapid stride. Look, I pray you, to Wright's speech in the Senate. He had ten substantial objections to the Act. See the floundering of the party on the subject of coarse woolens. See in short the numerous efforts made to defeat the measure. The truth is the party went for force and for the tariff [1]. I boarded with Gov. Dickerson who held us out at arm's length. He would

----

[1] When Van Buren, in 1828. voted for the "tariff of abominations," Senator Tazewell, of Virginia, said to him in the senate: "Sir, you have deceived me once; that was your fault; but if you deceive me again the fault will be mine." Calhoun, in 1837, retorted this sentiment on Silas Wright, "as the author of the tariff of 1832" (Debates 1836-'37, p 910). John Quincy Adams said that, as chairman of the committee of manufactures, he had carried through the Tariff Act of 1832 "in per-fect concert" with the Jackson administration. (Niles, 63, p. 172.) This tariff of 1832 reduced the rates on the revenue articles, but increased those on the protected.

make no concession, not the slightest. [1] And now this is
the party which moves for reduction, instant, rapid reduction.
They represent Pennsylvania, N. York, Maine, Connecticut,
New Hampshire, Rh. Island, a majority of the Manufacturing
States, and I would put their sincerity to the test. The South
should make loud calls upon them to press forward. Let us
test their sincerity. If they are sincere, we advance our interests by an instantaneous repeal. If they are not, we expose
them in all the nakedness of depravity. Cambreling's bill
should be considered as the first measure of the session. But
mark! it is a mere feint. They mean, if possible, to confine
the sale of public lands to actual settlers, and the revenues
from imposts will be found not more than sufficient to meet
their economical expenditures, and then the tariff must stand.
I want the *pea-viners* expos'd, if indeed they are *pea-vining* it.

A word to you *confidentially*. I see you have Reuben M.
Whitney in hand. Now, if you could get a view of his account
at the Bank of Metropolis, you would be *edified*. You know
I was on the D. Bank committee. I can disclose no secrets of
my prison house. But Kent and Southard and King of
Alabama were on that committee also. Moreover, the agreement between that Bank and the Treasury will shew you that
the pay of an *agent* was stipulated for on the part of the Bank
—its proportional part. These hints are for youself exclusively. If you can make them available without the use of
my name, I shall be pleased.

One word about the past. The double shotted ticket [2]
killed us. Added to the fact that our leading presses play'd
altogether for the Northern States. They substantially drop-
p'd Judge White, and took up Harrison. This caus'd the thin
turn out in tide-water Virginia, and lost us the vote of North
Carolina. I remonstrated, but the course could not be
altered. You were right and I wrong. If our mountaineers
could have been taught wisdom by defeat, we should have carried the entire South. It is too late now, however, according

---

(1) Mahlon Dickerson was one of Jackson's leading supporters,
but admitted that $12,000,000 was annually abstracted from the South
under the tariff law—I., p. 441.

(2) the following is the " Union ticket " voted by the Whigs in
Virginia, in 1836. Judge White was an old Jackson man, put up by
the Whigs of the South, but the Northern Whigs were for Harrison,

to the old adage, to lock the stable door. We must look to
the future, and there our vision is limited by darkness. I fear
that no union can be form'd between us and the latitudinari‚
ans of the North—but *Nous verrons*.

With sentiments of the highest regard,

I am truly Y

John Tyler.

Hon H. A. Wise,

P. S. My respects to Judge White[(1)] and Peyton,

———

who was not so publicly committed to the States rights doctrines of
Anti-Bank, anti-Tariff &c.

" The People Against Official Dictation.

REPUBLICAN

Whig Ticket.

FOR PRESIDENT.

Hugh Lawson White. *of Tennessee*

OR

William Henry Harrison, *of Ohio*

As the vote for the one or the other may prevent an
  election by the House of Representatives, and secure
  a choice by the people.
The first, a Republican of the old Virginia School—
  of mature wisdom—upright, honest, inflexible—and
  of great experience in public affairs.
The second, a Virginian by birth and education; attached to her principles and institutions—a gallant defend-
  er of his country in the field, and an experienced
  statesman.

FOR VICE-PRESIDENT

That tried Republican Statesman and Patriot,

John Tyler, *of Virginia*.

———

  "The recent demonstrations of public sentiment in-
scribe, on the list of executive duties, in characters too
legible to be overlooked, the task of reform; which
will require, particularly, the correction of those abuses
that have brought the *patronage of the Federal Government* in conflict with the *freedom of elections*."

[*Jackson' Inaugural Address*.]

Williamsburg, Dec. 26,<sup>th</sup> 1838

My Dear Sir :

Your letter of the 22d, is now before me; and as well for the promptitude with which you answered mine of the 19<sup>th</sup> as for the readiness with which you yielded to my request, be pleas'd to accept my thanks.  I hope Col. McCandish will be permitted to walk over the turf without a formidable competitor, altho' we had some talk of Poulson's intention to be a candidate.  There is, however, no annunciation of him in the public press.

Turning from this to other subjects, I am highly gratified to have it in my power to say that Mr. Coke<sup>(1)</sup> has no intention of opposing your re-election.  He has long made me his confidant in the matter, and from the first he has laugh'd at the idea of *his* lending himself to that party to which he was

---

Electors for President and Vice President;
William R Johnson, of Chesterfield,
John Urquhart, of Southampton,
William Collins, of Norfolk County,
Mark Alexander, of Mecklenburg.
Allen Wilson, of Cumberland.
James Saunders, of Campbell,
Joseph Martin, of Henry,
Robert McCandlish, of York,
William P. Taylor, of Caroline,
Robert W. Carter, of Richmond County,
Chapman Johnson, Richmond City,
William F. Gordon, of Albemarle,
John L. Marye, of Spotsylvania,
John Janney, of Loudoun,
Charles J. Faulkner, of Berkeley,
John B. D. Smith. of Frederick,
Joseph Cravens, of Rockingham,
Brisco G. Baldwin, of Augusta,
Henry Erskine, of Greenbrier,
John P. Matthews, of Wythe,
Robert Beattie, of Smythe,
Joel Shrewsbury, of Kanawha,
Moses W. Chapline, of Ohio."

(1) Richard Coke, a Jackson man in 1828, a nullifier in 1833, a Whig in 1838, &c.  Born Nov. 16, 1790; died March 31, 1851.

formerly obnoxious, and which would use him for no other purpose than to obtain your defeat, and who would speedily be brought, if he were elected, to look out for an oponent to him.  The solicitations seem to proceed from the administration gentry of Mathews and Gloucester.  To the first, he responded some weeks ago.  To the last, he is, I believe, preparing a response designed to be published—Rely upon it that from him "the party" will receive no countenance in this move but the mere externals of civility.  *We here* are warmly for you, and among *us* I include Mr. Coke's own brother, who is one of our most respectable citizens.

As to Mr. Rives and his movements, I have long been appriz'd of the billing and cooing which was going on between him and some of the prominent members of the Whig party.  This had its origin as far back as last winter— but I have not believ'd, until very lately, that any serious impression could be made by him upon our ranks.  There is a large mass of the Whig party in this State, who have gone in all sincerity for what they protess to go for, viz. an abridgement of the executive powers.  They recognized in Mr. Rives one who sustained Gen'l Jackson in all his high handed usurpations and openly proclaimed the doctrine that the executive power was a unit, and who sustain'd that unit even unto the point of blotting out the just censure of the Senate, for his most daring and inexcusable conduct.  Mr. Rives is, therefore, obnoxious to them, and altho' matters may be so arrang'd as to re-elect him, yet I doubt not that the gain of Conservative support will be counterbalanced by the loss of Whig votes at the polls. I shall, however, be a vigilant observer of the scenes of the winter, and trust to get through them without either compromitting my principles or experiencing harm.  Be assured that I shall take all things patiently and smoothly, and resting upon the people, who I know are with me, bear myself accordingly.[1]

As to Harrison or Clay, I await the decision of the convention to meet at Harrisburg.  With both I have been very well acquainted.  The first was born within seven miles of my birth-place, and the last within 20.  They are both Patriots.  The last undoubtedly most highly distinguished by his

---

[1] See Vol. I, 588; letter to Thomas R. Dew is printed as written in 1836.  It ought to be 1839.

talents, and who, amid numerous errors, has yet contrived to build for himself a fame which will greatly outlast the times in which we live. I have admired him always, and he knows it.[1] The first is a noble scion of a patriotic stock, whose family connections in Virginia are among the numbers of my best friends. Mr. Clay is undeservedly obnoxious to many in the Whig ranks While Tom Ritchie held sway, he poisoned the public mind against him. He taught the Demagogues to declaim against him and to slander him. For saying this some years ago, that same Tom Ritchie clapp'd his hands and set the pack on me. For a time they bark'd most furiously, but in the end they gave up the business upon that score, and open'd upon other scents. So goes the world—the political world at least. But the prejudices then engendered against M^r Clay still have their influence over the minds of many.

As to the Vice Presidency, I dream not that any Southern man with *Southern principles* is to be selected This has already been tested in my own case[2] My election was certain if Northern and Western men had come to my aid. I saw that they would not, nor will they now assist any Southern man to that station. Be assured that I look not to it, nor to any honor which does not lie in the gift of the people of Virginia. If honor comes to me from any other quarter, it comes unlook'd for.

Of one thing be you assur'd, that I am with you and for you always. The task which you have before you is full of difficulty. I can only say to you in the language of our State motto, *perseverando*—and wishing you health and happiness, and tendering you the salutation of the season,

I am truly and faithfully y^rs,

JOHN TYLER.

---

(1) Mr. Clay won the gratitude of the South by ~~his~~ introducing the compromise tariff, which was followed by his surrender of the bank "as a practical question" and of internal improvements His leading supporters for the presidency were Southern men and original Democrats. Among the Democrats were Tyler, Leigh, Botts, Bell, Lewis McLane (Jackson's former Secretary of State); nullifiers like Waddy Thomson, William C Preston, Gen. Duff Green, George R. Poindexter, &c, The North used Scott as *a tertium quid* to defeat his nomination. I. 593; "Parties and Patronage," p. 62.

(2) Mr. Tyler refers to his nomination for the vice-presidency, in 1836.

TO HENRY CLAY.
Williamsburg, Sept. 18, 1839.

Dear Sir,

In conversation with a friend of mine a few days ago, in which you were chiefly spoken of, he made his advocacy of you in the coming Presidential election to turn principally on the point of your opinion in relation to the power of removal from office. I informed him that I had over and over again heard your opinions expressed in debate upon that question, and that I had no hesitation in stating that you were decidedly against the power as an original question, and against its exercise as practiced by the last and present administrations, and in proof of this referred him to the register of debates. He said that he regarded it as a matter so intimately connected with the preservation of free government, that he could not and would not trust a reported speech, since that might have received the interpretation of the reporters and could not therefore be relied upon with accuracy; but went on to remark that if I could write you and receive from you a clear but succinct exposition of your opinions on this question, and it corresponded with my statement, he would not only support you but do all in his power to advance your election. He is a man of decided influence, and is now the Delegate to the Legislature from this district. Do I request of you too much in asking of you a few lines upon this subject? Your letter will only be used to satisfy the gentleman referred to, whose good opinion it is highly important to conciliate. I do not doubt his full and unconditional redemption of his pledge.

There is another matter to which I desire to invite your attention as much for my own gratification as to enable me to satisfy others. I remember that in a day or two after the proclamation was issued, I waited upon you, believing as I firmly did that you were the only man in the Union who, at that perilous moment, had influence enough to save the Union. The conversation turned on the Proclamation, and you unhesitatingly pronounced it *ultra-federal black cockade* (1) (I

---

(1) Mr. Clay began political life as a supporter of Mr. Jefferson. When with Mr. Adams he formed the National Republican party in 1828, he claimed to be a true Jeffersonian. He called the Democrats "Federalists," and in 1833 denounced the heresy, advanced by Jackson in his proclamation, of a consolidated people, "as ultra Federal black cockade."

use your language.)  You afterwards expressed to me your dissatisfaction with the Force Bill; and when afterwards you declared in the Senate that had you been present, you would have voted for it, am I mistaken in the fact that, in a conversation afterwards with me, you ascribed that declaration to the circumstance that the Northern members required you to make it as the condition of their support of the compromise Bill?  I have frequently so stated it.  I bear in distinct recollection your antipathy to the measure, as is fully evidenced by the fact that your compromise Bill made it a dead letter. In short, I have never heard you do other than declare that the govt. was the creature of the States, a compact among equals, and when we have differed it has been more in construing the constitution than on fundamental principles.  Thus have I always regarded you as a republican of the old school on principle—who had indulged, when the public good seemed to require it, somewhat too much in a broad interpretation to suit our Southern notions.

If any apology is neccessary for this intrusion on your time, ascribe it solely to the great solicitude I feel for your elevation to the presidency.  You are aware of my position in this part of Virginia, where nine in ten are what are called states-rights men.  It is natural for me to desire to arm myself fully for the approaching conflict,—while, you may be assured, that nothing that you may communicate will ever be used to your prejudice.

One word more—I have but just returned from the North where I was sorry to find so many opposite opinions prevailing.  I am however nothing daunted by what I see or hear—and cannot but conclude that you will receive the nomination at Harrisburg, and will not doubt but that our divisions will cease.  I said to Mr. Crittenden at Frankfort that I should regard your election as certain, if in accepting the nomination you would emphatically declare your determination to serve but a single term.  If you have leisure, will you read three numbers under the signature of *Civitas* published in the Richmond Whig early in this month?

I write you without reserve, and in doing so furnish you the strongest evidence of my esteem and confidence.

                    Truly and faithfully

                         Yrs,
                         John Tyler.

DR. WAT HENRY TYLER,
(Eldest brother of President Tyler.)

P. S. You can, if you think proper, throw your answers to the foregoing enquiries into separate letters.

————

TO HENRY A WISE.

Vaucluse<sub>(1)</sub> , March 23, 1840.

Dear Sir:

Your letter from Phil<sup>a</sup>. of the 4<sup>th</sup> In<sup>st</sup> was not received till yesterday. I am glad to hear that you have obtained effective medical aid in that city.

\* \* \* \* \* \* \* \* \*

You ask me if I am not "going to give you my help." To do what? To put out one party and to put in another. And *cui bono* ? I admit that the administration party is the most profligate, corrupt and slavish that ever dishonored and degraded any country, but what can be said of the Whigs? I fear that I should be considered uncourteous, if I were to say to a *Whig leader*, what I think of his party. But I will say this at least, that as to so much of it as there is in Virginia, it is impossible for me to feel either respect for or confidence in it. I have seen it deserting its best friends in favor of its worst enemies; I have seen it support Mr. Rives. to the neglect and exclusion of all those on whom it called aloud, only two or three years since, to aid in putting down that very Mr, Rives. I have seen it turn, with indifference and most strange ingratitude, from those who *built it up*, by exposing the enormities of the Proclamation, the Protest, the Force Bill, the Expunge, the profligate waste of the public money and the shameless prostitution of the public patronage, and take to its warmest embraces the strongest advocate of the Proclamation, of the Protest, and of the Force Bill, an unblushing actor in the slavish and debasing expunge, a sharer in the abused patronage of the executive, and an uncomplaining witness of the waste of the public treasure. And all this too, without any disavowal on his part of one slavish principle, without repentance of a single fault, or atonement for a single wrong. Never did I witness party degradation equal to this. Who would be willing to trust a party thus ungrateful, and thus false to every just obligation? John Tyler was sacrificed by

————

(1) The residence of Mr. Upshur in Northampton County, Va.

the party which brought Rives into office, and yet the same party with whom, and for whose sake, Tyler fell, have endeavored to put the heel of this same Mr. Rives upon his head.[1]   By what terms, Sir, shall we designate such conduct as this?   Who can hope to win the favor of such a party, by deserving it?   Who can expect to escape its persecutions and curses by serving it faithfully?   After all that it has done—I speak of it in Virginia,—it would not be at all surprising if Mr. Van Buren himself should become its chosen leader.   As mere parties then, and in reference to party conduct, a hair makes the difference between Whigs and Democrats   And as to *political principles*, God knows, I expect nothing from either of them. With professions of State Rights doctrines, loud and ostentatious, until credulity is shocked and good taste disgusted, what has either of them *done* to sustain the principles it professes?   I see the same great leading error in both.   With State Rights forever on the tongue, both are incessantly engaged in withdrawing the attention of the people from their State government to that of the U. States.   The consequence is that Federal politics absorb all other considerations.   The Federal Gov$^t$. is regarded as all that is good and all that is evil in our condition; the states are overlooked; the beneficent action of their governments upon our rights, our interests and our daily comforts, is forgotten; they sink to nothing in the scale of public importance, and their dignity, their rights, and their powers perish under the neglect of their own people. To such an extreme has this error been carried, that we can not elect a single State officer, from the constable of a village to the Governor of a State, without reference to Federal politics.   Now tell me, which of the great parties will come forward in good faith to build up the States once more, in their

---

(1) Upshur was at this time Judge of the General Court of Virginia, and had just published his powerful review of Judge Story's work on the Constitution, completely demolishing the Judge.   Calhoun said that "this review left nothing more to be said in behalf of the theory of the States-rights men," and once expressed the regret that Upshur could not have been matched against Webster. "In eloquence he was his equal and in reasoning his superior." ( Judge William Archer Cocke, M. S.) Judge Upshur had been a Jackson man in 1828, but was now a Whig on the theory that Whig meant " State-rights." For Mr. Tyler's contest with Rives, see Vol. I.

just dignity and importance, and thus restore the true and only bala ice of the Constitution? Neither of them;—my life upon it, neither of them. And yet until this shall be done, how vain and worse than foolish are all our contests about Federal men and Federal measures! You may change your rulers, but the disease of the system will still remain. The tendency of all power to the Federal Govt will be as strong as ever. A virtuous President may be chosen, by whom power may not be abused, but its mass will be forever increas-ing, until at length some unscrupulous incumbent of the office will find it great enough to overwhelm, not the rights of the States only, but the rights and liberties of the people also. And all this too, in the *name* of States Rights and Lib-erty.

You see then that I look upon Federal *elections* as compar-itively unimportant. I, and the "corporal guard" who think with me, do not believe that the abuses of which we complain, are to be corrected in Washington. Reform, to be worth any thing, must commence in the States. Do you think that the late unspeakable outrage in the case of N. Jersey, would have been committed, if the rights and powers of the States had not sunk into contempt? Never; and now where is the Whig or Democratic Legislature that has come forward to vindicate its *own* State in that of N. Jersey! Not one; "none so poor as to do reverence" to a disfranchised State! If you would keep the Federal Govt. within its proper sphere, and check its abuses and usurpation, make the States strong enough to be felt, and dignified enough to be respected. Surey, they ought to have sufficient power to control their own agent. This is the aim of my despised "corporal guard;" and now I retort your question, "are you going to help us?"

As to the unfortunate condition of the monetary system, to which you allude, the Fedl Govt did not produce, and cannot relieve it. The error is in the Banking system of the States; in the ridiculous requisition to keep a certain amount of specie always hoarded up in their vaults. Specie is *not* the true basis of credit, as I could easily show, if necessary. To hoard it up in Banks, does not strengthen their credit at all, but on the other hand, it produces precisely the same effect upon the exchanges of the country which you Whigs attribute to the "specie clause," without any of its attendant good. I dislike that clause, as much as any of you do, being thoroughly

convinced that it is altogether false and empirical. I allude
to it as a strong illustration of the folly of looking to the
Fed¹ Gov' for remedies which it cannot apply, and overlook-
ing those which are within the power of the States. The evil
under which we labour is not a *defective*, but a *deficient* cur
rency; our circulating medium is *good* enough, but there is
not enough of it. How can the Federal Gov' remedy this?
The States can do it in five hours, but they never will do it,
while their people are. persuaded that nobody but Mr. Van
Buren produced the evil, and that nobody but Genl. Harrison
can cure it. If the people would elect their delegates themselves, instead of suffering them to be virtually chosen by the
candidates for the Pr esidency; if they would choose Legisla-
tors for the States who are best calculated to serve the States,
instead of choosing them by a standard found only in a distant and in effect *foreign* Government, they would have much
less of hard times to complain of, and would be much better
served at Washington, as well as at home.

I owe you an apology: your short paragraph on political
matters did not authorize this tedious homily I find I grow
garrulous as I grow old, but yet I have not said half that I
wish to say. However, I will merely add that I have great
respect for, and great confidence in, Genl. Harrison. If the
Whigs should elect him, as I sincerely hope they may, I have
great hopes that he will do as much as a President *can* do, to
restore the government to its purity. But if the States be
not also restored to their proper place and influence, the ma-
chine, without a balance and without a regulator, must inevi-
tably soon fall to pieces, or to be consolidated into one mass.
The latter, by far the worse evil, is by far the more likely to
occur.        *      *      *      *      *

We have no news here The *canvass* waxes warm.[1] I
understand, but I can form no conjecture as to the result.
How much have all you gentlemen to answer for, who are
persuading the people to think that the sub-treasury is the
cause of their present distress, and thus preventing them from
discovering the true course of the evil, and the proper quar-

---

(1) Mr. Upshur had been a Crawford man in 1828, and was a nullifier in 1833; and like nearly all the nullifiers, outside of South Carolina, was a Whig in 1839.

ter to which to apply for relief? So it is, and so republics
are ruined.

Very respet. Yours,

A. P. UPSHUR.

If the speeches of Buchanan and Clay on the Sub-treasury, should fall in your way, I should be obliged by your
sending them to me. My newspapers have contained no part
of the discussion on that subject.

———

TO HUGH S LEGARE.

Washington City, Feby. 26th, 1840.

Dear Sir:

It is true I have been spouting loud and long, and
if any thing or motive could induce me to cry out daily, it
would be the graceful flattery of your letter. Are you not
amazed at every day's history of our public affairs? I have
lost all my old confidence in Men—How weak is the strongest, how foolish the wisest! Whither do we tend? Shall our
civilization, think you, reach the Pacific before it is crushed or
turned back by some folly or wickedness of the weak and
wicked Demagogues that swarm all over the land? I have
dreamed that our arts and letters might yet break over the
Rocky Mountains and taking their way across the Pacific
wake up the people of Asia from their long sleep. This must
yet be. There is a God in Israel. The effects of our Misrule
are now beginning to be felt. The Bankrupt Merchant feels
it when he closes his door. The thrifty trader feels it in his
diminished sales. The rich planter and farmer in their reduced prices. The laboring poor in no employment and
short allowances. The whole *people feel* rather than *think* that
they have been cajoled, cheated and *fooled*. Now from all I
know, derived from newspapers and correspondence extend-
ing thro' almost every state, the end of the spoilers is come.
I gather facts from men of cool, calculating temper—Such
will tell you that N. York and Pa. are both sure for the
opposition. Four of the N. England States beyond a doubt,
and a fair chance for Maine, New Jersey, Del, and Maryland,
all considered safe for us. You see what is going on in Va.
and N. Carolina. Now for the West—there I am at home;
and now remember what I predict, Ohio, Ky., Ind$^a$., Ill. and

Tennessee will all give every one of their electoral votes for old *Tipp.* A convention assembled on the 21st and 22d of this month in the Capitol of Ohio to nominate a Governor and electors for the Whigs. There were upwards of *Fifteen thousand Delegates present.* Many of my letters before me say 20,000, 19 in 20 of these are hard working landholders and mechanics who travelled from 50 to 150 miles, and some, 200 miles to attend. This Army of voters have nominated your unworthy friend for Governor,—so I leave Babylon after *June,* never I hope to return. Depend upon it Harrison will be Prest. and Congress I hope may be regenerated, then I should like to see you here. Then you and such as you will find a vocation. I have more to say hereupon some other day.

I have looked after the North American and shall have it to-morrow. Had I known your pen had been at work there, I should have devoured it long ago. Why should you shrink within your briefs and pleas? Write—Write—speak, you know you can do both better than one in a million of those whose scribbling and babbling have filled the world. with books and talks, Appropos—my scrawl will be no mean example of "that same," unless I say here God bless you. Pray write me often—Why not—If I print my *say* concerning old Tipp I shall send you a copy that you may see how small a thing can be puffed in these days of little men. Again, good night.

Most truly Y<sup>r</sup>. friend,<br>THOS. CORWIN.

———

TO THE FRIENDS OF "HARRISON AND REFORM"!

[Extract].

June 12, 1840.

It would afford me unspeakable pleasure to be able to partake in what I trust will be the frank, joyous and triumphant festivity of such an occasion. Rejoiced as I am at any manifestation of a proper spirit of resistance to the insolent Cabal, who aim at perpetuating by the worst means the power they are abusing to the worst ends   It is in the South especially that I exult at the awakening of the Spirit. These men have not only treated us as they have the rest of the country, they have attempted to do a great deal more. They have reserved for us the broadest and grossest of all the insults they have been in the habit of offering to the understanding of the people, in the shape of grimace and imposture. They suppose Southern *gullibility* to be proof against anything; they actually wish to make us believe that a man born and educated in the South, who sacrificed himself as a politician in the West in defending the rights of the South—Well knowing at the time that that would be his fate—is not to be trusted by the South on that very subject. This is not all. Not only are you to repay a benefactor and a friend with hostility and most criminal ingratitude, but you are called upon to put your faith in one who is known to you only by the breach of his promises.    *    *    *    *    *

Now I do not mean to imitate the example of the adversary. I do not charge Mr. Van Buren with any purposes hostile to our interests or institutions. I do not believe he entertains himself or would (unless instructed, as in 1828,) forward any such, and I disdain to charge him with them for popular effect. But I act on the defensive and I maintain that the impudence of those who would have us sacrifice Genl. Harrison to *him*, on the sectional ground referred to, is equalled only by the injustice, the glaring and unpardonable injustice with which you are required to repay a friend for his fidelity to you and to the Constitution, at one of the most important epochs of our history.

As for Mr. Tyler, if he do not obtain the unanimous vote of the South, I shall begin to fear that faction has entirely bereft us of the clear judgment of which more than any other people on the face of the Globe, we now stand in need.

I have the honor to be, gentlemen &c.

HUGH S. LEGARE'.

---

TO HENRY A. WISE.

Williamsburg, April 28, 1840.

My Dear Sir:

Your letter of the 20th informing me of the deposit of a hickory cane with you for me by the Secretary of the Tippecanoe club of Tip County, Indiana, along with a letter from that gentleman was received on my return home after a short absence. You will be pleased to keep it until I see you or until some one coming directly here can take charge of it. An opportunity of this latter kind may be presented in Baltimore through some one going from there to the convention.

Have you ever known so total a rout as the *admon* party has experienced from Richmond to Hampton and in Norfolk town and county, Princess Ann, and Nansemond. In Gloucester the struggle was rendered severe by the absence of more than 20 Whigs, chiefly merchants who had gone north, and dissatisfaction with Smith who had diminished the zeal of many by having declared last fall that he would not support M^r. Clay if nominated,

There will be a strong rally this Fall, and I do not doubt but that we shall carry the county by a respectable majority. I am not informed of the result in Mathews, but I left that side of the river in the best hopes that the Hudgins' influence was departed.

So far I have heard of the results in but few counties—Prince Edward, Powhatan, Nottoway and Hanover are revolutionized, and I hope that other counties have followed in their train.

I feel deeply the death of Judge White. He was a pure man and a patriot, and that in these times is the highest compliment that can be paid any man.

Be pleased to give my respects to M^r. Botts and congratulate him for me on the results in his District.

Very truly Y^rs

JOHN TYLER

TO HENRY A. WISE.

My Dear Sir:

Williamsburg, Nov. 25, 1840.

The great battle has been fought, and General Harrison goes into the Presidency upon a majority controling and decisive, Virginia has proved recreant but not our part of it, that is certain—for *Wise's District*, as *par excellence* it has been called, has come up to the polls with a majority, which with decent aid from the middle country, would have carried the State. The Tide-water has in truth had to maintain the contest almost alone, and Whiggery has found in its ally Conservatism but poor support. I had put my heart with much more confidence on the Southern states than on Virginia, altho' knowing our strength on the Tide, and being flattered by reports of changes in "Little Tennessee," and large acquisitions elsewhere, I had brought myself to believe that all would be well with our mother state. She has again wheeled out of line, and unites herself with New Hampshire in preference to affiliating with Maryland, N. Carolina, Georgia, Mississippi, Tennessee and Louisiana. Will she not now be brought to her senses and come speedily to reject the false priests who have ministered at her altars?

I have been very desirous to see you and converse face to face, but the near approach of the session of Congress bids fair to preclude this.

In desiring your views I wish to prepare myself for playing my part as may best become me, should it be required of me to play any part. Let me also say, I scorn to flatter, that I regard you as having been as much instrumental in bringing about the present state of things as any man who lives, and your views of the future should be as much sought after as your opinions in the past. Give me your views then as from friend to friend, and be assured that you have no one in whom you can confide with greater security than in

Yʳˢ Truly and faithfully,

JOHN TYLER

TO HENRY A. WISE.

Williamsburg, Va. Dec. 20, 1840.
My Dear Sir:

It was not until after my former letter was written and committed to the mail that I came to be informed of your absence from home on a visit to Philadelphia, and the Newspapers of the following week brought the intelligence of your marriage. Let me now congratulate you on that interesting event, and tender through you to Mrs. Wise my best wishes. [1] It has occurred most opportunely, since the leader of the House of Commons should evermore be under mild and softning influences, which coming in aid of tact and argument will lead him oftentimes to pour oil on the waves of a tumultuous debate and bring back the House to a sense of dignity and justice. By the by, should you be left by the new admin-

_____

(1) Mr Wise married the daughter of John Sergeant, of Philadelphia, afterwards prominent in the Bank question.

istration in your present political position, you will be presented in a new light before the Country. Heretofore the
assailant of men in power and of public abuses, you will in
future lead the reform party and conduct them to safe conclusions, and I take it that this new position is one of much
greater difficulty than your former one. There are so many
jarring views to reconcile and harmonize, that the work is
one of immense difficulty, and in your ear let me whisper
what you already know, that that branch of the Whig party
call'd the Nationals is compos'd of difficult materials to manage—they are too *excessive* in their notions, I mean many of
them, and are accustomed to look upon a course of honest compromise as a concession of something which they call principle, but which dissected is nothing more than mistaken conviction. However, you will understand the elements with
which you will have to deal, and I doubt not but that you will
reconcile and control them.

I agree with you fully in the importance you attach to
General Harrison's first step.--It is one, however, of great
difficulty. I hope he may meet and overcome it. His language should be firm and decisive to one and all. There
should be no caballing, no intrigueing in his Cabinet. Every
eye should be kept fixed upon the official duty assigned, and
never once lifted up to gaze at the succession. He should
play Henry VIII in this respect, so that each and every man
should know that there was one above them who would toler-
ate no official interference with the aspiring Plantagenets.[1]
Taking up your suggestion of men of business for the Cabinet,
my mind has been turn'd to a good friend of ours, who unless
I mistake him, would make an efficient minister. I mean
Bailey Peyton. He has two essential ingredients, intellect
enough to know what is right, and firmness of purpose to
pursue it. But I can do no more than suggest.

It will be my duty to be in Washington sometime in February. Gen. Harrison will be in Virginia in January—so the
papers state, and will remain here until it will be time to be

---

(1) In a letter written after the election and shortly before this
(the late Dr. J. S. H. Fogg, of Boston had the original in his collection) Mr. Tyler said that "The introduction of either Clay, Scott or
Webster into the Cabinet would excite the jealousy of the others
and produce discontent and final rupture."

in Washington.  I may accompany him thither.  In view of
my visit may I ask you to do me the favor to call at Brown's
hotel, of at such other place as you may deem better, and en-
gage me two rooms, a parlor and lodging room adjoining.  I
would not disappoint the anxiety, which I know to prevail in
some quarters to see me, and therefore I designate the most
public position.  If I go into a private boarding house, I would
prefer to be located at my old Landlady's, M$^{rs}$ McDaniel's.
Now if this matter devolves on you any inconvenience to
comply with it in person, do me the favour to address a note
to Brown expressive of my wishes.—I learn that numberless
application are making for quarters by citizens from every
part of the country, and hence my solicitude at this early day.

In conclusion I have only to say write me when you
please and *as you please*, being assured that whatever you communicate will be with me as a seal'd book,

Truly and faithfully  Y$^r$ H$^{bl}$ Serv$^t$.,

JOHN TYLER.

---

TO HUGH S. LEGARE.

Castle Hill, Dec. 25, 1840.

My Dear Legare :

I had the pleasure of receiving some days ago your letter
of 3$^d$ inst.—Tho' I can well appreciate, as I sympathise, in
your feeling in regard to the Charleston affair, I think you
greatly over-estimate its importance.  Your reputation is *national*, as your services and exertions have been, and is not to
be affected, therefore, by anything transacted in a *corner*.
Belonging as you do to the *nation*, you must place yourself in
a position which will bring you more constantly before its
view.  New York, Baltimore, or Virginia is your true destina-
tion, and you must make your arrangement for connecting
yourself permanently with one or the other of them.—It is
only within the last day or two, that I have heard anything
from Washington of an authentic character, in relation to the
negotiations going on there for the formation of Genl. Harrison's Cabinet.  It is now considered certain that Mr. Webster
will be the new Secretary of State and Crittenden, Attorney
General.  So far, all is *arrete'*.  The filling of the other Cabi-

net offices awaits, it is thought, the arrival of the General in Washington, on his route to   *   *   *   where he is to spend with a nephew, (now the proprietor of the   *   *   * (1) the month of January and first half of February.  The designation which has been made of the two Cabinet ministers already named, sufficiently indicate the principle on which the remaining appointments will be made.  Mr. Crittenden is the *alter ego* of Mr. Clay in the Cabinet.  Mr. Webster answers to himself there.  Between these two rivals' interests, in reference to the succession, there is, doubtless, to be an equal partition of the portfolios, as John Gilpin

"—hung a bottle on each side.
To keep *the balance* true."

But as happened in the case of the " train-band Captain of famous London town," a luckless collision may shatter the "bottles twain" at a blow, and leave the broken necks, still, "dangling at the waist," as the sole trophies of the arrangement for a ministerial *balance* between the two family competitors for the succession.  I wish it may not be so; but if what I learn of the incipient jealousies already manifested between the friends of these two gentlemen be true, there is some danger of it.  Mr. Sergeant, I understand, is spoken of for the Treasury Department, Mr. Bell for the War, Mr. Ewing for the Post Office, and who for the Navy, I have not yet heard. From all these negotiations for office, I have been glad to learn that the Conservatives have stood sedulously aloof, content with the consciousness of having performed their duty to the country, and leaving to those who may desire them more, or may consider themselves better entitled to the employment, all the personal advantages of the triumph.

I give the substance of all which the few correspondents I have at Washington have communicated to me.  With the exception of what relates to Mr. Webster and Mr. Crittenden (which is considered as certain and definitely decided,) the other arrangements, I presume, are as yet but matters of suspicion and conjecture, with more or less probability, however, in each of them.

In regard to the Senatorial election here, you will have seen that it has been *suspended*, by a refusal of the Senate to

---

(1) Where the stars appear above the copy has been eaten by mice.

go into election on the day proposed by the House of Delegates. It is thought, however, that a day may be agreed on
about the middle of January for proceeding to the election,
when the prevalent opinion is that I shall be returned. Of
this, however, I am neither very confident nor very solicitous.

Let me hear from you frequently and fully. My wife
and children join me most cordially in all the good wishes of
the season to you, and I remain most

truly and faithfully yours,<br>W. C. Rives

———

TO FRANKLIN MINOR.<br>Richmond, January 15, 1841.

Dear Frank:

You say nothing of Tom's views as to my correspondence with Gov. Seward. He has maintained a studied
silence, which induced me to apprehend he was not very favorable to my interest. I sent him a copy. His paper is
rather a poor concern, I think, and seems to have disappointed public expectation altogether. He has approved Webster's
appointment as Secretary of State, and is quoted by the
*Intelligencer* as a sign from Albemarle, where I should suppose
there cannot be more than one hundred votes who would
approve it. It is universally disapproved here by our party,
and letters have been written by everybody who could write
to Washington entreating our friends there to avert so heavy
and disastrous a calamity. If not averted it knocks us into a
cocked hat in Virginia and everywhere. The editors of the
*Whig* (or rather the senior of the concern), I believe, is the
only Whig here who approves, and his article a few days
since, like Tom Wood's, will seem to undo what the whole
party was trying to effect. The vice-president and all the
Southern Whigs at Washington think as we do on this point.
Tyler wrote me he would come and stay with me during
Harrison's visit here, and I shall try then to get Webster put
into some dark corner, or thrown overboard entirely. He is
a Federalist of the worst dye, a blackguard and vulgar de-
bauchee; and but for his splendid talents would be in a jail
or on some dunghill. He won't do and the men who cling to
him can't stand. You ask who is to go to the Senate No. 1.

I  answer Rives, I  suppose.  You  ask  as to No. 2. *Non sum
informatus.*  Many have spoken to me about running for both
places.  I have invariably answered that I did not seek either,
and wished it distinctly and emphatically understood that I
would not be in anybody's way, nor embarrass my friends.
If after so broad a declaration they can agree, as I suppose
they will on some other, of course I shall not be the man.  If,
however, they find difficulty, as some of our friends apprehend, *I may* be chosen as a dernier resort.  I thank you for
your advice.  Do you observe any symptom of too much ambition?  I thought I had been very modest and self denying,
and surely the ground I take and have taken for two years
as to proffered promotion to the Senate entitles me to a verdict of acquittal from a charge of restless ambition.  I try
to be, as far as vain mortal can be, devoted to the public
good, while I cannot help feeling gratified by the confidence
of my countrymen and their desire to promote me.  I do not
mean to run ahead of the public wish on this head.

    We are all well except myself.  My health has not been
good for a month, though it is mending.

                    Love to all,          THOMAS W. GILMER [1]

-----

    (1) This letter, published with others of a similar character in Vol.
II, p. 704, is reproduced here for its connection.  Mr. Gilmer, who had
been Speaker of the House of Delegates, was now Governor, and the
election of two Senators was pending in the Legislature.  It resulted
in the choice of William S. Archer and William C. Rives—two Whigs
who had been lately Democrats.  William H. Campbell, Mr. Gilmer's
predecessor in the Governor's office had also been a Democrat, but
was now a Whig; and such was the history of John M. Patton and John
M Gregory, his successors.  It was literally true that, until Clay raised
the party whip a year later, the Whigs of the South were more rampant States-right men than the Democrats, whom indeed admiration
of Jackson had made to a certain extent *Nationalists.*  This was
especially shown in the case of the two brothers Nathaniel Beverley
Tucker, professor of Law at William and Mary College, author of
the " Partisan Leader " etc., and Henry St. George Tucker, professor
of Law at the University of Virginia.  The former, a Whig, was an
advocate of secession as the ultimate right, while the latter, a Democrat relied on the Supreme Court as the arbiter between the States.
It is but right to say in allusion to the reference to Webster contained in this letter, that President Tyler always said that Webster
excelled every member of his cabinet in gentlemanly deference to
him, and that in practical matters there was never any clash between

TO J. F. STROTHER.

March 3, 1841.

My Dear Sir:

Understanding that you have been kind enough to think me worthy of the seat in the United States Senate which is to be conferred by the General Assembly to-day, I take the liberty of expressing to you candidly my wishes and feeling on the occasion. This is one of those honors of the State which is neither to be sought nor declined, yet there are peculiar reasons which induce me at this time not to embarrass any one in casting his vote, nor would I accept the distinction at the hands of a reluctant Legislature. It is a distinction moreover which should belong to the State and not to mere party.

I am informed that some doubt has been expressed as to my opinions on the subject of a United States Bank and the distribution of the proceeds of the public lands. If you hear it repeated, I will be obliged to you to do me the justice to state that my opinions have undergone no change on these questions. I have always regarded a National bank as both unconstitutional and inexpedient, and I am still in favor of distributing the *surplus* proceeds of the public lands. When this last subject was under consideration in the House of Delegates, some years since, I was in the chair and gave a silent vote. I then thought, however, as I now do that it would be unwise and dangerous to distribute the *gross* proceeds of the lands, thereby creating a vacuum in the treasury which must be filled from other sources of revenue.

I have alluded to these subjects now because I am unwilling under any circumstances to be misunderstood or misrepresented, and because I am in a position which deprives me to a great extent of the means of explanation or defence.

With many thanks for the generous confidence, which, though almost a stranger to you, I have received at your hands,

I remain your humble servant,

Thomas W. Gilmer.

---

them. His conduct was simply unexceptionable. Gilmer had been unfavorably impressed by Webster's conduct in Richmond the October before, when he made his celebrated "October speech." During his stay, as I have heard from several who saw him, Webster succumbed to frequent potations.

TO HENRY A. WISE.

Philada. April 6, 1841.

My dear Sir :

I wish you were here for half an hour. The death of
Gen'l Harrison makes a great change, but what it will be exactly, it is hard to say. One only thing concerns me particularly, and induces me to write to you, tho' I have but a moment
to spare. My settled determination, as you know, was to
resign, and the time, about the middle of the month. This I
feel obliged to abandon, and undergo the burthen of the extra
session. The general anxiety and alarm, and the really critical condition of our country, in relation both to *foreign* and
domestic affairs, seem to require of every man to remain at
his post, and give what help he can, however feeble. To
withdraw at such a time, would be desertion. I have made
up my mind to submit to what duty demands, however irk-
some. Therefore, in your arrangements at Washington, com-
prehend me if you can. Perhaps M^rs Rouckendorf could
accommodate us.

It appears from the papers that no measures were taken
to inform Governor Tyler of the President's illness 'till Fri-
day last. Information of his death was forwarded on Sunday.
He will not, of course be in Washington for some days. This
is much to be regretted. The moment the President was
taken sick, information should have been sent to Gov. Tyler,
and repeated day by day, that he might have been at Washington, or, if that would have caused excitement or remark in
the neighborhood, say Baltimore—I am obliged to stop.
Love to Sarah.

Yours very truly,

JOHN SERGEANT.

———

TO HENRY CLAY.

April 30, 1841.

My Dear Sir:

Your letter of the 14th was received some days
ago, and its acknowledgment at an earlier day has been prevented by pressing engagements. At its date you had not
probably seen my address to the people of the U. States,

LETITIA CHRISTIAN
(First wife of President John Tyler.)

which was designed as an exponent of the principles on which I should administer the Gov't. Considering the brief time allowed me and the extreme pressure on my time, it will not be expected that I shall come before Congress with matured plans of public policy connected with deeply interesting and intricate subjects. There are some points so simple in themselves as to require but brief consideration. The repeal of the subtreasury and, if necessary, additional burthens for the relief of the Treasury. The wants of the Treasury will be made manifest, and the state of our military defences requires immediate attention. There is not a seaport town that does not hold its existence at the will of a great naval power. Altho' I am not apprehensive of a war, yet I cannot but feel solicitude as to the ability of the country to repel invasion. If these shall be the only matters attended to at the extra-session, great good will have been done. The pressing wants of the Treasury will have been relieved, the war on the currency will have ceased, and the banks be placed in a condition to afford partial relief. Should Legislation stop here, the loss public monies would be restored to the custody provided for them by the Act of 1789, which law has been abrogated by the course of Jackson and his successor. To these objects the late President's proclamation concerning Congress seems exclusively to have looked. It will however, be for Congress to decide whether other measures shall claim its attention. The citizens of this District should undoubtedly not be forgotten.

My opinion on the subject of a distribution of the proceeds of the sales of the public lands, was promulgated some three winters ago in a report submitted to the H. of Delegates of Virginia. I made the basis of that distribution an abandonment of that course which has for some time prevailed, of annual appropriations to harbors and rivers, a course wholly indefensible in any view in which I can regard it,—thereby substituting a wholesome, sound, and agreeable action in place of one unequal and therefore unjust, not to say anything of its want of constitutionality—and without which substitution the loudest and most violent complaints will be urged against the distribution at this time.

As to a Bank, I design to be perfectly frank with you— I would not have it urged prematurely. The public mind is in a state of great disquietude in regard to it. The late exposures at Philadelphia have not been calculated to put it at rest. The misnomer given to that Bank by the injudicious policy pursued by those who obtained its charter and the late disclosures have furnished the demagogues with new weapons to assail those who advocate a Bank charter,—whilst the close division of votes by which, if at all, it will pass through Congress will encourage the *ultraists* in efforts to destroy it, before it can go into operation. I apprehend a strong protest from the minority and an avowed purpose to cancel it, the charter, at a future day. Should this be done, are you sure that capitalists will adventure their capital in it? The fact is before the world that Jackson tore the charter of the old Bank into tatters, and his followers will go forth as agitators, and the result of their agitations may prove disastrous. If, however, you see nothing in this of force, then I desire you to consider whether you cannot so frame a Bank as to avoid all constitutional objections—which of itself would attach to it a vast host of our own party to be found all over the Union. I make these suggestions for your consideration— and make them in that spirit of frankness which will always characterize my course towards you. I have no intention to submit anything to Congress on this subject to be acted on, but shall leave it to its own action, and in the end shall resolve my doubt by the character of the measure proposed, should any be entertained by me.

My attention is turned to the removals from office after the manner that you suggest, and I hope that to the recent appointments you have nothing to object. The P. office at Lexington shall be attended to I derived very great pleasure in affixing my signature to the Commission of Mr. Denalds for the appointment of naval officer at New Orleans.

I tender you assurance of high esteem and regard,

JOHN TYLER.

---

TO PRESIDENT TYLER.

Boston, July 14, 1841.

Dear Sir:

I take great pleasure in acknowledging the honor of your letter of the 8th inst. and thanking you for the confidence which it implie s.

Mr. Hall has thus far been retained by me in the office

of measurer, from respect to the very considerations which are referred to in your letter, and I shall most certainly re-gard those considerations as greatly enforced by a truthful, deference to your opinions. It is, however, proper to state that Mr. Hall has been intimately connected, and his politi-cal conduct closely *identified* with the measures of the last Administration. He was a citizen of *Maine* and a Represen-tative in Congress from that state, when yielding his claims to re-election, to a more popular, or a less patient Competi-tor, he was transferred to *Massachusetts*, and the *Custom House* of this Port. Finding him here, I did not feel called upon to inquire into the propriety of his original appointment. I knew him to be of the *old Republican* family, and that he had enjoyed the confidence of a beloved Brother of mine, formerly Governor of Maine, by whom he had been appointed to the office of Sheriff of a County, previous to his election to Con-gress. With this motive, therefore, to prepossession in his favor, it was my hope to find nothing in his recent course beyond an honest difference in opinion, to which the Rule, so justly, yet so liberally laid down by the Executive, could ap-ply. As an officer, I believe him capable, and to have been *as faithful*, as the required allegiance to *party*, and the sup-posed higher obligations to party discipline over mere official duty would allow. Strong representations, however, have been urged against him of *active interference* in the recent election, and of *betting* on the result. I am not certain that injustice may not have been done him in this respect, and have thus far, suspended any action in reference to the dis-position of his office, that I might have opportunity by calm and leisure examination to be made better satisfied with the facts in the case. The Rule of the Executive, thoroughly approved by my own judgment and reiterated in a Circular which I found occasion to, issue an extract from which I do myself the honor herewith to submit to your notice, has been the *law* of my conduct. I shall be gratified to find, upon fur-ther inquiry and indulgence to Mr. Hall, that he has not made himself obnoxious to the application of those just prin-ciples, to his situation, which should exclude him from the right to appeal to your kind consideration. I trust, I need not add the assurance, that I can have no higher gratification in the matter, than in pursuing that course in reference to him, which I shall feel, upon a full knowledge of all the circumstances, will be most like to meet your entire and cordial approval.

Allow me, Sir, to express the sentiments of faithful esteem and respect for you personally, and of the highest considera‑ tion for your public services and character, with which I have the honor to be

Your obedient and obliged Servant,

LEVI LINCOLN.[1]

———

TO DANIEL WEBSTER.

Philadelphia, 14 Sept. 1841.

Sir:

As a citizen of the United States deeply interested of course in its government, I take the liberty, without knowing anything of your wishes or intentions, to deprecate the resig‑ nation of your office.

If you allow me any further claims, as a *Whig*, I w'd say that I cannot imagine any reason why the President's refusal to sign a *charter* should injure him with that party—or why your remaining in office should be considered inconsistent with your course in the canvass. I am aware that a large portion of the Whig party, perhaps more than half of it in the cities, was and is in favor of a Corporation; but it was considered previous to the election, as one of the measures upon which there was not a party union; and Sir, so far as I could see, *you* were not in favor of a corporation. Being opposed to a charter myself, I could yet agree in all yr. doc‑ trines as proclaimed on the house tops. You held that the regulation of the Currency belongs to the Federal Govern‑ ment; and so believed the Whig party—but it does not follow that the party was in favor of *giving up* to *private* individuals, this immense power—I could not have believed, a *priori*, that any public man of large experience would have been willing to throw away all we have learned on this subject.

———

(1) The letter is given as an instance out of many in which Pres‑ ident Tyler stopped the Harrison appointees from proscription. See *Parties and Patronage.*

The course of the Whig press here has been in strict conformity to the supposed plans of Mr. Clay. I have in vain endeavored to get into the papers here or into the Nat. Intelligencer any argument against Mr. Clay's course. Altho' in private conversation the Editors w'd admit *doubts*, their papers allowed no expression of dissent. For one reason, because they are very ignorant of the subject, but principally because they considered that the confidence of the majority of the Whig party in this city was especially given to Mr. Clay. To make an appearance of unanimity, they excluded the opinions of the minority, (if indeed it *be* a minority), and do not represent the feelings of the Whigs.

Even if the Whigs were unanimous, it were rashly encountering a fearful risk, to place so vast an interest as the Currency on a *party* foundation. One principle of the Whig party was that *their* President s'd be in truth the President of the Nation.

If the President will now advocate a *substantive* plan which shall provide for the *permanent* settlement of this question, he will be impregnable. But if, like Mr. Van Buren, he stand on a *negative*, he will fall.

If I can spare time, after Washington shall have been a little thinned out, will have the pleasure of offering to you in person the thanks of one citizen, for your adherence to the post of duty, and it seems of present danger.

Your obed<sup>t</sup>. servt.

E. LITTELL. [1]

————

TO PRESIDENT TYLER.

Washington,

21<sup>st</sup> Dec<sub>r</sub>. 1841.

Dear Sir:

I called on Saturday last to make my respects to you, and also to bring before you the name of General Carroll, of Tennessee for the Mission to Mexico, but found that you were engaged with your Cabinet.

I learn from General Carroll himself as well as from his friends here, that the Mission would be acceptable to him. Of his qualifications and services I need say little. Few men

————

(1) Subsequently editor of "Littell's Living Age."

are posessed of stronger common sense and such thorough acquaintance with human nature; with these he associates the requisites of a mind well informed and good manners. I speak from personal knowledge.

Of his services to his country at a most critical and dangerous period you are of course well informed. It is known to all, that next to General Jackson he stands highest in the roll of merit for defeating the British and saving N. Orleans and giving a glorious termination to the late war.

His standing in his own state has been evinced by the many honors that she has bestowed on him, and among others, that of having conferred on him the highest in her gift, by electing him as her chief magistrate.

To these public reasons in his favor I will conclude by adding, that he has been affected with rheumatic pains in consequence of his exposure in the public service, and that he has been advised by his physician, that a residence in a mild, equitable climate such as that of Mexico, would be probably of great service to him. I have said more, I fear, than I ought in favor of one, whose claims must be so well known to you. If so, you must put it down to my anxious desire to serve one who has so well served his country, and whose appointment to the place he desires would afford me so much gratification.[1]

> With great respect,
> I am etc.
> J. C. CALHÓUN.

---

TO PRESIDENT TYLER.

Philad<sup>a</sup>. Feb. 22<sup>nd,</sup> 1842.

Sir:

As I cannot suppose that the charges of conspiracy to defraud the United States brought against M<sup>r</sup>. Biddle and others, including myself, have escaped your notice, I venture to hope that you will spare a moment to glance over the en-

---

(1) The President appointed Waddy Thompson, who had been promised the office by Harrison and was especially backed by Judge Beverly Tucker, Upshur and others. He was at the same time a special friend of Henry Clay, and supported him for the Presidency in 1844.

closed opinion of Judge Randall, honorably discharging me.

In regard to the first specification, Judge Randall says : "*have been unable to discover, in any part of the evidence exhibited in support of this charge, a single fact or circumstance that would justify me in inferring such an intent*" to commit crime.

As to the second, the Judge says: "*In the conduct of the defendant I see no just cause of censure.*"

Feeling deeply interested that the fair reputation which I so fondly hoped I had built up by so many years of anxious and devoted exertion to the interest of an institution once greatly beneficial to the county, but which has since fallen from causes over which I had no control and after I ceased to have any share in its management, should be preserved from the stigma which a charge of criminal conspiracy to defraud is calculated to impress upon it, I trust that you will pardon this trespass upon your time.

I have the honor to be,

With great respect,

Your ob<sup>t</sup>. Serv.,

S. JAUDON.

------

TO JUDGE N. BEVERLEY TUCKER.

Washington, April, 1 st, 1842.

Dear Sir:

Everything connected with the Surveyor Generalship of Illinois and Missouri has given me pain. The removal of Gen. Milbourn, altho' he fell under the influence of the rule promulgated in March 1841, was unfortunate, and the rejection by the Senate of Dr. Reed who was known to be a friend of the administration and exhibited strong testimonials of character. He had been assailed by the Ultra Press on both sides, and his rejection arose from erroneous impressions made on the minds of some Senators by his and my enemies. Upon the strength of your letter I unhesitatingly appointed Mr. Brown to Reed's place, and now Reed is restored and Brown out of employment, and this has been done as an act of justice, and upon the application of some of the Senators who formerly voted against Reed. And now what can I do to place Mr. Brown in a proper position before the country? An appointment to some other office will readily repair all and every imaginary wrong, and render unnecessary any further publication in the newspapers.

Do you know Samuel Merry, the receiver of public monies at St. Louis, [1] who and what is he? And if he is not the proper sort of man, how would Mr. Brown like the place? You have inspired me with entire confidence in him, and I wish him to know it.

Lord Ashburton's arrival is daily looked for. We shall do our best to preserve peace, but shall plant our feet firmly on American ground, and maintain it at the hazard of all consequences.

Gen. Thompson will receive special instruction for Mexico.

Be assured, my dear Sir, of my constant regard and esteem.

JOHN TYLER.

---

TO CALEB CUSHING.

London, 18 May, 1842.

My dear Sir:

I shall have but a moment's time before closing the parcel for the steamer to thank you for your two obliging favors of the 23$^{d}$. inst. which were highly instructive and interesting to me, giving me much light on several points, which I had not well understood before. I will take the earliest opportunity of writing to you more at length on some of the topics touched in your letters. Meantime I shall give my best attention to everything to which you may call it, whether of a public or private nature. A day or two after I received your letters, I met Lord Aberdeen at dinner at Lord Stanley's. After dinner Lord A. and myself being nearest each other, we fell into conversation on all the questions between the two governments. I told him that great discontent already existed in the United States, relative to the operation of the Convention negotiated by himself and Mr. McLane, on the subject of the colonial trade; that the convention was cutting down the tonnage; and that we were not satiisfied with the principles on which it was founded. He remarked by way of reply: " Well, perhaps we can do some-

---

(1)  Judge Tucker had been U. S. District Judge in Missouri. See on this office, Vol. II. p. 53.

thing about that matter also." I introduced Mr. A. Smith, the recently appointed Texian *charge d' affairs*, to Lord Aberdeen at the Foreign office on the 16th. He brought me a letter of introduction from my former Congressional associate, President Houston. The ratification of the treaty between Texas and this government is not yet exchanged, but I do not know that the *charge d' affairs* anticipates any difficulty in that matter. I write this letter in great haste, at the last moment and remain, as ever, with great regard.

Faithfully yours,
EDWARD EVERETT.

May I beg you to make my grateful acknowledgments to the President for his continued confidence and his favorable opinion. He finds me but a poor private correspondent; but in truth the public business employs nearly all my time. I hope I shall not always be so much occupied.

————

TO CALEB CUSHING.

(Confidential)                London, 2 August, 1842.
My dear Sir:

I have hastily thanked you already for your two very kind and instructive letters of the 23d of April. I should feel more compunction at being no better a correspondent, were I not confident that you will make due allowance for the multitude of my engagements and the oppressive amount of my correspondence. The American Minister being a kind of upper clerk to all his traveling countrymen on Public affairs, I have nothing to add to what is contained in my dispatches. The centre of interest, as far as the relation of the countries goes, is at Washington, and by this time I suppose what was matter of speculation, when you wrote, has passed into history. It is, therefore, useless to dwell on that point. I understand that Col. Robinson, the gentleman sent by the Treasury, has arrived, although I have not seen him. I am afraid it is an unpropitious moment to come here for money. The neglect of Penn$^a$ to make provision for the interest of her loan has given the *coup de grace* to American credit.

There is a real and unaffected distrust very widely diffused in the community; and those who do not really feel it, but have suffered as holders of State stock,—believing that their best chance of payment by the states would be to compel the United States to assume the State debts as a condition of relief to the general government,—pursue the policy of decrying the credit of the general government till some such arrangement is made. I am told that if any capitalist showed a willingness to take our loan, he would be deterred by the combination of those opposed to it, and yet money here is so plentiful, and seeks investment so anxiously, that I have no doubt any amount could be borrowed at 3 pr. cent on a security commanding full confidence in this market. What a disgraceful state of things ! We are harrassed here with rumors of changes at home; for however unlikely the individual reports, it would seem impossible that explosion and separation, if not recomposition, should not result from such terrible confusion of the elements as exists at Washington. I hope the President will continue to have the support of Mr· Webster, yourself, Choate and other friends, who have thus far stood by him. With your aid I think he may weather the storm; without it, I fear it must prove too much for him. General Duff Green is here. I occasionally see him, but not frequently, nor do I suppose I possess his confidence, having never felt sure that my own could be safely given to him. He entertains, I believe, an undoubting conviction that Mr. Calhoun will be a candidate for the Presidency, having the best chance of success; such is his language, I am told, with those who see him more nearly than I do.

If this letter reaches you before the adjournment, pray make my most respectful remembrance to the President. I rejoiee to hear that he retains his health and spirits, amidst the unexampled cares and burdens of his station. All is quiet in France. The death of the Duke of Orleans seems, for the present, to have strengthened the dynasty of Louis Phillipe; that it has shown that it is able to meet the first encounter of a very rude shock. Genl. C. talks of going home in the summer of 1843, but I imagine that depends very much on circumstances. I shall always feel greatly indebted to you for a letter, and I beg you believe me, with sincere regard,

faithfully yours,

EDWARD EVERETT.

## TO CALEB CUSHING.

(Confidential)                                     Phil[a]
                                              23 Sept[r]. 1842,
My dear Cushing:

I rec'd your favor of the 20th inst. by the mail of yesterday. On the day before, I met Mr. Marks on Chestnut street, and he informed me that Mr. Forward *had gone* to the Rip Raps. with the view, as I understood, of getting the period of his stay in the cabinet extended to the first of Dec[r]. Yesterday I met with Mr. Tyson, who told me that Marks informed him of Mr. Forward's intention to resign.

For your sake I trust that the matter will be settled one way or the other *instanter.* Our friends here are in spirits. They have united the Democracy, and hope to carry the City; but this I think scarcely possible. I am staying with my brother-in-law Lieut. Emory, on Schuylkill 7th Street, 4 doors below Market, where I shall remain until Monday or Tuesday. If you come here in the meantime let me know. If not, let me hear from you. I enclose a letter from a friend of mine, the Postmaster of Harrisburg. He is a Democrat and I dont want to see him removed. Will you be pleased to look into the matter and advise me thereof either here or at Harrisburg, where I shall stop one day *en route* home?

Thanks for your attention to my friend Denny's interests.

                              Very faithfully,
                                   Yours,
                              W. W. Irwin.[1]

———

## TO DANIEL WEBSTER.

                                         Aug. 8, 1842.
Dear Sir:

I have delayed sending in this paper to-day from a desire that you should look over it before it is sent. The other gentlemen saw its outlines on Saturday when I deeply regretted your absence. Suggest, if they occur to you, any amendments on a separate paper.

———

(1)  Irwin was one of the "Corporal's Guard," and brother-in-law of Robert J. Walker, Senator from Mississippi.

How deeply do I regret that I cannot have your full concurrence in this procedure. But a Clay Congress can only
be met in the way proposed, nor can the independence of the
Executive or the good of the country be otherwise advanced.

If you could return it to me immediately after reading
and suggesting changes, it would enable me to have it copied
and off of hand this evening.

Most truly Yrs,<br>
JOHN TYLER.

TO H. A. WISE.

Washington, 24 Sept., 1842.

Dear Sir:

Mr. Forward has at length made up his mind 1. not
to go down to the Rip Raps at all; 2. not to resign, at any
rate at present; 3. to *talk with the President* on the subject
after his return to Washington, but not to go out if he can
help it until after the meeting of Congress.

The reasons of this are partly what you know by your
conversation with Mr. F.; partly his inveterate habit of pro-
crastinating and *do nothing* by which the Department has been
disgraced ever since he entered it, and by which it is now in
a pitiable condition of delay and disorder; but chiefly, as I
think, for another reason as follows:

Mr. Marks is agent to negotiate the loan. He expects a
commission, of course. I think also there is some other interests of his in the matter. You know that *money* was the
beginning, the middle and the end of all Mr. Forward's views
as imparted to you, to Irwin and myself

Under these circumstances, all our ideas of organization
this autumn are of course defeated.

I think it is the duty of the President, in the first place,
to forbid Marks having anything to do with the loan, and cut
off that limb of corruption.

In the second place, as to the Treasury Department, it is
disgraced by Mr. F. Whatever has been done there (except
the Currency Report written by Mr. Webster) has been done
by the clerks and heads of bureaus, and can be done by them
better without him than with him. Of all the other Departments the administration has been admirable during the last

---

(1)  Secretary of the Treasury.

years of that ignominious. His Treasury Report came to Congress a fortnight (unprecedented) after time; his Tariff Report after three months delay. He got us into a scrape about the loan bill; he created all the fuss about no law for revenue after June 30th·; he would not issue a circular until driven to it, and if you can get a favor, a fact, or an idea from him, it is more than I ever did; for I never saw in him anything but weakness and ignorance. Under these circumstances is he to go out with a Foreign Mission? Not with my good will.(1)

As for myself, I beg not to be further thought of in connection with the Department. I propose to leave Washington on Monday, the moment I have seen your Address under way, and to go straight home to enter upon a canvass for Congress, or, if in consequence of what I wrote to my friends about not remaining, they have made other arrangements, then to retire in good humor with them into private life, and wait for better times.

I have written by the same mail to the President.

I am,

Very faithfully yours,

C. CUSHING.

(1) Mr. Forward shortly afterwards resigned, but Mr. Cushing, who was nominated his successor, was not confirmed, whereupon John C. Spencer was nominated and confirmed. He brought the Treasury to the highest point of efficiency. The national debt stood Jan. 1, 1842, at $15,028,486,37, with charges created by Van Buren for several millions more—Sumner's "Currency." In October 1845, the debt stood at apparently $17,075,445,52, but at that date there was a balance available of $8,000,000 in the Treasury. See R. J. Walkers' Report, December, 1845. See "Parties and Patronage" p. 91. Mr. Corwin's Treasury Report, 1850-51, shows that the Tyler administration averaged annually $3,481,158,95 less than Van Buren's in its expenditures.

TO GEN LESLIE COOMBS.

Washington, Decr. 29 th, 1842.

Dear Sir:

In a conversation, this morning, with the Hon. Thomas F. Marshall, of Ky., he reminded me of an expression once made by me "that there was no time when I could have been waked up at 6 o'clock in the morning that I would not have answered, if inquired of, that Mr. Tyler would not sign an Act to incorporate a U. S. Bank." I remember the expression well, admitted that I had used it often in a general way, and repeated it to him with the qualification that at one time, shortly after I heard of Genl. Harrison's death, and after I had seen Mr. Tyler's Inaugural declaring he would follow the example of the Republican fathers, and before I had seen Mr. Tyler after these events, I hoped that he would follow the example of Mr. Madison, and upon the principle of *stare decisis* sign a bank bill; but this I was led to infer only for a short time from his inaugural address, before I had seen and conversed with Mr. Tyler himself. That in a short time after I had seen the inaugural I visited Mr. Tyler, and he at once dispelled my doubts and hopes. He avowed to me, in our first conversation after he became President, his continued opposition to a U. States Bank on constitutional grounds, and said he was too old in his opinions to change them. Mr. Marshall then informed me that my name was actually quoted as authority for the fact that Mr. Tyler would have signed a Bank bill. I denied that I had ever doubted, except as I have herein described, as to what Mr. Tyler would do on that

(1) This letter shows how idle the charge was that Mr. Tyler was persuaded to veto the Bank bill. Mr. Wise was for a bank, but, in his speech in Congress on the Treasury Note bill several months before, he said it was unfair to press such an issue. After Harrison's death, his desire for a bank so far got the best of him that he wrote Mr. Coombs the letter described, But he did not see Mr. Tyler till three weeks after Harrison's death, nor did Gilmer, who was busy with his canvass for Congress. Mr. Tyler had to act, as he says, "in the absence of all his prominent friends."

subject; and informed Mr. Marshall that I knew of no one to whom I had spoken or written my opinions as to what he would do, about the time that any doubts whatever or rather hopes existed in my mind, except yourself. That shortly *after I had seen the inaugural,* and as I was confident, *before I had seen Mr. Tyler,* I had written to you from my home (Accomac) my then hope that the Whig party would meet with no embarrassment from Mr. Tyler's course. He then informed me that he had seen that letter from me to you, and that it had been referred to as proof that I had said Mr. Tyler would sign a Bank Bill, which was wholly inconsistent with my general public declarations on the subject. This immediately determined me to write to you for my letter, or a copy of it.

After this letter which I am now writing was commenced, Mr. Marshall brought to me the enclosed for you, which discloses the further fact *that he now is in possession of my letter to you and has it in this city to be sent back to you to-morrow morning. and that the disposition of it has been submitted by you to his discretion.* I was very much surprised to find this state of facts; especially as when you wrote to me you did not notify me that you expected an answer for the public; as I wrote to you in the unguarded confidence of a private correspondence; as you have since and lately written to me for permission to publish the letter or use it publicly or privately at your discretion which permission was refused by me on the ground that it was not written for the public eye, that I had retained no copy of it, and did not remember, as I do not now particularly, what it contains; and as you have never notified me that you had placed my private letter to you in the hands of Mr. Marshall or any one else to be used in his discretion, though it seems you were here in Washington where I was and where you had opportunity of daily interviews with me at the time! Mr. Marshall does not feel himself authorized to give me the original letter, or a copy of it. He sends it back to you by to-morrow's mail. I retained no copy of it, and would be obliged if you will send me the original or a copy so that *I* may now use it in *my* discretion. In making this request I should, perhaps, send back your own letters to me; but, if they are not destroyed (which I fear is the fact), they are in Accomac, safe under lock and key, and the key is here in my pocket. If it is your desire, they, or copies of them, shall be sent to you hereafter, unless they were destroyed by me as soon as answered and cannot now be found. They are at all events safe from the inspection of any eye except my own. With the hope that you will gratify my request, I am Sir,

Your ob<sup>t</sup>. servant,

HENRY A. WISE.

––––––

TO GEN. LESLIE COOMBS.

H. Reps: Dec. 30<sup>th,</sup> 1842.

Dear Sir:

I have shown to Mr. Marshall a copy of my letter of yesterday to you. He requests me to add, that, on yesterday after he put into my hands his letter to be enclosed to you, he informed me that "he learned I had written a letter to you in which *Mr. Tyler was committed to a U. States Bank;* that he regarded this as a fact which properly belongs to the public, in order that truth might be arrived at and justice might be done to all parties concerned in the public controversy about it; that whilst you were here last Spring, he requested you to furnish him the letter or a copy in reference solely to that fact, and that you, from this place, wrote for my letter to you to be sent to him here from Kentucky, which was done." I am satisfied that this was done upon his application to you, and not by you as volunteer; but still I was not notified of the transaction, and no care was taken to furnish Mr. Marshall with such parts only of my letter as related to the *Bank fact* deemed of *public* importance. All that was said of *men,* by name, in private confidence and of private import was sent with that which alone was inquired after.

Your ob<sup>t</sup>. servant,

HENRY A. WISE.

N. B.—I have shown this letter to Mr. Marshall.

––––––

TO CALEB CUSHING.

Private                                                        Pittsburgh,

24 March, 1843.

My dear Cushing:

Your favor of the 16<sup>th</sup>, reached Washington some

days after I had left, but was forwarded to me by Mrs. Irwin and I have just rec$_d$ it.

My decided opinion is that you ought not to run, unless your election is so certain as not to admit of a doubt.

Neither the Administration, the country nor your personal friends of whom I am proud to be one, can afford to have you sacrificed. You must lead, and guide, and control the Democracy of New England. That is your destiny, if you do not balk it. You are not and cannot be a Whig in the new fangled sense of the term. In my judgment, it is synonimous with Bourbonism or the ultra federalism of the black-cockade, and anti-war school, remorseles, vindictive, uncompromising and behind the age. It has doomed every Tyler man and every man who has had the coolness to think and judge and act for himself, in that conflict and disruption of parties which characterized and disgraced the 27$_{th}$ Congress. With the Democracy there is a place of refuge, with Whiggery none. For the sake of Mr. Tyler, whom I love, I would not have you defeated; for your sake, I would not. If you run and fail, it will be the severest blow his administration has ever received.

The political friends would howl for very joy, and hell itself would get drunk on the occasion. If you are elected, it will indeed be a glorious triumph for you and all of us, but once more, I say, be well assured of success, before you take the field. You have asked my opinion, and I have given it to you with perfect candor. A few days before I left Washington, I saw Proffit. He was sick in bed. I had several interviews with him. We parted with the understanding that he was to see the President on the morning of the 16th in reference to himself, an hour having been fixed by the Pres't for that purpose, and was then to report the result to me at my lodgings. I have not seen him since, for he did not call, and I was under the necessity of leaving on the 18$^{th}$, having been occupied every moment of the interval in getting ready. I therefore know not what has been decided upon in regard to him, but I trust in God every thing has been arranged to his entire satisfaction. The administration owes him much, and should take care of him.

I return to Washington about the first of April, and will sail on or before the 19th. When and where can I meet you? for, if possible, I should like to see you once more before leaving the United States. I sail from New York, my wife goes with me. When I last dined with you at the President's you mentioned the case of your friend our Consul at St. Thomas, to whom the Danish Govt. has refused an exequatur, and said you would furnish me a memorandum. Let me have your views of the whole matter, for I learn it was made the subject of negotiation by my predecessor. Command me in all things, and believe me to be ever faithfully,

Your friend,
W. W. IRWIN.

----

TO CALEB CUSHING.

Private and confidential,
Washington,
Monday, Mar. 29-43.

My dear Sir:

I thank you for your letter which I received two days ago. I believe you have decided right, in withdrawing your name for the present as a candidate for Congress. If there should be again no choice, a different aspect of things might present itself.

So backward and cold is the season, that it is hardly likely I shall get North earlier than the first of May. In the mean time I want to see you much, and think it necessary you should come here for a day or two. I suppose you care nothing about being at home next Monday; and therefore suppose you set out for the South on receipt of this. Important things, in which you are concerned are to be thought about and talked about. I believe the President intends to offer you a Department. I wish you to have *this*, then again there is *China*, if Mr. Everett should decline the mission. (1)

It is high time some of these things were settled. I pray you come and see us soon as you can.

The picture has arrived from North Bend.

Yrs. truly,
DANIEL WEBSTER.

----

(1) Edward Everett was nominated for the Chinese Mission, but declined it, and thereupon the President in the vacation appointed Caleb Cushing. Benton, in his "Thirty Years View" misstates the case But Congress had no power to limit the President's right of nomination in the way suggested by the bill.

TO HUGH S. LEGARE.

Charles City County, Va., May 16, 1843.
My Dear Sir:

Your letter of the 12th May was received by yesterday's mail, and I am quite concerned at the information you give in relation to the Sandwich Isles. You will remember the message sent to Congress by me during the last session recommending the Mission to China, and the establishment of a Consular agency at the Islands, in which I said that we could not witness their occupancy by any Nation, without entering against it a solemn protest. I had hoped that a declaration so emphatic would have been respected by G. Britian, and regret now to learn the contrary. The levying taxes or exactions upon trade by her agents in the Islands is the exercise of sovereign power over them. Should we not enquire without delay into all the circumstances and address a strong note to the British Govt. upon the subject ? We should also lose no time in opening a negotiation relative [to] the Oregon.

I note what you say relative to the Chinese Mission. I confess I am surprised to learn that all the money has been withdrawn from the Treasury. It has been done, I must frankly say, without my knowledge, except to the extent of Mr. Cushing's outfit and $6000 to Mr. Fletcher Webster, in order to purchase articles agreed upon as necessary to be shipped, and some advanced to himself which was regarded as right and proper; even this amount was greater than I deemed strictly necessary as I said to Mr. F. W. after it had been drawn, but cared but little about it as he had to account for it at the Treasury. This is all that I have been made acquainted with. I hope, nay, I cannot doubt, but that whatever else has been done has been properly done.

I think it altogether proper that whatever has been done before your accession to the Department should appear plainly on the books, and I doubt not but that Mr. W. would take such steps, if you would give the slightest intimation as would be agreeable to you.

I am well aware of the heavy burthen upon you by the occupancy of the two Departments and will, at as early a day as I can, afford you relief.

The Register of Wills in Alexandria has died, and it becomes necessary to appoint a successor. Do me the favor to make out a Commission for Mr. Bernard Hooe, who will hand you this, and be assured of my constant regard and esteem.

JOHN TYLER.

P. S.    Had you not better appoint Dr. Martin your chief clerk without further delay? He would be a decided acquisition to you. Do preserve *this letter on your private file*, as I have not time to copy.

———

### TO HUGH S. LEGARE.

Charles City County. May 21, 1843.

My Dear Sir:

Your last letter only reached me twenty-four hours ago. In regard to Dr. Martin, my embarrassment is even greater than your own. I considered his appointment not only due to his deservedly high standing, but to sound policy. It would have an effect equally substantial with the appointment of a Democrat to the Head of the Department, and was calculated to make all things smooth and easy. I had, of course, no knowledge of any bitterness of attack by the Doctor on Mr. Webster. I look'd upon the substitution of Mr. F. Webster in the Doctor's place as a thing perfectly natural in itself, and that Doctor M. seeing it in the same light had been entirely reconciled to it. When Mr. F. Webster left the Department, it seemed to me that the way was open to Doctor Martin's restoration whose talents and business habits were highly estimated by the country. I exceedingly regret that Mr. W. places his appointment on the footing that he does. Since writing the foregoing Mr. Cushing has arrived, and to him I have talked confidentially. He says that he had inquired of the Doctor whether he had written anything personally offensive to Mr. Webster for the *Globe*. His reply was, not since the establishment of the *Spectator*. Now I am exceedingly reluctant to give up Doctor Martin for the place,

and I still think that Mr. Webster may be induced to waive
opposition.

I certainly should be unwilling to do anything personally
offensive to Mr. W.  I have desired Mr. Cushing to converse
with him on the subject and let us know the result.  If, however, he is obdurate, then we must look to something else.  We
want a Diplomatic Agent at Buenos Ayres and I know no
man who is better suited to it than the Doctor.  My intention
is to nominate such agent for the Chargéship next winter.
Intimate this to the Doctor, and see how he will like it.

I shall return to Washington early in June.  With truest
regard.

JOHN TYLER

Mr. Cushing informs me that the balance of the appropriation for China, deducting $13,000, 7 to himself and 6000
placed in the hands of Mr. F. Webster, has been he believes,
transferred to our Bankers in London.

J. T.

Young Green, Duff Green's son, has long since been promised the Secretaryship to Mexico.  That cannot be altered; so
do make out his commission and send him at once to Mexico.

PRESIDENT TYLER TO J. B. JONES. [1]

Sept. 13, 1843—I write you hastily and on a torn sheet of
paper—but I am anxious to make a suggestion relative to
your course touching the Syracuse convention. It has seemed
to me for some time that the Calhoun Press of the North, if
there be one at all, looked altogether to our papers to carry
on a war with Van Buren.  Now whatever may be done in
New York and elsewhere, I think your Press should preserve a
dignified reserve.  Publish the proceedings and say nothing
about them—or but very little, as that "you fear they may
have a disastrous bearing", or something of that sort.  We
have nothing to hope from either faction, so let them fight it
out.  Prudence, my Dr Sir, prudence is the word.  There
will be no harmony in any convention, nor do the parties desire it.  They will run upon their own hooks, under the
belief that a Whig cannot be elected and that some Democrat

(1)  Editor of the Washington "Madisonian."

will succeed before the H. of R., composed as it is of a large majority of Democrats. *Verbum sap.* Hold off as much as possble and let your fire be directed at Clay. He broke up the Whig party for his own selfish ends. Use my name as little as possible in your paper.

I have no other paper at hand.

---

### SAME TO SAME.

Washington, Jan. 16, [1844]—Your paper leans too much to Clay. Beware of the men around you. You should preserve an exact balance. All opposition to Van Buren should rest on his unavailability. What you say of Mr. Rives and the *Globe* is just, but you should have expressed your regret that Mʳ Rives had spoken before the issue was in fact made.[1]

Many things may yet occur to change ₜthe direction of public opinion. It is also fatal to connect my name with Mr. Webster as in the commentary on the Columbus convention. Remember always that mine is an isolated position.

There are several persons who want to control the *Madisonian.* Hold firmly the reins.

---

### [2] SAME TO SAME.

My own opinion is that we had better now leave off abusing Mr. Clay altogether. He is dead and let him rest. More attention should be paid to the proceedings of Congress, and the paper should contain the earliest intelligence of important matter elsewhere. Long editorials had better be avoided.

All the papers of city give the result of Edward's trial. Yours does not. Your subscribers want the earliest intelligence on all matters at home and abroad.

(1)   This means that the abuse of the *Globe,* as the organ of the Van Buren wing of the Democratic party, had driven Mr. Rives back to the Whigs.

(2)   This letter is without date, but was probably written shortly after the election of 1844.

# Annexation of Texas.

In a letter published in the " Norfolk ( Va.) Land-
mark" of Oct. 31, 1884, Robert W. Hughes, Judge
of the United States District Court for the Eastern
District of Virginia, speaks of the "stupendous work
done by Virginia in developing the Union by the annexation, through Tyler, of Texas, and the conse-
quent acquisition of the Northern states of Mexico,
surpassing even her boon to the Union, in 1787, of
the North-western Territory, and only parallelled by
the act of another of her statesmen in the annexation
of the entire French dominion on the continent."
Another representative of Virginia, Ex-Governor
William E. Cameron, in a recent publication, is enthusiastic in his praise of the genius, character and
splendor of Mr. Tyler's statesmanship as manifested
in the overwhelming success of his administration
and the annexation of Texas, "which Mr. Tyler had
made distinctively *his* issue. "

It is a fact that all the really great men of the
country have been annexationists. Hamilton and
Jefferson, who agreed in nothing else, were annexationists. Calhoun, Benton, Walker, Jackson,
Biddle, Clay, Adams, Tazewell and William H.
Seward believed in the policy. The last, writing
to Mrs. Brewster, daughter of Hon. Robert J.
Walker, declared that " if the bold and enlightened
policy" (advocated by her father) " could have ruled

in his time, the Republic would have been the continent of North America." "It will," writes Seward,
"be accepted hereafter." [1]

Mr. Tyler took up the question of annexing Texas
early in 1841 (Vol. ii., p. 126). It was frequently dis-
cussed[2] by him and his friends, Gilmer, Wise, Upshur, Cushing, &c. Gilmer had visited Texas in
1837, where he was employed by that government as
agent to obtain a loan. In his letters to his wife at
that period, Gilmer dwells on the advantage of annexing the country. In the debate in 1837, in the house
of representatives, Wise also had taken strong
grounds for the same measure. In the debate upon
the nomination of Waddey Thompson, in 1842, Wise
had grown fiery upon annexation. In the winter
of 1842-3, President Tyler, with the co-operation of
Webster, had the plan of a tri-partite treaty for the
acquisition of Texas and California. [3] In January,
1843, Gilmer wrote a strong letter for the papers,
urging the importance of annexing Texas. [4]

In the meantime, Webster (spurred on by the
President), who was "favorable," but afraid of his
abolition constituents," [5] had negotiated the independence of that country in an able correspondence with
Bocanegra, Mexican secretary of state.

(1) MS. in Gen. Duncan S. Walker's possession.

(2) See Reilly's Letter, Niles lxxiii. Reed's Letter in this volume
to author, &c.

(3) Vol. II., p. 261.

(4) See Niles' Register for this letter.

(5) Anson Jones' "Official Correspondence."

But the senate, anxious to obtain a favorable adjustment of the claims against Mexico, chose to disgust Texas by rejecting the treaty which Webster had negotiated. Soon after, on July 6, 1843, Van Zandt was instructed [1] to withdraw the offer of annexation which had been pending since 1842.

Houston, the President of Texas, soon looked to England for aid in the struggle for autonomy. Anson Jones, Texan secretary of state, says that England's interest in the independence of Texas was "to build up a rival power to the United States." [2] The holders of Mexican bonds had also an interest that way, to which were added the active efforts of the "World's Convention" of abolitionists in 1843, who wanted to abolish slavery in Texas in order to attack the institution in the United States. [3] The question was not—as von Holst put it—the danger of a free state on our southern border, but one engineered by an organized band of abolitionists to carry on war against the South. Ashbell Smith attended the World's Convention, and heard from the lips of the speakers the most blood-curdling propositions, and said that it was well known that they promoted the fitting out of Mexican war steamers, in order to bring Texas to terms. [4]

---

(1) Anson Jones " Official Corespondence. "

(2) Ibid.

(3) These were the charges of Anson Jones, by no means unfriendly to England.

(4) " Reminiscences " of Ashbell Smith, formerly Texan secretary of state.

In a confidential letter, [1] dated Washington, Aug. 28, 1843, President Tyler wrote to Waddey Thompson, our Minister at Mexico, that "we feel here the greatest desire to know the precise basis on which the existing negotiation between Texas and Mexico is conducted," that "information had been received from the Texan Minister in London that Great Britain was the chief mediator, and that her meditation is founded upon proposed stipulations in the highest degree detrimental to the United States"—stipulations "equivalent to making Texas a dependency of England." He urged Thompson to be on the alert, "Communicate all you gather, and keep us duly advised." On Oct. 16, 1843, Upshur, at the President's direction, made an offer to Van Zandt, the Texan Minister of annexation. In the August before, the Mexican Minister to the United States had announced that any act of annexation by the United States would be considered a declaration of war. In a dispatch dated Dec. 13, 1843, the Texan government directed their Minister to reject the overture, as certain to break off the truce brought about by the mediation of Great Britain, and involve them in hostilities. The Texan congress, however, passed strong resolutions instructing Houston to negotiate. And in the United States the President exerted every effort to overcome Houston's scruples. Upshur took means to sound the senators, and in January he was able to officially state that two-thirds of the senate did approve of a treaty to annex Texas. [2] About the same time Houston was assured by Jackson, who

(1) MS.
(2) Vol. II., p. 284.

was posted by A. V. Brown and Walker, from Washington, that 39 senators were in favor of the measure. [1] The fact that pledges had been given was current rumor. [2]

Houston pretended to give way to the pressure, but made his terms such as he knew this government would not accede to. Van Zandt had already asked Upshur to agree to furnish troops to protect Texas preliminary to the treaty, and Van Zandt states that, while Upshur did not officially reply, he informed him (Van Zandt) verbally that he would protect Texas with arms only during the pendency of the treaty before the senate, after signature. [3]

Murphy, our agent in Texas, carried away by his zeal, volunteered to give the desired assurance, and thereupon Houston dispatched General J. P. Henderson to the United States to co-operate with Van Zandt. Murphy was promptly disavowed by John Nelson, and, though Calhoun, his successor, held to Upshur's original position, the Texan commissioners, instead of going home, signed the treaty. It was a

---

(1) Ibid., p. 258; Yoakum's Texas, ii., p. 425.

(2) Clay heard the report, in February, 1844, that 42 Senators were pledged to support a treaty for annexation, if negotiated,—Vol. II. p. 306; For confirmation of Upshur see Tylers statement, Vol. II.,, p. 396; Van Zandt's, Vol. II., p. 278; Thomas H. Bailey's Ibid., II. p. 284; Gen J. P. Henderson's letter March 30, 1844, Jones, Official Correspondence;" C. A. Wickliff's statement (Debates in Kentucky Convention, 1849) ; Hon, T. B. Cropper's who said that Senator William S. Archer, afterwards an opponent of the treaty, had "importuned and urged the lamented Upshur to form" the same " if report upon the best authority be true"—Richmond *Enquirer*, July 2, 1844.

(3) Yoakum, ii., p. 426. See I I., p. 290.

game of bluff on the part of Houston, but, as Anson Jones says, he was completely beaten.[1]

Mr. Calhoun, in 1836, had advocated the annexation of Texas, but he says that he did not take in the debate at that time the prominent part assumed by Walker, Preston and others. [2] Gilmer talked with him about annexation in 1842, but Calhoun's attitude was that of quiescence. Gilmer wrote to him in December, 1843, for his opinion, which proves that up to this time he had taken no part in the so-called "Texas conspiracy." [3] The President had exchanged no views with him; [4] and Upshur could not do so; as he was under injunctions of secrecy from the President. Some one, 'tis true, appears to have written Calhoun from London about the movements of Lord Brougham and the abolitionists, and this

[1] Can no instructions be given by a President but such as are absolutely in contemplation of peace ? If not, then no instructions of any kind can be given, since any instructions may terminate in war. If the President has a right so initiate a treaty for annexation, surely he has a right so employ the military to prevent the treaty from becoming abortive by action of a third power, who in the interim of the action of the Senate of the U. S. might inaugurate war and take possession. This is not trenching on the war powers of Congress, but an act of necessary implication from granted powers. How different the conduct of Mr. Lincoln, who, in 1861, declared war, suspended the writ of habeas corpus, and enforced an embargo; but in his message at the extra session in July, 1861, he said that "his trust was in Congress," and that "whether his measures were legal or not, they were ventured upon under what appeared to be a popular demand and of public necessity." After inviting Texas to negotiate, President Tyler felt himself honor bound to protect her against any attacks brought on by the invitation, as far as he could.

[2] Calhoun's Speeches," IV., p. 369.

[3] Gilmer's Letter in this volume.

[4] Vol. II., p. 413.

letter, it seems, Calhoun transmitted from his home
in South Carolina to this government. [1] But the
Texan Minister, Ashbell Smith, wrote the President
direct, and Mr. Tyler imputes, in the letter to
Thompson, quoted above, his information about matters in England entirely to Smith. [2] Nor is it
reasonable to suppose that the President, aided by
the accredited organs of the government, should
have had to depend upon a private person for information. Upon being called upon to supply the place
of Nelson in 1844, Calhoun protested,[3] as he says,
with his friends against accepting office; and after
accepting, he did not reach Washington for three
weeks. Had the Texan minister, J. P. Henderson,
been more speedy in arriving, the treaty of annexation would have been concluded by John Nelson.[4]
Calhoun afterwards advised the President, when the
treaty was defeated, to let the subject and all other
subjects go over with it to Polk's administration.[5]
Had this advice been followed, Texas and the West
would have been lost.

The *Intelligencer* announced the treaty in its issue
of March 16, 1844. A. V. Brown had sent Gilmer's
Texas letter to Gen. Jackson, who had returned an
enthusiastic endorsement, dated February 12, 1843.
Afterwards, in the early part of the session of
1843-44, he was in active correspondence with A. V.

(1) Calhoun's "Speeches, " IV., 369.
(2) See also Vol. II., 479, Mr. Tyler's letter to the *Intelligencer*.
(3) Vol. II.. 330.
(4) Ibid., 413.
(5) Ibid., 331.

Brown, R. J. Walker and Houston about Texas. [1] After the public announcement by the *Intelligencer* of the annexation, Jackson's letter of Feb. 12, 1843 was published [2] in the Washington *Globe* of March 20, 1483, with correct date. And two days after an article appeared in the Richmond *Enquirer* made up chiefly of the commendatory notes which Walker had received about his Texas letter, and including the letter of General Jackson, but with its date misprinted [3] 1844, instead of 1843. Blair, of the *Globe*, was sick, but his daughter, Mrs. E. Blair Lee, wrote to Walker [4] on April 13, 1844, that "her father would earnestly advocate the reannexation of Texas." On April 25, Blair wrote an editorial, defending the treaty, and speaking of Calhoun's correspondence as having nothing to do with the merits of the question. [5] But in a few days, when Van Buren came out against Texas, Blair in an editorial, dated May 1, 1844, changed [6] his ground, and pronouncing the cor-

(1) Ibid., 285; Jackson's Letter, in this volume.

(2) Benton says that Blair declined to publish Jackson's letter when requested by Brown, but it is not so. Jackson, so far from wishing to recall his letter to Brown, of February 12, 1843, wrote to Houston in January, 1844, urging him to negotiate, and kept up the fight in public and in private letters. See Yoakum's "Texas" ii. p. 425; Vol. II., p. 285; and see his letter to Lewis in this number, where he assumes responsibility for the treaty rejected by the senate.

(3) Benton makes out of this misprint a great conspiracy, but the *Globe* two days before had published the letter with correct date.

(4) See her letter in this volume.

(5) See the *Globe*.

(6) Mr. C. A. Wickliffe, in the Kentucky Convention of 1849, said that the very men who urged him to get Texas were subsequently the most forward in denouncing annexation.

respondence "as evidently intended to defeat the treaty," attacked it bitterly. The senators, too, being compelled to follow the commands of Clay and Van Buren, who had come out against annexation at this time, broke their promises and caused the treaty for annexation to be rejected.

This treaty, as Anson Jones showed, was in every way advantageous to the United States. It guaranteed to the United States all the immense public lands of Texas for the assumption of the national debt of $10,000,000—a sum afterwards, in 1850, paid by the United States for the relinquishment of the claims of Texas to a portion of the same territory, viz.: two-thirds of New Mexico. Texas, under the joint resolutions, retained the land, and, after paying the debt, has still an immense tract remaining.

After the rejection of the treaty, the Texan government declared that "we must regard ourselves as a nation, to remain for ever separate."[1] France and Great Britain proposed to Houston to guarantee the independence of Texas, if Texas would give a formal pledge not to unite with any other nation. In September, 1853, Houston instructed Anson Jones to forward the authority required. But Jones, who was then secretary of state and also president-elect, disobeyed the order, and, instead, sent leave of absence to Minister Smith. [2] And yet, in May, 1845, Houston, in a speech made at New Orleans, tried to make people think he had only "coquetted" with England to bring about annexation. In this aspect

(1) Jones' Official Corr.

(2) Williams' "Sam Houston "; Jones' Official Corr.; Vol. II., 335. 401, 432, &c.

he paraded before the public till Anson Jones made an *expose'* in 1848. Then Tyler said certainly the right thing, that Houston's "billing and cooing with England was as serious a love affair as any in the calendar.,"

Mr. Tyler accepted a nomination from his friends in 1844 for the great purpose of driving the Democratic party from the support of Mr. Van Buren, who totally to the surprise of Gen, Jackson, came out against annexation. The Democratic party felt the move and nominated Mr. Polk, to whom Mr. Tyler had tendered the position of Secretary of the Navy, after Gilmer's death. Tyler knew from the first he had no chance of an election, and so expressed himself. But his friends were much stronger than his enemies were willing to concede, and enabled him to control the situation, at any rate.[1] After Mr. Tyler was assured, in every possible way, that his friends would be treated as "brethren and equals," he withdrew his name from the contest, and Mr. Polk's election was from that time rendered next to certain. Mr. Clay, who had taken, in the canvass, a position

(1) Those who ridicule Tyler for accepting the nomination have nothing to say against Birney, the abolition candidate, who had a much less following than Tyler. M. M. Noah knew all the facts, as he was once a friend, but when Tyler refused to give him the consulate at Liverpool because he was an editor, he garbled a conversation, but admitted that Tyler said that "he entertained no hopes of an election himself."—Niles, 64, p. 394. (1843) That Mr. Tyler had a just conception of his strength, see his letters to Gardiner, Wise, &c. Vol. II., 317, 341. See also Walker's letter to Polk in this volume; John Tyler, Jr's. paper in Lippincott's Magazine, 1888, p, 420; "Parties and Patronage," p. 81.

on the fence as to nearly every public question, was defeated, and fairly so. [1]

At the session succeeding Polk's election, the Texas question was taken up and carried through. In his note of Oct. 19, 1843, first proposing annexation, Upshur referred to the treaty form as the "most proper" under the requirement of secrecy then prevailing, to avoid the intervention of Great Britian and France. He left it to be inferred that there was another mode by which the subject might be approached. So, too, in June, 1844. after the treaty for annexation was rejected, and the President recommended joint resolutions of congress, Tyler said that he *had* regarded the treaty form as the "most suitable."

Mr. Ogden, in the Texan congress, proposed joint resolutions for annexation in that body in December,

---

(1) If Clay by his letter to Miller, lost the abolition vote in New York and Michigan, without the letter he would have lost Delaware, Maryland, North Carolina and Tennessee—the last Polk's own State —which were all carried for Clay by slender majorities. The Whig writers and those who adopt their views do not seem to remember that the argument is as broad as it is long. Moreover, in the canvass, the Whig stump speakers in the South pleaded that if Clay was elected, he was the man of all others to procure a speedy annexation— See remarks of A. H. Stephens, Duncan, &c., Cong. Globe, 1844-45 p. 190, Appendix 495: "Parties and Patronage, p. 86, Before Clay's Raleigh letter the South was a unit for annexation. See Upshur's letter, II., p. 284, and "Democratic Address of Virginia," Ibid., p. 324. Milton Brown claimed that his resolution was "an original Whig proposition, and received only a reluctant support from the Democrats,"—A. V. Brown's "Speeches," quoting Milton Brown, p. 219. Senator William S. Archer, of Virginia, Whig Chairman of the Committee on Foreign Relations, admitted that his own Whig constituents were strongly in favor of annexation.—Cong. Globe, 1844-45. Appendix, p. 326.

1843.   In the United States, Robert J. Walker, who in 1836, had proposed in the senate the resolutions recognizing the independence of Texas, pointed out, in his celebrated Texas letter, published in January, 1844, three ways by which foreign territory might be constitutionally added—1, by treaty; 2, by joint resolutions of congress; 3, by act of any state, with consent of congress.   At the session in 1844-'45 a good many propositions were urged, but the joint resolutions proposed by a Whig named Milton Brown prevailed; [1] and the President's prompt action in preferring them to the senate's proposition, tacked on as an amendment, prevented the result which Houston pictured to Minister Murphy.   This was the establishment of a rival power whose growth would absorb California and Oregon. [2]

Dr. H. von Holst, in his "Constitutional History of the U. S.," objects to the constitutionality of the mode by which Texas was annexed.   But I am content to place George Bancroft's opinion and argument against his. [3]

Dr. von Holst pronounces[4] Calhoun's statement to Packenham, that his letter was the occasion of the

---

(1) Willoughby Newton of Virginia, wrote to the Richmond *Enquirer* in 1845 : " I in company with the gallant Whig members from Tennessee, Georgia and Alabama, voted for the Texas resolutions. . . . . To vote against them would have been to violate what I had every reason to believe to be the will of a large majority of my constituency.   In the late election I urged the election of Mr. Clay, because . . . he of all men was best calculated to settle annexation peacefully."

(2) Williams' " Life of Sam Houston."

(3) Bancroft's " History of the Constitution of the U. S.," II., p. 162

(4) Dr. H. von Holst's " Life of J. C. Calhoun," p. 232.

treaty for annexation "a lie." But Calhoun never said what von Holst imputes to him. He declared; only that Packenham's letter had confirmed the President's "previous impressions", and made it his "imperious duty to *conclude* the treaty, &c." Nor did Calhoun tell a lie when he wrote that the United States had "hitherto" declined to meet Texas' wishes, &c. Of course he meant "previous" to Upshur's overture in October, 1843, the treaty concluded in April being really begun then. It was a fact that the United States had declined the overtures of Texas in 1837 and 1842. What the private persons— Calhoun and others cited by Von Holst—had said or done, was not the action of the U. S. government.

Dr. Von Holst lashes himself into a fury of indignation over the Texas question, but his whole work is a preposterous tissue of absurdities, and cannot well be otherwise, since his main reliance is on Benton, who wrote nothing correctly.

In concluding this paper, I however notice two other charges. The first is that Mr. Tyler had no power to ask for a joint resolution in his message to the House of Representatives in June, 1844, after the Senate had already rejected a treaty. Concurrent powers under our form of of government are not uncommon. The State Courts have concurrent power with the U. S. Courts, in many cases. The foreign trade and the imposition of duties can be determined not only by the treaty power but by the legislative. And in the same way, as shown in Walker's letter, there exists as many as three methods of adding territory. The failure of one does not inhibit the use of the others.

The other point is, that most Northern writers, in their maps of successive acquisitions of territory by the United States, limit "Texas" to her present boundaries and describe the rest of the vast territory acquired by Texas and properly included· within her territory when annexed, as "Mexican Cession." Now the United States took Texas with full knowledge of her claim to the Rio Grande, and from its head waters to the forty-second parallel of North latitude. They afterwards, in 1850, admitted her title by paying her for two-thirds of New Mexico. It is true the Mexicans denied the validity of the Texan claim, and assigned the *Nueces* as the Southern boundary, and the Free Soil party adopted the same view, because Texas was a slave territory and the Mexican law prohibited slavery. But the United States were in honor bound to do what they could for Texas in the negotiation with Mexico. To be logical their maps should be constructed either to represent the Texas acquisition as bounded by the *Nueces*, or give the full claim of the Texas congress to all the vast country as far north as the forty-second parallel.

# Letters.

TO ANSON JONES [1]

15th March, 1843.

[Extract]

The late view I have presented to the President on the subject of English efforts in Texas has aroused him (Tyler) very considerably, and if matters were settled here he would undoubtedly make a move. Mr. Webster will leave the State department very soon. Though friendly to us, he is very much in our way at present. He is timid and wants nerve, and is fearfnl of his abolition constituents in Massachusetts. I think it likely Upshur will succeed him; if he does, it will be one of the best appointments for us. His whole soul is with us. He is an able man and has nerve to act.

I regret Cushing's rejection. Though from the North he was with us. If Wise is elected again, he will do us as much as if he went to France. He is a perfect thorn in the side of old John Quincy Adams.

The President, though much abused, is gaining ground; the Democrats and moderate Whigs are falling into his ranks and coming to his support. Our principal strength in this country is with the Democrats. Our own success depends much on the political turns in this country.

The President said to me the other day in a private interview: "Encourage your people to be quiet and to not grow impatient; we are doing all we can to annex you but we must have time." If the President concludes he can make capital by the move or can secure the ratification, he will make the treaty as early as he can afterwards; but the opposition is so great that he moves cautiously indeed, and I think very prop_erly.

I. VANZANDT.

(1) **Texan Secretary of State.** This extract is from Jones' "Official Correspondence."

TO ANSON JONES. [1]

Washington, D. C., 5th April, 1843.

[Extract]

I had a conversation with the President on Monday last upon the subject of our foreign relations  He said he was clearly of the opinion that it was high time the war should cease, and that he was for action in the matter and had so said to Mr. Webster ; but that Mr. Webster had not acted so promptly in the matter as he desired; that he would return from Boston in a few days when he would again call his attention to the matter.  He said Mr. Webster's reasons were that he was greatly absorbed in their own affairs across the water.  I fear there is not the best understanding among all the secretaries at this time (I speak this of course confidentially ).  Mr. Tyler certainly feels embarrassed from the opposition which surrounds him, and any attempt to force matters too strongly would possibly produce an explosion which is certainly much to be dreaded.

I. VANZANDT.

TO J. C. CALHOUN

Washington, Dec. 13, 1843.

My dear Sir:

At the instance of a mutual friend I venture to drop you a line not to speak of the chances, calculations and chapter of accidents of a presidential election.  (For these I have

(1) From Jones' "Official Correspondence; "

(2) This letter was found lately among Mr. Gilmer's papers in his own handwriting, and marked " copy, "  The answer to it was published in Vol. II., 296,  Negotiations had already commenced, and the " mutual friend " was Upshur, who was beating up recruits for the treaty then under secret consideration.  It will be seen that in the Texas matter the administration approached Calhoun, not Calhoun the administration, as Benton and those who have copied after him have asserted.

very little appetite)—but to remind you of a conversation we
had nearly a year since on a subject which as I then predicted
is beginning to attract general and deserved attention. I allude to the annexation of Texas to our Union. I have not
doubted for some time that this question would soon assume a practical shape and that its results would ultimately,
if not immediately, enure to the peace, permanence and pros-
perity of the Union. If the question were free from some
prejudices ( which by the way apply with equal force to a
portion of the Union as it is) it would not be approached for
a moment as one of only local importance. It is indeed a
great American question and involves the first principle of
American independence. The efforts of European powers
which have been or may be made to establish an influence in
Texas prejudicial to our commercial interests and republican
institutions will probably aid in giving this question a national aspect somewhat sooner than would be hoped from its
intrinsic merits.

You remember I asked you last winter to turn your mind
to this subject in all its bearings and to be ready to meet it.
As a candidate for public favor, I would not have you or any
other to be committed on this question in advance—I do not
therefore approach you as one of those now in the public eye
as candidates for the chief magistracy, but as an illustrious citizen whose opinions would derive no additional force from
any station, as I believe they would not be influenced by a desire to obtain it. I have no doubt you have bestowed much
reflection on this particular subject. While I am not at liberty (nor am I informed) to speak of the precise state of this
question at present, I will say to you that negotiations have
been commenced, the object of which is to annex Texas to the
Union. On a question of such magnitude it is not meet that
a voice which for more than thirty years has been heard with
so much interest on all public question, should be silent. I will
esteem it a favor and so will many others, if you give us the
benefit of your counsels now. They will be regarded as
confidential, if you chuse—or otherwise. You are familiar
with the negotiations, correspondence etc., between our government and Spain from 1805 to 1819 with regard to the
boundaries of Louisiana under the treaty with France. The
effect of annexation on the interests (domestic and foreign) of

our country, however, is the point to which public attention
will be chiefly directed. The test will be practically applied
whether the compromises of the constitution are to be regarded or the Union endangered by violating rights secured under
the compact of 1787.

Excuse this liberty, I beg you, and allow me to subscribe
myself,

With sincere esteem and very high consideration,

Your friend &c.,

THOMAS W. GILMER.

TO GOV. WILSON SHANNON.

[Confidential]

State Department

Washington, March 6, 1844.

Sir:

I am instructed by the President to apprise you that,
confiding in your intelligence and integrity, he has this day
nominated you to the Senate of the United States as Envoy
Extraordinary and Minister Plenipotentiary to the Republic
of Mexico, to succeed the Hon. Waddy Thompson, who has
asked and obtained leave to resign.

In communicating to you this evidence of the high consideration in which you are held by the Chief Magistrate, I
deem the occasion a suitable one to say that the relations between the United States and Mexico, which have long been of a
very delicate character, are rendered particularly so at the present juncture by the anticipated negotiations for the annexation
to this Union of the Territory of Texas, in the issue of which
the President feels a deep and anxious interest; and which
he assumes,—and in that assurance offers you the difficult position that may enable you to advance this leading object of
his policy,—that you entirely and cordially endorse.

I take leave further to suggest that the public interests
may require your immediate assumption of the duties of this
mission, and that it will be therefore advisable that you should

hold yourself in readiness to enter at once upon its duties, should you decide to accept the appointment and should your nomination be confirmed, of which there seems to be no doubt.

Please advise me of your views on this subject.

I have the honor to be,

Very respectfully, Sir,

Yo: obedt. serv't,

JNO. NELSON. [1]

TO THEOPHILUS FISK.

Columbia, Tennessee, March 20th, 1844.

[Confidential]

My Dear Sir:

I have received your kind letter of the 9th instant. The information which it conveys as well as the proposition made I need not assure you was wholly unexpected. In responding to your inquiries I am frank to say that my personal feelings toward the President are as they have ever been of a friendly character. Knowing him personally as I do, I have often felt it to be my duty as well as inclination, since he has occupied his present exalted station, to vindicate and sustain him in his course on the bank and some other subjects of great public importance against the rude and violent assaults of his political enemies.

You desire me to intimate to you whether it would meet with my approbation to be tendered a place in the cabinet, and whether I would accept the office of Secretary of the Navy made vacant by the late melancholy and lamented death of Gov. Gilmer. I have implicit confidence in the sincerity of the declaration which you make, when you say that "this inquiry is not made to gratify an idle curiosity merely upon slight authority." A situation in the cabinet is one which I have never sought or desired under this or any pre-

(1) John Nelson was the Attorney General, and acted as Secretary of State after the death of A. P. Upshur, and until Mr. Calhoun arrived.

ceding administration. If I believed that I could, by accepting, render any great public service which others could not more ably perform, it would be my duty not to hesitate. Believing, however, that there are many others whose services the President can command who could render more service to the country than I could, I must express my disinclination to yield to the wishes which you so earnestly express, and my sincere desire that some other may be selected. Declining therefore the proffered honour, I have to express my acknowledgment to the President and other friends who may have thought of me for so distinguished and important a station.

I may add that all the public preferment which I have at any time enjoyed I have derived directly from the hands of the people; and since I have been in retirement, I have often declared to my friends that, if I ever again filled any public place, I expected to receive it from the same source. This is well known to my friends, Mr. A. V. Brown, Mr. Cave Johnson, and others of the representatives in Congress from this state.

I most anxiously desire that Mr. Calhoun may accept the department of State which has been tendered to him by the President and Senate. Entertaining the most exalted opinion of Mr. Calhoun's talents and patriotism, I am quite sure that there is no citizen who could better, if so well, fill the important station to which he has been called, in the present posture of our foreign affairs, and especially in reference to the Texas and Oregon questions. Were I to occupy a place in the cabinet, there is no man in the country with whom I would be more pleased to be associated. I hope the country may have the aid of his great mind in bringing these questions to a favourable settlement. Should he undertake the task and be successful, as I have great confidence he would be, it would add to his already just claims upon the public consideration and would entitle him to the lasting admiration and gratitude of his countrymen. Hoping that the President may have no difficulty in filling the office of Secretary of the Navy by the selection of some other than myself,

I am with great respect,

Your friend & obt. Serv't,

JAMES K. POLK.

TO R. J. WALKER.

April 13, 1844.

My dear Sir:

My father desires me to say that he had dictated to me this morning about hal fof an article upon Texas, when, seized with such violent pain, he was obliged to desist. He hopes to finish it for Monday's paper. He will earnestly advocate the reannexation of Texas.

It is a matter of great regret to my father that he has to be extremely quiet and thereby deprived of the privilege of seeing his friends, but it is deemed necessary to his recovery by his physician and my mother.

Yours faithfully,

E. Blair Lee. [1]

TO HENRY A. WISE.

Washington, 11th May, 1844.

My dear Sir:

I spoke to Gen'l Bagley about attending at Baltimore tomorrow evening, but he left me uncertain, whether he would or not. I shall endeavor to see him this evening, and hope he will consent to go. Walker is invited and so is Hammet from Mississippi, but it is uncertain whether either will attend.

Since you left, we have had dispatches both from Mexico and Texas. The former is pressed and threatened by the French, and will be little disposed to give us trouble. The internal Provinces are in a very unsettled and unquiet condi-

[1] Mrs. Lee was the daughter of Mr. Blair, editor of the Washington *Globe*. In accordance with this letter Blair said editorially April 15, 1844 that "the Globe would earnestly advocate the reannexation of Texas to the United States." On April 26, Mr. Blair was still an earnest advocate, and even said that the correspondence of Calhoun, lugging in slavery, had nothing to do with the merits of the question. And yet on May 1—Van Buren's letter opposing annexation being received in the meantime—he attacked the treaty as the "worst" possible form to effect the annexation, and denounced the correspondence.

tion.  The information from Texas confirms the previous impression, that her government will throw her into the arms of
England, if we reject her hand.  Of this, I hold there is not
the least doubt.  I cannot but hope, that the Whigs will see
the gulf into which they are about to fall, and to save themselves will approve the treaty.  If they are not destitute of
sagacity, such will certainly be their course.

The riot in Philadelphia is the legitimate fruit of fanat-
icism and the spoils principle, and that of the numerical majority.  When will you be in the city again ?

With great respect.<br>
Yours truly,<br>
J. C. CALHOUN.

TO CAVE JOHNSON

Nashville, Monday night, May 13th, 1844.

Strictly confidential.

My dear Sir:

At the urgent solicitation of Major Don-
aldson, General Armstrong, and one or two other friends who
wrote to me, I came to this place on yesterday.

To-day General Armstrong and myself visited the Hermitage.  On our way up we met Donaldson with a letter
from General J. for publication in the Union, reitering and
reaffirming his views upon the subject of the annexation of Texas.  He urges immediate annexation as
not only important but indispensable.  He speaks most af-
fectionately of Mr. Van Buren, but is compelled to separate
from him on this great question and says both he and Mr.
Benton have by their letters cut their own throats politically
He has no idea that Mr. V. B. can be nominated or if nominated that he can receive any Southern support.  He is not
excited but is cool and collected, and speaks in terms of deep
regret at the fatal error which Mr. V. B. has committed.  He
says, however, that it is done and that the convention must
select some other as the candidate.

The truth is, and should no longer be disguised from
yourself and other friends, that it will be utterly hopeless to
carry the vote of this state for any man who is opposed to

immediate annexation. The body of the Whigs will support Clay regardless of opinions, but hundreds, indeed thousands of them will abandon him and vote for any annexation man who may be nominated by the Baltimore convention. If such a man shall be nominated, we will carry the state with triumph and with ease. If an anti-annexation man is nominated, thousands of Democrats, and among them many leading men, will not vote at all, and Clay will carry the state.

The Texas question is the all absorbing one here and swallows up all others at present. It is impossible to arrest the current of the popular opinion and any man who attempts it will be crushed by it. What you can or will do at Baltimore God only knows. My earnest desire is that you shall harmonize and run but one man. Gen'l. J. thinks that Mr. V. B. being sensible that his opinions are not in harmony with those of the people will withdraw and hopes he will do so. For myself I attribute Mr. V. B's. course to Col. B—ton.

General J. says the candidate for the first office should be an annexation man and from the Southwest, and he and other friends here urge that my friends should insist upon that point. I tell them, and it is true, that I have never aspired so high, and that in all probability the attempt to place me in the first position would be utterly abortive. In the confusion which will prevail, and I fear distract your counsels at Baltimore, there is no telling what may occur. I aspire to the 2d office, and should be gratified to receive the nomination, and think it probable that my friends may be able to confer it upon me. I am however, in their hands and they can use my name in any way they may think proper. General Pillow and Col. Laughlin left here last night. Wm. G. Childress leaves to-night and Major Donaldson on to-morrow night. They can give you more in detail the state of things here. I repeat that I wish my friends to place my name before the convention no matter what the result may be.

I deplore the distraction which exists in the party. It has all been produced by at most half dozen leaders who have acted with a view to their own advancement. Add to this the Texas question, and I have great solicltude for our safety as a party. Surely there is patriotism enough yet among these leaders to save the party. This can only be done by uniting upon one candidate, and he must be favorable to the annexation of Texas. I have stood by Mr. V. B. and will stand by him as long as there is hope, but I now despair of his election even if he be nominated.

The idea which has been suggested of running three candidates, Mr. Clay the Whig, a Texas annexation Democrat in the South, and an Anti-Texas annexation Democrat in the North, ought not to be entertained for a moment. If that is attempted, it insures Clay's election. We would have triple tickets in almost all the states, which would enable a plurality, less than a majority, to give the electoral vote of the state to Clay. I shall expect you to write me daily after the receipt of this until the convention is over.

Your sincere Friend,

JAMES K. POLK.

P. S. I learn that General Jackson's letter will not appear in the *Union* of to-morrow; the paper having no space for it. It will appear in Thursday's paper unless he changes his mind about its publication and withdraws it, which is not probable. W. G. Childress can give you its contents in detail.

Yrs. &c.,

J. K. P.

TO HENRY HORN & J. K. KANE.

[Extract].

*Confidential*.

Columbia, Tennessee,

July 2nd, 1844.

To Mess. Henry Horn & J. K. Kane,
   Gentlemen.

*     *     *     *     *     *     *

It may not be uninteresting to you gentlemen, to learn that the whole South-West is in a *blaze of enthusiasm*. There never was a time when there was half the excitement in this part of the country that we now have. It extends over the whole South West. We now entertain *no doubt* of carrying Tennessee by a large majority. Our friends at the North need have no fears of this state, or of a single state in the South or West. We will sweep everything before us We *feel* it—we *know* it. The excitement on the Texas question is carrying and sweeping down every resistance.

\*     \*     \*     \*     \*     \*     \*     \*

Your obt. St.

Gid. J. Pillow.


TO J. K. POLK.

Washington City, July 10, 1844.

Dear Sir:

On the 4th July last two important meetings were held by the friends of Mr. Tyler in different parts of Philadelphia, at which it was resolved to run separate Tyler electoral tickets and for Congress and State and County offices, and this course it seems was to be adopted througout the Union. Our friends in Philadelphia and also in New Jersey and New York have written to me in great alarm. Yesterday, altho' it was a most disagreeable duty, I called on Mr. Tyler, resolved if possible to ascertain his ultimate views. I had a conversation with him of several hours, in which he disclosed to me confidentially all his views. He said he knew he was to retire to private life, in any event, on the 4th of March, and that he would *at once* withdraw, but that were he to do so *now*, it would not aid the Democratic cause, for that his friends were so exasperated by the assertions of the Globe and other presses, that if he withdrew they would either remain neutral, or many of them join Mr. Clay. That they considered themselves proscribed and invited not to join our party. He stated his deep regret at this state of things, and his great anxiety that Polk and Dallas should be elected. After some remarks from me as to the injustice of holding you and Mr. Dallas responsible for the course of two or three papers, he remarked that his friends numbered about 150,000, that they were chiefly Republicans who voted for the Whigs in '40, and that if a different course were pursued toward them; that if they could be assured on reliable authority that they would be received with pleasure and confidence by you and your friends into the ranks of the Democratic party, and treated as brethren and equals, that he would at *once withdraw*, and that his friends with all their influence and presses would then, he had no doubt come in, and uniting everywhere zealously and efficiently with us, render our victory certain.

Of General Jackson he spoke in terms of deep affection, Mr. Van Buren also he said would be disposed to do him justice if left to his own impulse, but that he was or at least had been misled by others. I returned him many thanks for the confidence he reposed in me by this disclosure of his views, and which, as a political opponent, I had no right to ask at his hands, and concluded by assuring him that no honorable effort would be omitted on my part, to produce an honorable and cordial union between the Democratic party and him and his friends.

Now I think that the importance of this union and co-operation *cannot be over-rated.* In my judgment it would be *decisive* in your favor, and is right in itself. Now it is a delicate matter for you to act, but could you not write a private letter to a friend, which could be shown in confidence to Mr. Tyler expressing such views as you entertain of his services to the Democratic party, and welcoming his friends as brethren and equals back into our ranks ?

Could not General Jackson write a letter to some friend which might be published, expressing his views of Mr. Tyler's services to the party, and expressing the opinion that his friends upon his withdrawal would be welcomed back with cordiality and joy by the Democratic party, and be placed on the same platform of equal rights and consideration with any other portion of the Democracy ? I deem this a matter of such high importance that, if it concurred with your own views, it would seem to me to justify an interview at your earliest convenience with General Jackson, to whom you can show this letter. If anything is to be done, the sooner the better, as it will prevent committals to Mr. Clay, and rally the confidence of our friends.

Your two letters, the one to the Committee and the other to Mr. Kane have done us very great service. They could not be bettered in any way.

I finished a few days since sending 140,000 copies of my

JULIA GARDINER,
(Second wife of President Tyler.)

Texas letter and Texas speech to North Carolina and Indiana and still the demand is unabated, such is the interest taken in those states in the Texas question.

I shall be here until the 12th of August doing what I can for the good cause, and where, if there is anything requiring my attention, you can write to me.

Yours most truly,

ROBERT J. WALKER,

P. S. Since writing the above I have received further news from Pennsylvania. Mr. Muhlenberg, our candidate for Governor, thinks the greatest distraction and distrust in our ranks would be produced by running Tyler tickets in Pennsylvania. In addition to a letter which might be published, could not General Jackson write a private letter to Mr. Blair assuring him of the importance of bringing about Mr. Tyler's withdrawal and the invitation of his friends into our ranks? Already, I think, Mr. Blair is becoming more inclined to this course.

R. J. W.

———

TO J. K. POLK.

Washington City, July 11, 1844.

Dear Sir:

Since writing to you yesterday I have seen a private letter of General Jackson to one of his friends in this city. The letter is most kind and respectful to Mr. Tyler, and says all that could be desired, expressing also a deep anxiety for his withdrawal. It speaks, however, of Benton as crazy and therefore will not do to be published or even shown to Mr. Tyler. Besides it is strictly a private letter, and ought not to be and will not be used in any way. Now I say in confidence for your eye alone, and cannot doubt but you will unite with me in opinion, that any letter General Jackson may write for publication on this subject should contain no allusion to Benton, nor any attack upon any portion of our party. Mr. Tyler can be praised consistently as to the Bank, Texas, &c., without assailing any member of our party.

Yours most truly.

R. J. WALKER.

TO JAMES K. POLK.

Hermitage, July 26th, 1844.

Col. James K. Polk.

My dear Sir:

I have been surrounded with company since Gen'l Pillow was here that until this night I had not a moment to write you.

I read Mr. R. J Walker's letter with great attention, and altho' I have full confidence in him and in his high order of talents—still I could not help being surprised in his display of the great want of common sense in his suggestion that I should write a letter for publication to show that all Tyler men on Mr. Tyler's withdrawal from the canvass should be received and be upon the same level with all other Democrats in the selection for office, merit and fitness being the only enquiry. Why my dear friend, such a letter from me or any other of your conspicuous friends would be seized upon as a bargain and intrigue for the presidency, just as Adams and Clay's bargain. Let me say to you that such a letter from any of your friends would damn you and destroy your election. [1]

I have suggested to Major Lewis that Mr. Tyler now withdrawing from the canvass would give great popularity—and as he can have no hope of being elected, that his own sagacity with his fondness for popularity will induce him to withdraw—no letter from you or any of your friends must be written or published upon any such subject.

(1) The ethics of this letter is hard to understand. Clay was charged in 1825 with electing Adams, to whom he did not speak, in return for the position of Secretary of State and the succession. Mr. Tyler naturally wished to protect his friends in office, and asked nothing for himself. But the letter which follows this from Jackson to Lewis gives all the assurances that Mr. Tyler demanded. And the portion in italics in that letter appeared in print *as from Jackson,* and was not contradicted. See Vol. II., p. 338, 342. Moreover, Polk did write letters to Walker full of assurances of friendship to Tyler's supporters, which were shown to Talmadge and others. See *Post,* Talmadge to Walker Hardly was the election over before Jackson, under the influence of Mr. F. P. Blair, advised Polk to turn out Tyler's friends.

I am now writing scarcely able to wield my pen, or to see what I write. With all our kind salutations to you and your amiable lady, I remain your friend.

ANDREW JACKSON.

P. S. Tyler's friends are a mere drop in the bucket, [1] and they nor nothing but such imprudent letter as suggested can prevent your election; therefore all you have to do is to be silent, answer only such letters that may call upon you for your political principles.

———

TO MAJOR W. B. LEWIS.

Hermitage, July 26, 1844.

My dear Major:

We have a hope soon to see you at the Hermitage. I hope this may reach you at Washington before you leave, and I have to ask you to see my friend Mr. Mason the Secretary of the Navy and know if there is any prospect of John Adams obtaining a midshipman's warrant. His school closes this day and he must be engaged in some business, if not in the Navy.

Great excitement here. Polk and Dallas gaining daily, and Whiggery going down. You know I have a great desire that Mr. Tyler should close his term with credit to himself.

———

(1) But see Jackson's own letter to Polk of Sept. 2, 1844, *Post*: "The withdrawal of Mr. Tyler will no doubt strengthen us in Ohio and Connecticut, where the course of Allen and Tappan against the Texan treaty had much weakened the Democracy, &c." It must be remembered that Walker as *Chairman of the Executive Committee* of the Democratic party, could judge the field better than Jackson, and his letter shows the greatest alarm. See, too, Talmadge's letters, *Post*, as to the effect of the Tyler vote in New York. The opinion of Mr. Muhlenberg's as the Democratic candidate for governor in Pennsylvania, should speak for Tyler's strength in that state. When Tyler's letter of withdrawal was received, the Chinese Museum in Philadelphia was crowded with six thousand of his friends. II., p. 342. Tyler's estimate of his strength is fully supported by many witnesses. See Joel B. Sutherland's letter in this volume. As it was, Polk had a close run with Clay.

It is certain he can not now be elected, and he has now a fair field by withdrawing, to add great and lasting popularity to himself by the act, and free himself from the imputation that his exertions to re annex Texas were to make himself President, and show that his energy in this case was from imperious public duty, to prevent a country so important to the defence, safety and great interest of our whole Union from falling into the hands of England, our most implacable enemy. On Mr. Tyler's withdrawal from the canvass every true American will say, Amen to his patriotism in the case of Texas.

Several of Mr. Tyler's friends yesterday visited me, and wished me to cause it to be made known to him their wishes, as his *withdrawal at once would unite all the Democrats into one family without distinction. This would render our victory easy and certain by bringing Mr. Tyler's friends in to the support of Polk and Dallas, received as brethren by them and their friends, all former differences forgotten and all cordially united once more in sustaining the Democratic candidates.* (1)

Mr. Tyler has a good many Democratic friends here, but who will all unite upon the Democratic nominees, and consider themselves pledged to do so. It is impossible now that Mr. Tyler should be elected, and if he does not withdraw he will be charged with conniving with the Clay Whigs to defeat the Democratic nominees. ALTHOUGH THIS WOULD BE UNTRUE, yet really it would have that effect and would do Mr. Tyler much injury. I told Mr. Tyler's friends I could not write to him on such a subject, but I had such confidence in his good sense and patriotism, that I was sure he would withdraw in due time, as I believed him to be a good Democrat, and that he would do nothing to promote Clay or injure Democracy. If you think it prudent, you can make these suggestions to Mr. Tyler. I think he would receive them kindly, be his determination what it may. His proper dignified course is a magnanimous withdrawal, with such reasons as his good sense may suggest for the occasion. These hints flow from a real regard for Mr. Tyler and a sincere wish that he may retire with much credit.

---

(1) The portion above (my italics) was published in the leading Democratic papers *as from Jackson.* This letter itself was shown to Mr. Tyler by R. J. Walker, and used as an inducement for Mr. Tyler's withdrawal. See Vol. II., p. 338. 342.

As I expected from the debates in the Senate and the influence of England over Mexico, that S$^t$ Anna would make an attempt to conquer Texas. Will the United States stand tamely by and see it done and sold to England for the debt of Mexico, after Houston was induced to believe that, if he would enter into a treaty of annexation, 36 Senators would vote for its ratification, or will our government take the real ground, having made every friendly proposition to Mexico on the subject, and being replied to by Mexico, that she would never consent to the separation of Texas from her, that the Treaty of 1803 is the supreme law of the land, that it never could be abrogated by a Treaty with any other nation without the consent of those citizens living within the boundary of Louisiana as ceded by France and without the consent of France? That all such treaties were null and void and of no effect? That by the treaty of 1803 the United States were bound to admit them into the Union and protect them in their rights, liberty and religion? That Mexico never had any rightful claim over Texas, or any of the territory within the limits of Louisiana as ceded by France to the United States? That the treaty of 1803 had laid the United States under National obligations to the citizens inhabiting Louisiana, which national faith and honor required to fulfill, and Texas having became independent and having required of us a fulfillment of our previous obligations under the treaty of 1803, the United States were bound in honor and national faith to carry out their obligations under that Treaty? That we would sustain our National faith, and that therefore the first attack made by Mexico on Texas would be viewed as an attack upon the United States, and would be resisted with all the power we could command and thus maintain our honor and obligations under the treaty of 1803? Will our Executive have energy enough to make this reply to Santa Anna and call Congress to sustain him? This ground can and will be sustained, as I believe, on principles of international law. Mexico never had any title to Texas. The citizens of Louisiana, now Texas, being thrown off by the Treaty of 1819, and when Mexico formed her confederated government in 1824, Texas agreed to become a member of that confederacy, reserving to herself the right of complete state government with her own State Legislature. When St. Anna by military force drove the confederated congress out of doors and put down the

Constitution of 1824, and coerced all the other states to submit to his will, Texas resisted this act of tyranny and despotism, and the battle of San Jacinto conquered the tyrant, gave
Texas independence, acknowledged by us, England, France,
&c. I ask where is the right of Mexico to claim Texas?

These are hasty hints, thrown out under great affliction,
worn down by company so that for three weeks I have scarcely had time to drink my coffee and eat my mush and milk,
but, hasty as they are, given in half an hour, you may
show them to Mr. *Walker* and the *President confidentially*, that
if Texas is invaded by the powerful army threatened, this or
some other noble stand may be taken to preserve her from
the grasp of Great Britain and relieve our national honor
from the stain of bringing Texas by our treaty under danger
and difficulty and meanly sneaking out of the difficulty ourselves. My friend, R. J. Walker, as well as myself have been
in great part the cause as well as yourself, Major, in inducing
Houston to agree to enter into the treaty. Had I time and
strength, I would make it a clear case that now we as a nation
under the obligations of the Treaty of 1803 are bound to protect Texas as part of Louisiana ceded to us by France, but Mr.
Walker's mind will at once grasp every ramification of this
subject and will be able to present to the President in bold
relief all its strength. I write in haste. There is no time to
be lost, or Texas, if not already lost to us, may soon be, unless there be some hope of aid from the United States. I
have written General Houston as strong and positive a letter
as I can dictate, but let it be remembered that necessity creates its own laws, and necessity may cause Houston to yield
to the pressure of England and France.

Hoping to see you soon at the Hermitage, we all kindly
salute you with best wishes. I am daily growing weaker and
shorter of breath.

ANDREW JACKSON

TO ANDREW JACKSON.

Phila., August 20th, 1844.

[Private.]

My dear Gen'l :

I have just returned from Washington, where I was present when a committee from N. Y. waited upon President Tyler, with resolutions approbatory of his conduct, during his distinguished administration. The President listened to the address and resolutions with great attention and replied most eloquently and appropriately. He has recently received resolutions, addresses, letters from all parts of the Union, which were all highly flattering to him.

I need not enter on a detail of particulars here. It is sufficient to say that he has agreed to withdraw, and issue such an address as will, *I know*, meet the *hearty approbation* of the old Jeffersonian Republican Party. In Penna. I have been one of the most active of his friends. We will *now* go *into* the contest with all our might, and give Polk and Dallas a majority of 20 thousand. I travelled from Washington with the committee from N. Y. Them I *know most intimately*, and they' aver that as soon as President Tyler's address appears, that such force and spirit will be imparted to the good cause that they will *underwrite for the Polk and Dallas ticket in the Empire State.*

I have recently spent some time in the state of New Jersey and feel quite confident of success *there*. *Judge White*, President of the Tyler Democratic Convention that assembled at Baltimore, was at Washington, when I left a few days ago, and he gives it as his opinion, that as soon as President Tyler's friends shall go in for *Polk and Dallas*, that he is *certain* of Connecticut. I have just seen some friends from New Hampshire and Maine, who say there is no doubt of our ticket in those states. I have reason to *know* that the President's address will do a fine business for the Democratic Party in this state.

I met Mr. Southall from Va. at Washington; he was present when the Committee waited on President Tyler, and he said that Mr. Tyler's friends' active support would certainly secure a majority of at least 3,000 in Virginia.

About 2 months ago, I *gave some* friends the lock of hair that you were kind enough to send me from Sykesville on your way from Washington to Tennessee, to enclose in a breastpin to President Tyler *for his vetoes.* May I ask you to please forward me another lock in its place that I may prepare another *for myself.*

I saw our friend Major Lewis when last at Washington. I frequently *hear through* [*sic*] from you. I am glad that you possess sufficient health to keep up a correspondence on the good cause in which the country is at this time so *deeply interested.* Permit me in conclusion to say, that I *place you at the head of the patriots of this Great Republic,* having twice perilled your life for our liberties. I am willing to follow your lead while you are permitted to remain with us here below, nothing doubting that when you leave this world you will wing your way to the world of blessed repose prepared for the good men of every section of the globe.

After reading this, please send it to Col. Polk, to whom I send my warmest respects, not forgetting his amiable and accomplished lady. In the course of the contest, I think I shall be able to describe Mr. Polk and his claims to the Presidency, with as much knowledge of his excellent character and profound statesman-like views in relation to the great interests of the Nation, as any other public speaker north of Mason and Dixon's line. Please remember me kindly to Major D.

The mail is just closing.

Yours truly,

J. B. SUTHERLAND.

————

TO JAMES K. POLK.

Hermitage, Sept. 2nd, 1844.

Col. Jas. K. Polk,

My dear Sir :

The enclosed just received, and as requested by the author, I enclose to you. The withdrawal of Tyler I have no doubt will strengthen us in Ohio and Connecticut; we wanted strength in Ohio, where the course of Allen and

Tappan against the Texan treaty had much weakened the Democracy and where Col. Benton's speeches, as I am informed, had done us much harm with his abuse of Tyler. From all quarters accounts are gratifying. There are lively hopes of little Delaware and Rhode Island. If Col. Thos. Marshall's strength holds out to canvass Ky., as he intends, Clay loses the state. In one county adjoining Tennessee that gave Clay a majority, I am creditably informed, a very wealthy man offers to pledge one of his plantations that the county will give Polk and Dallas upwards of 500 majority. N. Carolina I view amongst the most doubtful states.

I think if the present enthusiasm can be kept up in the Democracy to the election and all be brought to the polls, you will carry the state by ten thousand. Let the Texan question be kept up and the vote of our Senators against the treaty with the German league [1] be fully exposed to the people. The treaty secured such important benefits to the growers of Pork, Tobacco, Rice and Cotton, and ensured, from the reduction of the revenue upon these articles, one cent a pound to the raiser of tobacco, perhaps more, and the additional consumption of these articles by 27 millions of people. This conduct of our Senators ought to be kept before the people, and this too, because Great Britain complained of it and would have had to reduce her tariff on these articles or lost this trade. *There never was such treachery to the laborer of the South and West, as the rejection of this Treaty.*

I have been greatly astonished that the Democratic papers have said so little about it. It must, when explained to our farmers, arouse them against Whigery. Have it laid before the people. I am quite low and greatly debilitated with shortness of breath that I cannot do more than walk twice across the passage without great apprehension.

My whole family join me in kind salutations to you and yours,

Your friend,

ANDREW JACKSON.

---

(1) See Vol. II., p. 325.

TO WILLIAM WILKINS. [1]

Washington, Sept. 7, 1844.

Dear Sir :

I have carefully abstained from all interference in regard to the Choctaw contract, feeling that the same was perfectly safe in your hands. I have no doubt but that the best possible arrangement has been made *thus far* to secure the great and only object on which my attention can rest, viz: the early emigration of the Indians. I have only now to request that such measures may be adopted in regard to the remaining contract for subsistence as will ensure the emigration. The object is one of too much importance to permit any other consideration to interfere with it. I felt it to be due to myself to make this single remark—and shall leave the mode of accomplishing it wholly to yourself.

With truest regard,

Yours &c.,

JOHN TYLER.

———

TO JAMES K. POLK.

Hermitage, Sept. 26th, 1844.

My dear Sir:

This day I am greatly afflicted, but I cannot forbear trying to enclose the within and others accompanying it. As you will see, *all's well* in N. York and Pennsylvania and Michigan, and I have no doubt of Ohio.

I have received a letter from Mr. V. Buren, who says Wright's accepting the nomination for Governor has secured beyond all doubt New York. Mr. Wright, he says, accepted with much reluctance, but he yielded the moment he was told it was the only way to ensure the N. Y. vote to the Democracy.

———

(1)   Secretary of War.

*Private.*

I have just received a letter from Mr. Tyler—Howard, our Minister to Texas, is dead—Major A. J. Donelson is appointed and the means forwarded for his speedy outfit and journey, and urging me to use my influence with him to accept. [1] Tell Donelson of this and hurry him home; the crisis is important. P. Tyler has sent a dispatch to our minister at Mexico to remonstrate against the invasion of Texas, to say, *cum multo in parvo,* that he will view it as war on the United States and present it as such to Congress. Tnis is the true, energetic course.

Yours in haste,<br>ANDREW JACKSON.

P. S. Congress will not be called.

A. J.

---

TO JUDGE WILKINS.

Oct. 15, 1844.

Dr. Sir:

Would it not be well to issue directions to Gen'l Worth to resort to all peaceful means to get the Indians remaining in Florida to migrate.

Yrs.<br>J. TYLER.

---

TO JUDGE WILKINS.

Sept. 4, 1844.

Dr. Sir:

I have received your letter of this morning covering one from Col. Totten as to the Florida Reef. The importance of the defences proposed to be erected there are pressing and urgent. I hope that all necessary steps will be taken without delay to give efficacy to the act of Congress. If a survey is necessary, the preparations ought to be completed so that the work can be entered on by the 1st of October.

Yrs.<br>J. TYLER.

(1) Mr. Tyler states that he selected Donelson " from the household of Gen. Jackson " in order to check Jackson's protegée Houston's intrigues with England. II., p. 430.

DECEMBER, 1844. On my arrival here had long interview with Mr. Calhoun, being the second on this subject. He still insists that the plan by treaty was best, adheres to provisions for annexation on terms proposed in the rejected (treaty), and thinks it best if a treaty impossible to have these terms proposed to Texas by joint-resolution of Congress. If this cannot be done, would take my bill with following amendments : 1st, Let it be done by joint resolution of Congress, instead of by Act of Congress as in my bill. 2nd, In third clause in my bill where Texas cedes North of 36°. 30, to the U. N. the soil and jurisdiction, insert "Subject to the Constitution of the United States and the decision in this and all other of the N. S. of all questions relating to slavery by the Supreme Court of the United States." 3rd, Strike out re-annexation and insert annexation. Mr. Calhoun is vehement on this subject, and says it is an implied censure of Mr. Monroe and all his cabinet in relation to the Florida Treaty. To the two first suggestions of Mr. Calhoun I cheerfully assented. To the 3rd I objected as weakening our position before Congress and the Country, and as approved by the historical records. Mr. Monroe himself, as well as Mr. Jefferson, Mr. Madison, and even Mr. J. Q. Adams admitted and proved as shown by me that Texas was once ours, under the Treaty of 1803, and it was conceded by the Spanish Minister on his return home in 1821 after negotiating the Florida Treaty; to get Texas again then is clearly re-annexation. Nevertheless, the word must be yielded; rather lose the measure. Mr. Calhoun approves decidedly of the six states, and the equilibrium, as secured by my bill. He says if the whole South would vote for it in both Houses of Congress, it would succeed, but fears that party will be stronger than patriotism and will divide the South. Thinks the united South could accomplish anything it ought to ask.

March 19, 1845. Mr. Webster introduced the Texas question. I showed him my original bill and stated Mr. Calhoun's three proposed amendments, in all of which . . . . Webster concurred. He continues opposed to the annexation of Texas, and especially to my bill with its six new

(1) From the correspondence of Robert J. Walker.

slave states, which he says would have revolutionized the Government.    He says the bill as it passed the House as to the annexation by Congress is the same plan as first suggested in my Texas letter, and differs only in details but not in principle from my bill.    He says its constitutionality can not now be questioned by any judicial power, but adds that Mr. Calhoun and myself may live to regret this dispensing with the conservative ⅔ vote of the Senate.    He says that in some contingency that may occur we may wake up some morning and find the Canadas and perhaps all British North America annexed by a joint resolution by a bare majority of the two Houses of Congress.    He differs with me as to Oregon.    Says our title is not demonstrable beyond the 49th parallel, that the Frazer River Country is British, and hopes I will not get the country into a war for 54. 40.    Says my plan of getting England to let us have all of Oregon will not answer—that she will not yield beyond 49, and that I cannot carry a mere *ad valorem* revenue tariff, and if I do it will bankrupt the Treasury and Country.    Thinks the tariff of '42 may be beneficially reduced, but prefers specific duties; wishes me great success in the department and increased reputation, and will most cordially support me and with great pleasure, whenever he can do so conscientiously.    Hopes we may have many conferences as to public affairs.    Expressed great admiration for Mr. Calhoun as a man and as a logician—thinks, if he had lived in the days of Luther and Calvin, or of Locke, Stewart or Reid, he could have demolished them all in in theological or metaphysical discussion.    To which I added, yes, he possesses also unsurpassed administrative powers, and as a statesman he is sublime even in his errors.

---

TO R. J. WALKER.

[Private].

Faycheedah, W. T , Dec. 9, '44.

My dear Sir:

In this remote region we have just got returns enough to settle the Presidential election.    I have never doubted the result, and it seems New York decided the contest in favor of *Polk*.    I am amused with the Whig papers in their awkward attempts to account for their defeat.    They have abused the Conservatives so much and under-rated their numbers and strength in such a manner that they dare not charge their defeat to them. They therefore talk about the foreign vote and abolition vote, &c. But let any one compare the vote in the strong Democraticic counties, where there are no foreigners or abolitionists with the vote in 1840, and the story is at once told. Those counties which gave Harrison such large majorities have now given Polk majorities equally large. These changes have decided the election. This is just as I always told you it would be.

After the invitation given by Polk and Gen'l Jackson through you for the Conservatives to unite with the old party, and that all past differences should be forgotten and they treated as if no such differences had ever existed, they did not hesitate to go into the contest. The result is seen.

In my position here I have thus far got along peaceably and quietly. I have seen but one instance to the contrary. There seems to be a general disposition to harmonize. A Southport paper has recently suggested the appointment of Gov. Dodge in my place. The editor says nothing personally unkind of me, and has made his suggestion without understanding my position or my relations to Mr. Polk and his leading friends.

Now, my dear sir, I wish you to write a letter in relation to Polk's and your views of the course of the Conservatives, &c., &c., &c., which I can show to a few, and it will have the effect to produce perfect harmony in the party here. But if, for want of light, a movement should be made to remove me, the party will be distracted, and there is no telling what the end will be. There is room enough in the territory for all, if they could so understand it. Write me on the receipt of this. Direct to me at Madison, where I shall be before this reaches you.

Very truly yours,

N. P. TALLMADGE [1]

P. S. Please to send the enclosed and forward it to its address, and a suggestion as to writing me a suitable letter would be well.

---

[1] N. P. Tallmadge had been a supporter of Jackson in 1836; but, like Rives and Legaré, he was a conservative in 1840, and voted for Harrison and Tyler. He represented New York in the Senate in 1841, and while he voted for the Bank bills, he did not approve the policy of the measures. Mr. Tyler appointed him governor of the Wisconsin territory, from which position he was removed by Polk, shortly after his inauguration.

PRESIDENT TYLER TO HIS DAUGHTER, MRS. WALLER. [1]

September 13, 1844.

I am still abused by all the papers in his (Clay's) advocacy, and he urged on that conspiracy in 1841 which was designed to ruin me personally and politically. His opposition to Texas, his attempt to revolutionize the government—through the abolition of the veto power—in short, his total want of principle of every sort renders him the most obnoxious man in the Union. Mr. Polk is, to say the least, a gentleman in principle and conduct. If he comes into power, his administration will be a continuance of my own, since he will be found the advocate of most of my measures. Mr. Clay leads the Federal cohorts; Mr. Polk the Democratic. My friends will be treated with regard and attention, and a rally on their part will secure the election. They have rallied *en masse* in Pennsylvania, New Jersey, Maryland, Massachusetts, Connecticut, New York, etc., etc. I hope Mr. Waller will seriously ponder before he commits himself to Clay.

---

TO JAS. K. POLK.

Hermitage, Decbr. 13th, 1844.

My dear Sir :

Having received from my friend Blair a letter describing the movements at the City of Washington, writing with a view that I might put you on your guard—first of all, the offices are filling up by Tyler, so that all his partizans must remain in office or you be compelled to remove them. I have said to my friend Blair that you have sufficient energy to give yourself elbow room, whenever it becomes necessary-

\* \* \* \* \* \* \* \* \*

There is much intrigue going on at Washington, and one that may divide the Democratic party and destroy you, and some of our imprudent political friends are at the bottom of it, viz: To substitute the *Madisonian* for the *Globe*—others to get Ritchie concerned with the *Globe* and Editor of it. As far as you are concerned, put your force against all these manoeuvres. The first would blow you sky high and destroy the Republican party. The second would be an insult to the

---

(1) This letter, as shown by its date, is placed here by mistake, somewhat out of its true order.

Editor of the *Globe* and separate him from you, whose administration he is determined to support. Keep Blair's *Globe* the administration paper, and William B. Lewis to ferret out and make known to you all the plots and intrigues hatching against your administration, and you are safe. The Major will be faithful, and I pledge myself for Blair; and you will be shielded and if attacked well defended by the *Globe*. Ritchie is a good editor but a very unsafe one. He goes off at half bent, and does great injury before he can be set right—remember his course on my removal of the deposits, and how much injury he did us before he got back into the right track again.

ANDREW JACKSON. (1)

———

Columbus, Tenn., Jan'y 4th, 1845.

I have received your letter of the 20th ultimo, and exceedingly regret that you feel yourself constrained by the circumstances which surround you to decline accepting a place in the Cabinet     *     *     I beg that you suggest to me the *person* in New York whom in your judgment I should select.—*Strictly confidential. Polk to Silas Wright.*

(1) Jackson had at this time returned to his old love, Blair, Benton, &c., and in this letter advises the slaughter of Mr. Tyler's appointees, seeming entirely to forget his own pledges through Major Lewis. It must be remembered that up to November, 1844, all the leading foreign missions were still in the hands of Whigs (notably, Everett in England, and C. S. Todd in Russia). Then at home nearly all the officeholders were also Whigs. During the months just preceding the election, these Whig office holders, counting sure upon Mr. Clay's success, abandoned their duties and were active in drumming up voters. Mr. Tyler removed some of the most rampant, and as he himself was no longer a candidate for office, the old charge of ambition for er-election fails. It is to be remembered in addition that the removals were made in vacation, though the names of the new appointees were sent in for confirmation when Congress met in December. Mr. Tyler in the last month filled a vacancy on the Supreme Court, which had been inherited from the preceding Congress and appointed Mr. Polk's own brother to one of the vacancies abroad. But he made no removals in these closing months, and he appointed no editors to office at any time.

See "Parties and Patronage," and Vol. II., p. 313.

Columbus, Jan'y 4th, 1845.

The first and most important duty which I will have to perform will be the selection of my Cabinet. I have reflected much about men whom it may be proper to call to my aid. There was but one individual about whom my mind was definitely made up—without any consultation with any one, as soon as I ascertained the result of the election—and that individual was Silas Wright of New York. I accordingly addressed him a letter early in December inviting him to take charge of the Treasury Department. To-day I received his answer declining to accept. In my letter to him I named the Treasury Department—because in my judgment it has become the most important of the departments and because of his eminent qualifications to discharge the duties of that station. I would be pleased to know your opinion—who would be a proper person to fill the offices of Secretary of the Treasury, and Secretary of State, as I think it probable that I will desire to take some one from New York to fill one of these important places.—*James K. Polk to Martin Van Buren.*

———

Washington, Texas, Jan'y 20th, 1845.

Colonel Pillow, a neighbor and a friend of yours, told me that he was in your confidence, and that your chief difficulty was to get rid of Mr. Calhoun. * * Any arrangement of your cabinet making it necessary for him to leave the State Department would be to take the side of Benton and Wright and to array all your influence against him and the measures to support which you were elected.—*Duff Green to Polk.*

Washington, Jan'y 24th, 1845.

Our annexation resolution passed this evening by a majority of twenty-two—the Tennessee Whigs voted with us, but we had to take it on Milton Brown's resolutions; the distinct friends of Mr. Wright stood out to the last—you never saw such excitement!

The general impression is that it will pass the Senate. Nothing but Texas has engrossed all minds since I last wrote to you.    *    *    No action on the Major's [William H. Polk?] case.[1] —*A. V. Brown to Polk.*

[ *Confidential.* ]

Lindenwald, Feb'y 10, 1845.

The Treasury is full and is likely to remain so, although I hope the tariff will be greatly modified.—*Martin Van Buren to Polk.*

J. C. Calhoun's letter to Polk, dated 27th Feb., 1845. apprising him of his resignation to take effect as soon as a successor is appointed and ready to assume the duties, "having been informed in the interview to which you invited me yesterday, of your determination to form an entirely new Cabinet." Endorsed by Polk, "Received March 1st."

TO ROBERT J. WALKER.

Faycheedah, March 30, 1845.

Mr. Macy says you suggested that I get letters from some Democratic friends against my removal from the place which I now hold. I cannot consent to go about for letters on such a subject. I trust I am too well known to Mr. Polk and all his cabinet to require such thing. And after what Mr. Polk wrote to you and F. O. J. Smith in relation to the Conservatives and the reunion of the old Jackson party, and after what my friends did in New York which carried that state and gave him the election, I do not deem anything necessary in relation to myself. I have never given myself one moment's anxiety about it, having entire confidence in Mr. Polk's good faith and justice in such a matter.

N. P. TALLMADGE.

(1) In the Polk correspondence, purchased by the Lenox Library, New York, is the following letter:—

"At Polk's own request, I asked Mr. Tyler in December, 1844, to give his brother, Wm. H. Polk, a foreign chargéship. He said there was a vacancy at Naples, and would gladly nominate W. H. for it, but he would like application to be made by the Tennessee members of Congress to fall back on, if necessary. A. V. Brown and others then took it up, and W. H. was nominated."—Letter of J.G. Harris to George Bancroft, dated Sept. 13, 1887. This letter confirms the published statement of Robert Tyler and John Tyler jr.—*Parties and Patronage, 88.*

TO R. J. WALKER.

Faycheedah, W. T., April 15, 1845.

( Private.)

To Hon. R. J. Walker. [1]

My dear Sir :

For the last two weeks I have heard rumors
of my anticipated removal. I have had nothing direct from
Washington on that subject. I have given them no heed.
For I never can for one moment persuade myself that Mr.
Polk, after the manner in which the remains of the old Jackson party were invited, can think of such a thing, especially as
the Conservatives were desired to unite with the old party
without reference to past differences, and as if these differences had never existed. They united accordingly, and in
New York their strength carried the state for Mr. Polk, which
gave him his election. I am aware that the Whigs have charged
their defeat to the foreign and abolition vote, but any one acquainted with the State knows that the great changes from
1840 were in those old Democratic counties where there are
neither foreign nor abolition votes. So much for the political aspect of my removal.

Aside from this, I never solicited the place. I was appointed to fill a vacancy. No one was removed to make room for
me. I was *unanimously* confirmed by the Senate. I have
come here not as a sort of pro-consul to return to Rome
when my duties no longer require me here, but I have come
to make Wisconsin my permanent residence. My interests
are all identified with the Territory and with the people here.
There is no public sentiment, I am well assured, in favor of
the change. On the contrary, there is no doubt of the almost universal sentiment in favor of things as they are. The
truth is, there has been so much turmoil under my predecessors that everybody is disposed to peace. My efforts have
been directed to restore peace to the Territory. Whilst my
friend, Dr. Lynn, was in the Senate, he often solicited me
to take this place, saying that he would assure me that his
brother, Gen. Dodge, and all his friends would be perfectly

---

(1) Polk appointed Walker Secretary of the Treasury despite
Jackson's advice to the contrary.

satisfied with my appointment, and peace and harmony would
be restored. I came here with those impressions and those
dispositions. I have endeavored to harmonize the Democratic party. I have succeeded at it. *     *     This was the
only appointment, as I told you at the time, that I would take
under any administration. *     *

N. P. TALLMADGE

———

ROBERT TYLER TO JOHN C. CALHOUN.

Philadelphia, April 19th.

[Private.]

My dear Sir :

I have been intending to write to you for a fortnight past, but have been delaying the execution of my design, because I desired to watch the developments made at
Washington and to obtain from them facts to sustain my
own decided conviction as to the course of policy which Mr.
Polk has determined to pursue.

We are again to witness precisely the same game which the
Albany Regency, with Van Buren as their exponent and tool,
played thro' Gen'l Jackson at your expense and that of the
country, played, by the Albany Regency, with Silas Wright
at their head, thro' Mr. Polk. The terms and conditions are
precisely the same. The policy has been agreed on after a
world of deliberation, for there is no earthly doubt that Mr.
Polk has been, since the day of his nomination, and is *now* in
the closest and most active consultation with New York politicians, and it is being slowly, cautiously and laboriously but
they hope (vainly) surely—perfected. This is my own decided conviction, altho' I admit that there is much of mere *suspicion* in my views. But I will relate to you certain facts.

Mr. Geo. P. H——may be regarded, altho' rather a
worthless man, as a credible witness to a fact which occurred
within his own knowledge, he being in point of fact an actor
in the matter. *He informed me* about ten days ago, that when
Van Buren wrote his Anti-Texas letter, that Cave Johnson, and
most all of the politicians in Tennessee, insisted that the
*Nashville Union* should endorse his letter and his positions.
The editor of the paper ( he being proprietor ) wrote an article endorsing Van Buren's letter, and brought it to him to be
inserted in the *Union.* He positively refused to permit

the article appear.   These men then threatened to establish an opposition paper to the *Nashville Union,* and abused him roundly.   All this occurred before the Baltimore Convention was held; and Mr. Polk was then a candidate for the Vice presidency.   Cave Johnson is now Postmaster General and the confidant of Polk.   The then editor of the *Union* is now recorder of the land office.   Mr. Polk, before Mr. Van Buren's letter against Texas appeared, had been a warm Texas man—the *Union* was regarded as his organ, Johnson &c. &c., as his peculiar friend.   This fact demonstrates that he was willing to give up Texas, anything and everything, to be nominated along with Mr. Van Buren for the Vice Presidency.   Since his nomination, since the day of Van Buren's letter, not one word did we hear from Mr. Polk on Texas, till by Walker's intrigues and treachery (and I believe with Mr. Polk's concurrence) the joint resolution with Benton's amendment passed the Senate. [1]   All this smells vastly of Hunkerism.

Let me mention another fact.   The country was dissatisfied, especially the Southern portion of the Democracy, that Mr. Polk did not cordially invite you to remain in the State Dep't.   This question was asked, why was Mr. Calhoun not continued as Sect'y of State?   The reply was that Mr. Polk wanted to avoid the cliques.   But lo and behold! it now appears (it is a truth) *that Silas Wright was offered the Treasury or any department he might choose,* that Benjamin Butler was offered the War Department, declined, and was made District Attorney for New York, given his choice of offices.   The *Morning News, Albany Atlas,* Wright's papers, asserted these facts.   Ritchie has endorsed them in his paper of the 15th April in a pretty significant manner, and I have them from private sources of the most authentic character.

Another fact.   Every appointment made for New York or Pennsylvania or Maryland is a restoration of *Hunkerism.* The transfer of the *Globe* is a farce.   You perceive that Ritchie has already attacked my father for sending on the joint resolutions to Texas.   Rest assured there is a faithful understanding among all—[*The rest of this letter is lost.*]

(1) It would appear that Mr. Walker's tacking Benton's amendment to Milton Brown's resolution was his own suggestion. Tyler and Calhoun thought the Senate would yield without this.

ANDREW JACKSON TO PRESIDENT POLK.

Hermitage, May 2, 1845.

I say to you in the most *confidential manner* that I regret that you put Mr. R. J. Walker over the treasury. He has talents, I believe honest, but surrounded by so many broken speculators, and being greatly himself incumbered with debt, that any of the other departments would have been better, and I fear you will find my forebodings turn out too true; and added to this, under the rose he is looking to the Vice-Presidency, and you will find that there is not that cordial feeling between him and Mr. Buchanan as ought to exist. He belongs to what is called the Dallas party—the real old Democratic party of Pennsylvania, the Lopers, the Horners, the Kanes, the Duane party, &c. &c. I write you this that you may have your eyes open, and whilst you have confidence, that you may discover whether it is well placed.

---

TO R. J. WALKER.

Washington City, Sept. 30, 1848.

Sir :

I invite your attention to two publications which appeared in the New York "*Evening Post,*" of the 28th of July, and were republished in the "*National Intelligencer*" of the 1st of August last, the one bearing the signature of *Benjamin Tappan* and the other of *Francis P. Blair.* Shortly after my arrival in Washington in February, 1845, I invited you to accept a place in my cabinet. After you had signified your willingness to accept the position tendered to you, I was upon terms of confidential and unreserved intercourse with you. That you might be fully informed in advance of the principles on which my administration would be conducted I submitted to you, for your examination, the Inaugural address, which I afterwards delivered to my fellow-citizens, and conferred freely with you in relation to public affairs. No opinions which I entertained upon any public subject, upon which we may have conversed, were withheld from you. The subject of the annexation of Texas to the United States was at that time under consideration in Congress.

HON. D. GARDINER TYLER.

Eldest son of President Tyler by his second wife, Julia Gardiner. Present proprietor of "Sherwood Forest".

Private C. S. A. 1862-1865. Presidential Elector 1888. State Senator 1891-1893. Representative in U. S. Congress from 1893 to 1897.

You were a member of the Senate, and took part in the proceedings which were had in relation to it. As it may become proper, that I should at some future period, take some notice of the publication of *Mr. Tappan* [1] and *Mr. Blair*, I request that you will furnish me with a statement of all you may know of my opinions, views or acts of mine, as well before as after my Inauguration as President, relating to the subject of the annexation of Texas to the United States. I desire that you will state any conversation which I may at any time have held with you, and any opinions I may have expressed to you, either individually or in Cabinet, on the subject of the annexation of Texas ; and also all that you may know, if anything, in relation to the matters set forth, by *Messrs. Tappan* and *Blair* in their publications, and whether you had any knowledge or information of the statements made by them, when the subject of the annexation of Texas was before the Senate, of which body you were at the time a member.

(1). See Vol. II., 404-416. See also Polk's *Diary*, Aug. 3, 1848, and Sept. 20, 1848: "Tappan, in his conversations and intercourse with me always professing friendship and the support of my (Polk's) administration, has acted hypocritically and most dishonestly." Tappan was the Senator who in 1844, for violating the secrecy of the Senate by giving to a newspaper man for publication a copy of the Texas treaty, was severely censured by that body (Niles' Register). Polk's reasons for discontinuing the *Globe* are given in his *Diary*. One was Blair's "failure to mention Polk's nomination as Vice-President by the Tennessee Legislature and a Democratic State convention: "and for two months after his nomination as President the *Globe* was cold in its support." Mr. Polk says also that arriving in Washington Feb. 13, 1845, he felt anxious for Congress to act upon the Texas question. "I believed that if no measure proposing annexation was passed at the session, that Texas would be lost to the Union. But I certainly never understood myself as pledged to select that mode if the resolution passed in that form. I never authorized Mr. Haywood or any one else to make such pledges to Senators. My cabinet was unanimously of the opinion that the selection made by Mr. Tyler ought not to be reversed and that it was to be preferred to the alternative of appointing commissioners. Neither Mr. Haywood or any other ever made any enquiry of me personally on the subject. * * * The whole story is an afterthought, and is designed to effect a political purpose, by advancing Mr. Van Buren's prospects for the Presidency."—Polk's *Diary*.

I desire that nothing I have ever said or done on the subject should be concealed from the public. The annexation of Texas was a measure of the highest national importance, conceived and consummated with pure and patriotic motive, and it may become proper and especially after the publications referred to, that the opinions, views, and actions of all the public functionaries entrusted at any stage of its proceedings with its management should be fully known. With this object in view, I address you this letter.

Yours respectfully,

JAMES K. POLK.

TO PRESIDENT POLK.

Washington City, November 6th, 1848.

Sir : I have the honor to acknowledge the receipt of your letter of the 30th of September last, and in compliance with your request to furnish you with a statement, so far as within my knowledge, of all your opinions, views or acts, as well before as after your inauguration as President, relating to the subject of the annexation of Texas to the United States, I proceed to reply as fully as memory will serve me at this date, detailing at the same time the progress of this question in the Senate of the United States.

On the 4th of February, 1845, the Committee of Foreign Relations of the Senate, to which had been referred the consideration of the joint resolution which passed the House for the admission of Texas as a state of the Union, reported in favor of the rejection of those resolutions. On the succeeding day Mr. Benton introduced his bill to provide for the annexation of Texas to the United States. A motion was made by an opponent of the bill to refer it to the Committee on Foreign Relations which had, but the day preceding, reported against the annexation of Texas. This motion was resisted by me, and failed by a single vote. Upon that occasion, on referring to the files of the Congressional Globe of that date, I find, by my remarks as there reported, that whilst my decided preference for the House resolutions was expressed, it was accompanied by the avowal, in the case of the failure of these resolutions, to take into consideration the bill of Col. Benton.

On the conclusion of this speech, I was addressed in the Senate chamber by Mr. Francis P. Blair, then the editor of the Globe, who seemed much gratified by my remarks, and requested me to retire with him for the purpose of an interview on the subject. We accordingly proceeded to the room of the Committee of the Judiciary of the Senate, when Mr. Blair stated to me that the House Resolution could never pass the Senate, designating the names of several Democratic Senators, who he stated as of his own personal knowledge never would vote for those resolutions, and requested me, as the only means of preventing the defeat of the measure, to agree to support the bill of Mr. Benton, assuring me, if I would do so, that it could be substituted as an amendment in the Senate to the House resolutions, pass that body, go to the House, and be concurred in and become a law.

I told Mr. Blair that I was bound in good faith to support the joint resolutions of the House, and besides I preferred them, as more prompt and certain, and as conforming to my own plan of admitting Texas as a state as proposed by myself in that form in 1844, 1835 and 1826. I told him that it was quite possible that Mr. Benton's bill might by a united Whig vote, with the aid of such Democratic Senators as were opposed to the House Resolutions, be substituted for them in the Senate, but that if this were done, the Whig Senators opposed to the annexation would then vote against Mr. Benton's bill, and as I feared also would several Southern Democratic Senators, and that in this way the great measure of annexation would be defeated. I then told him that there was one method which had occurred to my mind, growing out of the remarks made by the Senator from Missouri, under which the question could be saved; that Col. Benton in his speech that morning had made it an objection to the House Resolutions that Texas would reject them, and prefer his plan; that such was not my opinion, but I was willing to submit the decision to her judgment, and that I would suggest for his consideration, whether it might not be preferable to offer Mr. Benton's bill as a new section to the House Resolutions, presenting the alternative for Texas to decide which she would prefer, and that in this manner the friends of the House Resolutions might, in a manner perfectly fair and honorable, unite with Mr. Benton and his friends in supporting the whole measure thus associated and amended.

Mr. Blair seemed much pleased with this suggestion, and said he would consult Col. Benton upon the subject, and a day or two afterwards, he informed me that Col. Benton would support the measure in this alternative form rather than that annexation should be defeated.

It will thus be perceived that I was the first to propose the uniting of Col. Benton's bill with the House Resolutions as an alternative, which facts, together with my avowed preference for the House resolutions, will be found stated substantially by Mr. Blair in an editorial of the *Globe* of the 26th of March, 1845. Upon receiving this information from Mr. Blair I prepared the amendment, a copy of which is annexed, to offer as an additional section to the House resolutions, leaving the choice between Col. Benton's bill and the House Resolutions to Texas. The original amendment, as thus prepared by me, is now in my possession, and was shown to many of the friends of Texas at that date. I think this amendment was put in form by me on the 8th of February. Various efforts subsequently were made to ascertain with certainty whether the resolutions thus amended could be adopted, and I entertained hopes that the measure would succeed in that way until, I think, the 24th of February, when I was informed by Mr. Haywood of the Senate that there were several Democratic Senators who would not vote for the resolutions in that alternative form, which assurance he gave me as of his own personal knowledge as a settled and unalterable fact, and he stated to me that unless my amendment as proposed to be offered could undergo some modification, the great measure of annexation would be defeated, for the success of which Mr. Haywood expressed, and I believe felt, the utmost solicitude.

From these representations made by Mr. Haywood, while I then believed and still believe that the amendment in the form in which it had been drawn by me could not succeed without some modification, I asked Mr. Haywood to suggest the modification which in his judgment would carry the measure. He then assured me that if I would change my proposed amendment so far as to leave the alternative to the decision of the President of the United States in lieu of Texas, that Mr. Benton and his friends would all vote for the amendment, and that if I would support it he entertained no doubt but that the Senators friendly to the House resolutions would then give it their vote, and that in that form the measure could succeed.

He suggested also the importance of the amendment being offered by me, to which I assented, in case I became satisfied that the measure would succeed in that form and no other. I then changed my own amendment so far only as it substituted the President of the United States for Texas in deciding which should be preferred—the House Resolutions or the bill of the Senate, and after consulting with some of my friends in the Senate, became convinced that they would support it, and so informed Mr. Haywood, who assured me that Mr. Benton and his friends were still all determined to vote for the resolutions in that form; whereupon at 6 o'clock on the evening of the 27th of February, the hour being thus noted on the Senate Journal, I offered the amendment, convinced on that day for the first time that success was certain, and that in no other form could the measure be carried, and on that same evening my amendment was adopted by a vote of 27 to 25, and the joint resolutions of the House as thus amended passed the Senate the same evening, consequently, passed the House and became a law. It was not until the morning of the 24th of February, according to my recollection, that the suggestion of changing my alternative amendment was first made to me. This communication, as before stated, was made to me by Mr. Haywood, and I never communicated with you in any manner on that point, nor, so far as I know, did you have any knowledge of the change proposed, or of my determination upon the subject.

Indeed, notwithstanding my intimate relations with you at that time, being about to become a member of your cabinet, I did not feel disposed, as a Senator of the United States, to confer with you as to this particular form of amendment, when by its provisions you were to be made the umpire upon the subject, nor would I have ever consented to offer the amendment if you ever had expressed to me any choice between the two alternatives Nor did I know how you would decide the question; nor did anyone ever intimate to me that you had ever been consulted upon the subject, or that you had either formed or expressed any opinion in regard to the choice of alternatives. After the resolution, as amended by me, passed the Senate, you expressed to me your gratification at the result, and again when it passed the House, but with–

out alluding in any way to your opinion as to which alternative ought to be adopted, nor did I ever express any opinion
to you on that point, until the question was introduced at our
first cabinet meeting. Then I learned that President Tyler
had acted already upon the subject, and adopted the House
resolutions on the 3rd March, 1845, the last day of his official
term. At this cabinet meeting you presented the question
for the consideration of the cabinet as to what course ought
to be pursued by you in regard to these alternatives, giving
no opinion yourself upon the subject, and having formed
none, so far as was known to me. It was then suggested by
some member of the cabinet, but which of them I do not
recollect, that President Tyler having already acted upon the
subject and decided the question, which, by the law, he was
authorized to do, and dispatched the messenger with that decision to Texas, the question possibly might be regarded by
some as placed thus beyond your control. On that question
of power I am not aware that any decision was made by the
cabinet or yourself, because we were all at once unanimously
of opinion that it was best under all the circumstances of
the case to adopt the alternative presented in the House
resolutions, as the most certain to secure annexation. You
listened attentively and without interruption or expressing
any opinion yourself of the views given thus promptly and
unanimously by your cabinet. When you announced your concurrence in opinion with them, it was resolved that the Secretary of State should send a dispatch to that effect to Texas,
confirming the selection made by President Tyler.

I was confident then, as I am now, that you had never
committed youself in any way on this subject. If you had, it
certainly must have been known to some member of your
cabinet; and if you felt embarrassed by any such commitment,
you might very readily have relieved yourself by placing the
decision upon the choice already made by the President, your
predecessor, under the powers devolved upon him by law. I
will here add that I never heard even a suggestion that you
had committed yourself in any way on this subject or expressed any preference for the Senate or House resolutions,
until I read the letters of Messrs. Tappan and Blair in the
*Evening Post* of the 28th of July last.

I think it possible you may have stated to Mr. Blair either when Mr. Benton's bill was pending alone, or when it was

offered by me as an alternative, that if that mode of annexation were adopted, you would appoint the most able men in the Union of both parties as Commissioners, but that you ever did say that you would yourself select Mr. Benton's bill as an alternative seems to me absolutely impossible, and I have no doubt that this idea is the result of a misapprehension of your views on this subject, which might have arisen readily in case you had said that if Benton's bill were adopted as the alternative you would appoint such Commissioners. It would have been more satisfactory if the parties who labored under this misapprehension had stated the date of this alleged conversation with you, because the amendment as originally proposed to be offered by me, and which was drawn up and considered for several weeks and intended to be offered, left the decision of this alternative to Texas, and rendered it impossible that you should undertake to decide the question.

Nor was it until the 24th of February that any change in this alternative was suggested to me, nor until the 26th, that I finally agreed to offer it. It was offered by me on the 27th, and passed the Senate the same evening *without adjournment.* There could then have been but little time after the suggestion of leaving the alternative to the choice of the President of the United States for such a conversation with you, and still less time to have conversed with the several Senators friendly to that mode of annexation, and to have communicated your views to them, and still more extraordinary that this important fact should have remained unknown to me, and as I believe to every member of your cabinet, until divulged in the columns of the *Evening Post* in July last.

Very respectfully,<br>Your obed't serv't,<br>R. J. WALKER.

---

TO HENRY A. WISE.<br>Sherwood Forest, April 20, 1852.

My Dear Sir:

The *Pilot,* a small paper published in Portsmouth, containing a communication from some writer who was present at the late Democratic Convention, and who gives or pretends to give, a brief outline of your speech in that body in response to questions implicating your Democracy because of your support of my administration, has recently fallen under

my notice—and what less can I do than express to you the
great gratification which the article has afforded me? The
desire with all men to be understood by their contemporaries,
and their motives of action to be properly appreciated, is universal, and in that feeling I must confess myself to be a par-
ticipant—and yet I began to fear that I was to descend to my
grave without any shadow of justice being done me in *public*
places.

To you I have been constantly indebted for a fearless
and uniform exposition of my public conduct in all private
circles as well as in public assemblies—but these assemblies,
altho' public, represented more neighborhoods than states—I
speak of what has occur'd since we left Washington—but
you have at length spoken to the State at large, and from
what I learn, the State at large has responded by plaudits to
your sentiments. I rejoice at this not only on my own account, but also on yours. No man will ever hereafter taunt
you for the past, and you will stand in all the future in the
State at the head of the Democratic party.

Some things transpired after you left the country which
I shall take occasion one of these days to explain to you. I
desire now briefly to advert to one—very briefly.

Texas was the great theme that occupied me. The Delegates to the Democratic Convention, or a very large majority of them, had been elected under implied pledges to sustain Van Buren. After his letter repudiating annexation, a
revulsion had become obvious, but how far it was to operate,
it was not possible to say. A majority of the Delegates, at
least, were believed still to remain in his favor. If he was
nominated, the game to be played for Texas was all as one
over. What was to be done?

My friends advised me to remain at rest and take my
chances in the Democratic Convention. It was impossible
to do so. If I suffered my name to to be used in that Convention, then I became bound to sustain the nominee, even
if Mr. Van Buren was that nominee. This could not be. I
chose to run no hazard but to raise the banner of Texas and
convoke my friends to sustain it. This was but a few weeks
before the meeting of the Convention. To my surprise the
notice which had thus issued brought together a thousand
Delegates, and from every state in the Union. Many called
on me on their way to Baltimore to receive my views. My

instructions were—go to Baltimore, make your nomination, and then go home and leave the thing to work its own results. I said no more and was obeyed. The Democratic Convention saw and felt the move. A Texas man or defeat was the choice left, and they took a Texas man. My withdrawal at a suitable time took place, and the result was soon before the world. I acted to assure the success of a great measure and I acted not altogether without effect, and in doing so I kept my own secrets. You know the rest—to have divulged my purposes would have been to have defeated them.

One topic more. Something has been said about the administration of the finances. May I call your attention to Corwin's Report of 1850-1? You will see that by his admission the expenditures were cut down from 28 or 30,000,000 to 22,000,000 annually. Now then, if to this reduction you add the $8,000,000 of surplus left in the Treasury on the 4th of March, 1845, you know the fact that the government was administered for four years upon three years of the expenditure of the previous administration, and yet you know that the military arm was everywhere strengthened and a new impulse given to the industry of the country. I make no apology for troubling you with this brief narrative. You were abroad, and altho' if you had been here, I should have had no secret, yet it has so happened that I have not had the opportunity since your return, of conversing with you freely and unreservedly.

I have been unwell during the whole winter from the effects of a bad cold contracted as long ago as December. I flatter myself with now being in a fair way to recruit my wonted energies.

With best and truest wishes, ever yours,
                                    JOHN TYLER.

TO GEN. THOMAS J. GREEN,
                Sherwood Forest, Feb. 28, 1856.
Dear General:

I take occasion now to thank you for your kind reference to me in your remarks at the Richmond dinner. It would be indeed strange if my enemies could deprive me of the credit of having annexed Texas to the Union.

I presented the question, urged it first in the form of a treaty to the Senate, met the rejection of that treaty by a prompt and immediate appeal to the H. of R.—fought the battle before the people and conquered its two formidable adversaries with their trained bands, and two days before my term expired adopted and enforced the alternate resolution under which Texas took her place amid the fraternity of States. My successor did nothing but confirm what I had done.

Nor is that all—Texas drew after it California, so I may well claim that in regards to that whole subject. Mr. Polk was my *administrator de bonis non*.[1] True, I would not have negociated a treaty of peace without settling the slave question in that treaty—the omission to do which was a great blunder; of this I will talk to you when I see you. Accept the assurances of my constant esteem,

JOHN TYLER.

———

TO R. TYLER.

Sherwood Forest, Sep. 17, 1857.

My dear Robert:

In writing you the other day, I overlooked entirely the extraordinary letter of Genl. Pillow and particularly the assertion which he says Mr. Trist made as a reason to justify the bribe to Santa Anna, that I had expended $500,000 in the purchase of the Maine Press in order to carry through the Ashburton Treaty. The thing is really so ridiculous in itself that I was about to let it go for what it was worth, when a gentleman who came here yesterday said that it was a subject of conversation in companies where he had been, which reminded me that I had not adverted to it in my letter to you. The declaration of Mr. Trist is not only preposterous and absurd, but it is recklessly false. The largest amount appropriated by Congress for the contigent fund of Foreign Intercourse, called the secret service fund, for any year during my term,

(1) Mr. C. H. Raymond, the Texan agent at Washington said at the close of Mr. Tyler's term: " The diplomatic corps waited on the President this morning at the White House. He has had much opposition and many difficulties to encounter, and yet no President has closed his term with the affairs of the nation in a more prosperous condition than they are at this moment." *Jones' Official Corresp: Page 417.*

did not exceed thirty thousand dollars, and my impression is
that there existed often unexpended balances that lessen'd
greatly the annual appropriation, reducing it sometimes to
$15,000. But even if in this I am mistaken, yet upon the
supposition that the maximum of $30,000 was annually ap-
propriated, the whole amount of appropriation for my four
years would be but $120,000 which the luxuriant imagination of
Mr. Trist has magnified, according to Gen'l Pillow so greatly,
as to make $500,000 but a mere slice of it, a thing more than
poetic. Now as to the expenditures of that fund. A greater
portion of it is expended in the ordinary charges of diplomatic intercourse and the consular establishment, leaving
but little for any secret purposes of state. As to bribing the
Press of Maine, if that Press was of a character to be bribed,
it must have been content with a small *douceur* as none other
remained in my hands. The thing is supremely ridiculous.
When I left Washington I was careful to have placed in a
private drawer of the State Department, then in charge of
Mr. Stubbs, all the vouchers and receipts for disbursements
out of that fund under my orders—and if occasion shall ever
require it, all can be produced. No one will find a mare's
nest there, rely upon it. I write you hastily.

Yr. affec. Father,

J. TYLER.

Richmond, Va., Nov. 30, 1861.

My Dear Sir:

Yours of the 25 reached me in regular course of mail and
I lost no time in making enquiries for a copy of the enact-
ments of the congress at Montgomery and Richmond. The
clerk of congress flattered me at first with the hope that I
shd. obtain them, but reported to me yesterday that after dil-
igent inquiry he was sorry to say that not a copy was to be
had. I think it probable that during the session a new edition will be ordered in which event I shall not forget your
desire to have them.

I thank you most sincerely for the kind and complimentary manner in which you have been pleased to speak of my
agency in the great drama which is now being enacted. No
man could have been more earnest to avert the sad condition

of things which now involves us in the terrible realities of war than myself, but at the ₁Peace Conference I had to address "stocks and stones," who had neither ears nor hearts to understand  Blinded by lust of power, they have heedlessly driven the ship of state upon rocks and into whirlpools which have dashed it to pieces and engulphed its fragments, and seeing the ruin which they have brought about they seek to baptize despotism in the blood of freemen.  In this effort of desperation they will, I doubt not, be thwarted.  We have, however, to gird up our loins for trials and battles.

Your denunciation of the base tribe who would in times like these speculate on the public necessities meets a hearty response from me.  Be assured that I shall concur in all measures necessary to crush a spirit so abominable and demoniacal.  The convention will adjourn on Tuesday or Wednesday, after which its labours will be submitted to the people.  Congress in another week will be actively at work. We have not even a rumour from our armies worth mentioning.[1]  With sentiments of high respect,

I am Dr Sir, truly yours,

JOHN TYLER.

----

STATEMENT OF COL. BENJAMIN E. GREEN, SECRETARY OF LEGATION AT MEXICO IN 1844.

Dalton, Georgia, 8 Aug., 1889.

I am confident that there were no *written* instructions, in reference to the proposed treaty for the acquisition of New Mexico and California beyond the general proposal in Mr. Calhoun's letter to Gov. Shannon " to settle all questions of boundary with Mexico on liberal terms."  The *verbal* instructions were given to my father, who in his book, which I sent to you, refers to the subject (See page 85, Duff Green's *Facts and Suggestions*) as follows:

"Mr. Calhoun was tendered and accepted the appoint-
"ment of Secretary of State.  *  *  At his request I went to
"Mexico to aid in conducting the negotiation for the acqui-

----

[1] Mr. Tyler was a member of the State Convention of 1861 and of the provisional and regular congresses of the Confederate States and died January 18, 1862.

"sition of Texas, New Mexico and California, and upon
"handing me his letter of instructions—the letter addressed
"to Gov. Shannon—he remarked: "If you succeed in this ne-
"gotiation, our commerce in the Pacific will in a few years,
"be greatly more valuable than that in the Atlantic.

"Upon reaching Mexico, I found Santa Anna at the
"head of an army opposed to Herrera, who was at the head
of Congress."

This allusion to the condition of parties in Mexico does
not fully explain their relative positions. Gen'l Santa Anna had
for some time been seeking to regain his waning popularity
by abuse of the United States and by boastful pledges to
maintain the integrity of Mexican territory. The party of
which Gen'ls Herrera and Arista were leaders, patriotically
desired to cultivate friendly relations with the United States
and relieve themselves of the burden of New Mexico and
California, occupied chiefly by savage Indians, whose frequent raids the resources of the Mexican government were
inadequate to restrain. They wisely argued that the increase
of the native population of Mexico would not be sufficient for
centuries to occupy those territories and drive back the wild
Indians, while they had not, and never could expect to have,
the necesseary immigration from abroad to supplement the
slow increase of the native population. Gen'l Herrera was
connected by marriage with the most prominent American
merchant in the City of Mexico, and through him and the
Padre Orsoni, I was enabled to press these views on the
Peace party as also by means of a public correspondence had
with Bocanegra, Mexican Secretary of State, after Gen. Waddy Thompson's return to the U. S., leaving me as acting
chargé d'affaires  *  *

When my first note was published, the Padre Orsoni, (the
Pope's legate ) called to see me. He said he wanted to be
better acquainted with "el muchacho," ( the boy) who had so
effectually spiked Santa Anna's guns and given the veteran
statesman, Bocanegra, such a lesson in chronology. He was
a strong peace man and had wonderful sources of information. I cultivated him and we became "compadres." He
kept me well posted as to everything going on in Mexico and
was my channel of indirect communication with the Peace
party.

Late in 1844, Gov. Shannon arrived as minister, knowing nothing of the language, people, or parties. Soon afterwards my father came with the instructions to Gov. Shannon. I told them nothing could be done with Santa Anna, but all we wanted, with Herrera, if he should come into power as was then expected. I had some doubts lest Santa Anna's strength, waning under the effect of the Bocanegra correspondence with me, might be revived by the publication of Mr. Calhoun's instructions, but was assured, through the Padre, that it would not.

On consultation with Gov. Shannon and my father, it was decided that I should go to Washington to explain to President Tyler and Mr. Calhoun the condition of parties in Mexico. I expected to return immediately to Mexico, but out of courtesy to Mr. Polk, who was so soon to take Mr. Tyler's place, he and Mr. Calhoun thought best for me to await in Washington Mr. Polk's inauguration and the anticipated changes in Mexico.

Mr. Polk was inaugurated and almost simultaneously Santa Anna was deposed and banished. Herrera became President of Mexico, with Gen'l Arista and other peace men in his cabinet. Mr. J. D. Marks, for a long time U. S. consul at Matamoras, was an intimate friend and " compadre " of Gen'l Arista. As soon as installed, the Herrera administration sent Mr. Marks to Washington City, to make known, through me, to the Polk administration their desire to settle all questions, including that of boundaries, peaceably by treaty as had been suggested by the Tyler administration, and their willingness to cede New Mexico and California; but that they doubted their ability to sustain themselves in power against Santa Anna and the war party, if they received an ordinary Minister Resident in the usual form, as if nothing had happened. If the U. S. Government would send a special commission of two or more of their most distinguished men, they could keep down the war feeling, reconcile their people to the reception of such an extraordinary commission, and soon prepare them to expect and accept the solution desired by both governments.

All this was explained to Mr. Polk and Mr. Buchanan by me and Mr. Marks, and they fully understood that, while the Herrera administration would receive an extraordinary commission, they could not venture to receive any one with nothing more than the usual credentials of an ordinary Minister Resident, to soothe the dignity of the Mexican people, offended by the annexation of Texas.

For some reason the request for an extraordinary commission was refused, and it was decided to send Mr. Slidell to Mexico as an ordinary Minister Resident. Why, I can't say. I only know that it was known in Washington, before Mr. Slidell's commission was made out, that he would not be received. I do not know what influences led the Polk administration to turn the cold shoulder on our friends, Herrera and the Peace party, and to aid in bringing back Santa Anna, the acknowledged head of the war party. I thought then and think now that it was a great mistake.

---

STATEMENT OF DR. SILAS REED, U. S. SURVEYOR-GENERAL UNDER PRESIDENTS TYLER AND GRANT.

285 Marlboro St., Boston, Mass.

You will pleased bear in mind that I was a western man, living in a city on the frontier, where every Spring I had the opportunity of meeting and gathering valuable information from intelligent fur-traders who came down the Mo. river in their fleet of bateaux laden with furs, buffalo skins, &c., &c.

Thus I gained a knowledge of the Rocky Mountains and the Pacific coast prior to March, 1842, almost equal to what I have now, of those regions after spending most of the past fifteen years amid them; six of them as U. S. Surveyor-General of Wyoming T'y, under Pres't Grant, and the balance among the Silver mines of Utah, chiefly. I am now mining at Park City, Utah, the past six years, and am in much haste to return for the Summer (a digression you see).

Well, I had made my first visit to Boston with my wife to see her friends in 1839, and found such a total ignorance of the West, and especially of the great plains and the Rocky Mountains even amongst the most intelligent classes here, as to prompt me to talk so extravagantly (as it it appeared to them) of the possibilities of the near future out there, that I was urged to give them some of my "wild" ideas for the press, such as the completion of a continuous R. R. from Boston to St. Louis and Rock Island within fifteen years, and thence on to the Pacific in fifteen years more, making Council Bluffs the half way house on the straight continental line from Boston to the Pacific. And strange to say, both of these predictions have been verified  Thus, when Mr. Tyler half jocosely enquired of me in his son Robert's room in the White House what he could do to soften the asperities of Benton toward his administration, I at once replied that he could do it only by touching his heart and his pride by appointing Frémont, the cast-off son-in-law, the husband of his much loved and proud daughter, Jessie, and that in doing so, he would not only carry out the purpose of his great exemplar, Thomas Jefferson, in 1804, through Lewis and Clarke, but would serve the future interests of his country far beyond what he *then* could possibly conceive. At that moment, with great emphasis he brought his right hand into his left, and said, "*Doctor I will do it*," and he did do it against all the clamor and opposition of the head (Col. Abert) and higher grade subordinates, of the U. S. Engineer Corps. I then said, "This step, Mr. President, will lead to the acquisition, by purchase, from Mexico, of California and all her possessions in the Rocky Mountains, during your term, of, at least, from 10 degrees of north latitude up to the 42d degree, and both you and your friends must bend all possible energy to the accomplishment of this purpose within the coming three years," which was done, and I have always been surprised that he did not publish the substance of his treaty agreement with Mexico, when the *treacherous* Polk stood idly by and let the war begin by the battles of Taylor at Reseca de la Palma and Palo Alto.[1]

(1) See Vol. II, p. 692. I do not think any treaty was made formally with Mexico by Mr. Tyler, but the way was open to one when Herrera came in. See *Ante* Green's statement. In Polk's *Diary* occurs the following:

March 30, 1846. Polk sent for Calhoun to discuss with him the boundary question. "Mr. Calhoun said he had contemplated when Secretary of State, as a very desirable boundary, a line running from a point in the Gulf of Mexico through the desert to the northward between the Nueces and Del Norte to a point about 36° or 37°, and thence west to the Pacific, so as to include the Bay of San Francisco, and he said he would like to include Monterey also, and that for such a boundary we could afford to pay a large sum, and mentioned $10,000,000. I told him I must insist on the Del Norte as the line up to the Pass in about latitude 32°." Similar views, however, had been held hy President Tyler and expressed to Webster II, 261, 435, 449, as his southern boundary was to be the Del Norte.

Washington, D. C., 10 March, 1883.
My dear Mr. Tyler:

I have this moment received your communications of
the 7th of March, 1883, and, without waiting to read them
through, instantly thank you for what you have done for me.
I was on the point of addressing you a letter reminding you
of your promise to me, and now you have of yourself with
great goodness given me exactly the materials which I had
not in my possession and of which I really was in need. I
shall make immediate use of ycur communication and trust
you will be as well pleased with the proof of my constant re-
search after information as I am in receiving it.

Touching Polk, I do not wish to come out before the public
with a mere statement that Polk totally denied in the strongest terms the truths of the allegations against him. If I write
at all, I shall endeavor with what written documents I have
and with my memory to state the whole progress of the affair; but that the administration in power should itself have
made the decision and sent its messenger to Mexico seems
to me as natural as it was for Sir Robert Peel on going out
of his ministry to wait until he had accepted the terms of the
Oregon settlement and exchange ratifications, a thing which
he did and boasted that he did, having had just time to do it.
The question then with regard to Mr. Polk is narrowed down
to the question whether he should have sent some one to
overhaul Mr. Tyler's messenger, which might have been impossible if the messenger went with proper speed, or secondly,
whether he had made any promise direct, or implied that he
would do so. So far as I am concerned, I have to say that he
never made any hint to me in that direction, and that it seems
to me now that it would have been an unjustifiable interference with the legal and constitutional and proper act of the
administration of his predecessor.

Very truly your greatly obliged
GEO. BANCROFT.

---

Washington, D. C., 12 June, 1883.
My dear Mr. Tyler:

I have given close attention to your kind and instructive
letter on the subject of what I narrate in Volume I, on page
253 of my history of the formation of the Federal Constitu-

tion. I see no difference between "kept in the back ground" and "kept in reserve," but as the last was Madison's form of speech, of course, I prefer it. As to the word "prevailed" you very justly take exception to it and I have reconstructed the narration and corrected the error. As to the phrase "zealot for the independence of the states," Tyler may have been zealous, but the mention of this is out of place in relating his earnestness in favor of granting Congress full power over trade, so I have cancelled it. As to the matters that relate to the interior action of the mind of the one on the other, I take care to follow their own words, and so in stating Tyler's views on commerce, I have used his own account given in the Virginia convention a year later; a statement which has not been questioned by any one. I have represented Madison and Tyler acting cordially together; and I do not give any prevailing influence to either of them over the mind of the other; believing each to have acted from his own independent convictions.[1]

And now may I trespass on your goodness still further. In your essay which you sent me some months ago, you say that Polk wrote a note to Tyler encouraging him to go on and settle the Texas matter during his administration. I wish to know if there be such a note of Polk's; and if so, I should sometimes like to have a copy of it [2]

What was it that made Benton in his history so wrathful and exceedingly bitter on Polk? Or had he no personal grievances?

Very truly yours,<br>GEO. BANCROFT.

My address for the rest of the season, till the seventh of October, will be Newport, R. I.

(1) This portion of the letter had reference to a passage in Bancroft's "History of the Constitution," Vol. I, p. 253, regarding the calling of the Annapolis Convention. I showed Mr. Bancroft that the two Speakers, John Tyler and Benjamin Harrison, had been confounded; that Mr. Tyler was warmly in favor of granting new powers to Congress, while Harrison was not; that Mr. Tyler throughout the war, had thrown his whole influence in support of Congress; and that even if he had not done so, the term "zealous" conveyed a reflection which a biographer might use but a historian should avoid. See sketch of John Tyler, Sr.

(2) Mr. Bancroft misunderstood my letter. I said that Mr. Tyler directed Mr. Calhoun to wait on the President-elect and inform him of the President's intention to select between the alternative propositions, and that Mr. Polk did not object or protest. See Vol. II, p. 364-5.

TO THE EDITOR.

Sanford, Orange County, Florida,

March 3, 1886.

My dear Sir:

I was very much  pleased at the reception of  your letter this morning, and  feel well compensated  for the labor of  reviewing  " Drummond,"  when it meets such  complimentary notice from, such high sources as you present.

I think with you that the politics of  1840  were but imperfectly understood  in subsequent years by the many newspaper editors, and the general readers.  It was the unpopularity of John Q Adams which made Jackson president. I think we agree.  My review of your work has been sent to the *Sunny South*.  I expect it will published at an early day. The editor usually publishes my articles as  soon as they are received

I have no doubt  he  would be delighted to publish your article on Upshur.  I would say to him not to  hesitate one moment, and if you wish it, or deem it necessary, I will write to him about it.

I was a  student at William and Mary in 1840-1,  where I had an opportunity of  seeing Judge Upshur, whenever he held court in Williamsburg. He was the guest of Judge Tucker, and I very frequently joined them at tea, and  your father was often present.  Judge Tucker  extended his hospitable kindness to me by telling  me to  come in as often as I chose. The convention was always  charming to me.   Judge Upshur and your father were devoted friends.  I noticed  Judge Upshur's work  " A Brief Enquiry,"  in my sketches of  southern literature, and remark,  "Though a  small work, it is a  large and brilliant gem in our political literature."  I heard from satisfactory sources that Mr. Calhoun  pronounced it an abler work than Judge Story's "Commentaries on the Constitution," to which it is a reply.  Mr. Calhoun also  paid a high compliment to Prof. Dew's  lectures on the  Restrictive System, by pronuncing it the ablest political work in America.

Judge Upshur was extremely handsome, and his head, entirely bald, was a model of beauty.  I heard  him say one day to Judge Tucker, calling him Beverley,  " He wished he had as fine a suit of hair as he had; Judge  Tucker remarked to Upshur,  "If you had a heavy, thick growth of hair, I would send

for old Sam (a Negro barber), and have your head shaved
during your sleep; it is good fortune for any one with so
beautiful a head to be entirely bald as you are." He said-
"Tucker, I am going to get me a wig." "If you do," said
Tucker, "I will take it, and hide it, the first night I can get
into your room." You remember Tucker was the author of
"George Balcomb," and also of the "Partisan Leader." The
latter was not popular, while "George Balcomb" was. I
heard Tucker one evening jesting with Upshur, and saying
it was not known who was the author of the "Partisan
Leader," but that it was generally attributed to Upshur.
Judge Upshur replied, "Well, Tucker, it is not known who
was the author of 'George Balcomb," but as you are aware
that I am the author of it, I will publicly claim it, and leave
you the honor of the. "Partisan Leader.'" It was, however,
all pleasant joke, but I thought Judge Upshur got the advantage in a most good humoured way of his friend, Beverley.

I witnessed. while a student, a very striking event. In
open court, Upshur on the bench, a young man was arraigned
for trial under the charge of larceny; he was a soldier attached to the regiment stationed at Fortress Monroe. He had gone
out of the fort and committed the offense for which he was
indicted by a grand jury, and was committed to jail in Williamsburg. As the man was about to be placed on trial, with
leave to plead, some one from the Fort said he wished
to present an order from the Colonel. "What is it?" said
Judge Upshur. It was handed to the Judge, and was an order demanding the delivery of the prisoner to the bearer,
stating that he was demanded as a United States soldier subject to martial law, and that the court must return him
to the Colonel. Judge Upshur wrote on the order and
handed it back to the bearer: "The prisoner has been indicted for violating a law of Virginia; the penalty is the penitentiary; if the prisoner is found guilty, he will be sentenced
and conveyed to the penitentiary; if not found guilty, he will
be discharged;" saying, "Deliver this to the Colonel," and
saying to the commonwealth attorney, "Mr. Southall, have
the prisoner arraigned and proceed with the trial." Upshur
was much applauded; he was as quick as a flash, as determined as was necessary, and as firm as the old walls of the
Fort from which the prisoner had deserted. The jurisdiction
of the court was unquestionable, though some weak minded

Federalists differed from the light of the Bench.

When the review of your work appears, I will send you a few copies, I thank you very kindly for writing a notice of the review of " Drummond." I wrote a sketch some time since of Victor Hugo I did not notice it but I heard that it had been translated and published in France, and that an English paper noticed it. Do not consider me vain in relat-ing it; if it is so, it is unusual. I do not even know the names of the papers. If you have not a copy of my Civil Law, pub-lished in N. Y. by Baker, Voorhies & Co., I will send you a copy.

Yours sincerely, etc.,<br>WM. ARCHER COCKE.(1)

---

## FROM JEFFERSON DAVIS.

Mr. Tyler was greatly esteemed and admired by me, as well for his strict conscientiousness, his extraordinary talent, and graceful accomplishments. His conduct in regard to the United States Bank, which was the subject of complaint by some members of his party, furnished the highest evidence of a faithful adherence to principle. I well remember when he appeared before a committee of investigation of which I was a member, and which was directed to inquire into the con-duct of Mr. Webster when Secretary of State, in regard to the use of the secret sevice fund, that the ex-President de-clined the offer of the book containing the list of the war-rants drawn against the fund, saying that he was willing to state all which he could remember, but did not desire any aid to his memory. He then recited the warrants drawn, giving the name and amount in each case, and thus covered all which the record contained. It seemed to me such an ex-traordinary exhibition of memory that I took occasion to re-mark upon it, when he modestly replied that, supposing those disbursements would never be inquired into, he had felt more than the ordinary weight of responsibility in regard to them, and could not probably have so well remembered the expend-iture of any other fund. Thus did he exhibit a conscientious integrity more commendable even than his memory.

As an extemporaneos speaker, I regard him as the most felicitous among the orators I have known. It may not be

(1) William Archer Cocke was a nephew of Hon. William S. Archer, U. S. Senator.

unacceptable to relate an incident in support of the opinion I
have just expressed.  Once, when on my way to Washington
City, the steamboat on which I was travelling landed at Cincinnati.  Mr. Tyler was in the city; heard that I was at the
landing and unable to go ashore, being on crutches from a
wound received in Mexico, and kindly came on board the
boat to see me; found there a number of person who had
preceded him and to whom he was personally unknown.  In
being introduced to them he was addressed by the spokes-
man in a complimentary manner.  He replied so felicitously,
that had it been possible to suppose that the address was anticipated by him, it might well have been concluded that the
reply had been prepared.

JEFFERSON DAVIS.

# Tyler and the Offices.

_____ ᴀ

With most writers the Spoils System had its origin with removal from office. But this is beginning at the wrong end. The appointment precedes logically the removal, and the partisan appointment may sometimes compel a proper removal. Certainly no inefficient, negligent officer should be retained in any position of trust.

The responsibility of the "spoils system" so called necessarily rests with with the party, under whatever name it has been called, which has aimed to develop the power of the Federal Government. Every accession of power has increased the number of the offices, and of course this has given a wide field for the spoils. Now this field has been invariably filled, as fast as opened up, with partisan appointees. The present civil service laws are undoubtedly as good as far as they go, but no sane person doubts that the United States as at present administered have thousands of unnecessary offices and dependents. The reform contemplated had much better look to prevention of the evil than to its regulation.

The Federal party in the beginning created many offices and filled them with Federalists. The famous "Midnight Judges" are identified with the culmination of this period of spoils.[1]

The principles of the followers of Jefferson were for a restriction of the Federal power and Federal patronage. Mr. Jefferson showed himself conspicuously a civil service reformer in abolishing more than three-fourth of the offices, without making an appointment.[2] Mr. Madison and Mr. Monroe fol-

(1) " Parties and Patronage," pp. 5-30.
(2) Mr. Jefferson had the judiciary act and the internal revenue laws repealed, reduced the army, etc.

lowed in the same track. J. Q. Adams caused the
enactment of the Tariff of 1828 and many bills for
internal improvements, thereby swelling vastly the
number of appointees or dependents. Andrew Jackson and Martin Van Buren were thorough Federalists, and approved high tariff and internal improvement bills, in full co-operation with Mr. Adams, as the
latter himself says. In 1835 Mr. Calhoun made his
famous report and showed the enormous develop-
ment of the system. When Marcy announced the
doctrine of the Jacksonian government, "To the
victors belong the spoils," he announced the principle of Federalism as interpreted by Bayard and Otis
—the mouth pieces in Congress of the Federal party
in 1797— that "the politics of office seekers would be
the great object of the President's attention, and an
invincible objection if different from his own."[1]
Jackson's administration, it must be remembered,
was run by the high tariff men of New York led by
Marcy, Wright and Van Buren, of Pennsylvania led
by Dallas, and of Missouri led by Benton. There was
nothing Jeffersonian about Jackson and nothing
States rights. John Q. Adams himself says[2] that
"he carried through Congress in perfect concert with
Jackson's administration" the protective tariff of
1832, which provoked nullification in 1833.

The Crawford party of strict construction were
driven from the Jackson party, called the Democratic party, and whole states seceded, to form with National Republicans of the North the new party in
1834 called "Whig." The Whig party cried "Reform" and promised to reduce the government in
every way to the old Jeffersonian simplicity. They

(1) "Parties and Patronage," page 20.
(2) Ibid, 48, note 1. Niles 63, 172.

declared bank, tariff, and internal improvements "obsolete questions,"[1] and won the election in 1840. Then came the rupture of the party. A large portion of the Whigs—especially the Northern element—were secretly old Federalists; and led by Mr. Clay they renounced their Jeffersonian doctrines, and came at once into collision with President Harrison. Before the one-month Whig administration was out, matters had progressed so far that Harrison would hold no intercourse with Clay except by letter, and he himself bitterly denounced the lust for office, laying the blame at the door of the Federal Whigs "who," he said, "were bent upon seizing the reins of government"[2] John Tyler was not only a Crawford but a Southern man. In Virginia the State officers had not been disturbed by the change of parties until after 1834. Mr. Webster in his Richmond speech in 1840, declared that "Virginia, more than any other state, had condemned the doctrine of removals from office for opinion's sake." Miss Salmon in her pamphlet on the "Appointing Power," written from a Federalistic standpoint, shows nevertheless, that as late as 1859 the doctrine of spoils found little favor in the South. "The tendency of the North was in favor of proscription; at the South against it." James K. Polk in his *Diary* (1846) says that "it was Mr. Jefferson's plan to conciliate the North by the dispensation of his patronage and to rely on the South to support his principles for the sake of those principles." It is clear then that the whole *make up* of Mr. Tyler's position was against the spoils system.

A brief summary of facts which are stated more at large in my little work, "Parties and Patronage

(1) Schouler's History U. S., IV. p. 182.
(2) See speech of Mr. Watterson quoting Mr. Proffit, Cong. Globe, 1842, Appendix page 592.

in the United States," will show that his administration was one of reform.

On Mr. Tyler's accession to the Presidency he found that Harrison had removed very many office-holders, and promised away most of the offices. These removals by Harrison came before Congress for ratification at the extra-session in 1841, and many writers, like Miss Salmon, have been betrayed into thinking they were made by Tyler, as Harrison was dead. But Mr. Tyler was against proscription, as was shown by his making the retention of Messrs. Loyall and Whittle, two Democratic officeholders at Norfolk, the subject of his very first letter to Harrison, after the inauguration. ( Vol. II, 163, Note 1.)

After his own accession, the Maryland Whig delegation bitterly complained of Mr. Tyler's opposition to removals. ( Niles' Reg. 63, p. 79.) Granger stated that the Whig cabinet resigned in part because Mr. Tyler declined to make removals of Democrats. ( Niles 61, p. 231; "Parties and Patronage.") Tyler instructed the Postmaster-General to appoint no editor to office, and none were appointed. ("Parties and Patronage," 69.) He preferred to wound his own brother-in-law, Dr. Henry Curtis, who had received the previous promise of Harrison, to turning out of the Treasurer's office that competent officer, William Selden. For a a year after the Whig party ostracized him, Mr. Tyler continued to draw the majority of his appointees from their ranks. (Vol. II, p. 154. )

In March, 1842, he removed Jonathan Roberts, who had swept into the collector's office at Philadelphia the very scum of the city. Mr. Tyler evidently needed all the friends he could get, and he could not afford to make removals without cause. And he made none without it.

In two messages he urged Congress to regulate the civil service, so as to prevent removals. His friends, Gilmer and Wise, in the House of Representatives, urged Congress to require the President to give a reason, in writing, for every removal. They urged Congress to establish a press for printing all government work, thereby limiting political influences. These propositions were not given a hearing by Congress.

Mr. Tyler retained in office all the prominent Whigs filling foreign missions—Edward Everett, C. S. Todd, Henry Wheaton, Waddy Thompson, etc.—most of them till the end of his administration, and the rest until they voluntarily returned home. When Baldwin of the Supreme Court died, Mr. Tyler offered the post left vacant successively to John Sergeant and Horace Binney—two pronounced Whigs and political opponents. Nelson was finally confirmed in 1845.

After his withdrawal from the canvass in September, 1844, he removed a considerable number of Whigs who had remained in office up to that time, but only then for cause. Their zeal for Clay's election had carried them into all kinds of excesses. But Mr. Tyler, having withdrawn from the canvass, could not then be charged with personal motives. The appointments made by him to the vacant places were sent to Congress for confirmation at the closing session, which causes Miss Salmon to think that these removals were made at that time.

At the closing session, Mr. Tyler filled vacancies long existing. At Polk's own request, he appointed his own brother, William H. Polk, to office. But Polk returned the favor by turning out all Mr. Tyler's appointees. And that after he and Jackson had

promised to regard Tyler's friends as favorably as
any other portion of the Democracy. (See letters
preceding.)    Polk turned out all Mr. Calhoun's
friends also.    He turned out all the Whigs, complaining in his *Diary* under date April 22, 1846, of
being greatly embarrassed by the great number of
Whigs Mr. Tyler *had left in office.*

The Whigs, on other hand, while Mr. Tyler was
in office, actually tried to usurp the power of appointment and assume all the executive patronage.
They wanted to take away from him the appointment of the Secretary of the Treasury and the
Treasurer.    They persistently rejected his nominations, although, as in the case of Wise, many of them
had been often urged by Mr. Clay before to apply for
offices. (See Wise's address May, 11, 1843; "Parties
and Patronage," p. 76, Note 1.) They sometimes, 'tis
true, rejected his nominations, as in the case of Dr.
Silas Reed, and then convicted themselves of error
by unanimously ratifying it on a second nomination.
Congress let out all the executive printing to contract, but retained the disposition of their own. Congress made the President pay for his private secretary, and all the expenses of the White House, contrary to all precedent.

As shown by the testimony of M. M. Noah, an
editor and disappointed suitor for office, Mr. Tyler
did not expect to be re-elected President. ("Parties
and Patronage," 81, Note 2.) He had, in fact, twice
offered to announce in a public message his willingness to renounce the succession. (Ibid, 79.)    He accepted a nomination in order to force the Democratic
party to take a Texas man, to drop Van Buren, and
to compel a recognition of his friends.

It is curious that those who impute the worst of

motives to John Tyler for allowing his name to go
before the public make a hero of Birney, who did the
same thing and without half the following. Far from
desiring patronage, Mr. Tyler, by his vetoes, deprived himself of a host of opportunities to appoint his
friends to offices created by the bills vetoed. How
excellent Tyler's appointees were is shown from the
fact that no defalcation of any consequence occurred
during his four years. In money matters Webster
said that Tyler was critically exact. He reduced the
expenditures several millions below the average of
Van Buren's administration, according to the report
of even a Whig, Tom Corwin. He left a surplus in
the Treasury. And that, too though he negotiated
twice as many treaties as President Van Buren. ("Parties and Patronage," 90-92. ) In a word, Mr. Tyler's
principles as a States-rights man made him necessarily opposed to the spoils system. Senator William
B. Giles had long before observed that the spoils
system was the incident of a strong national government, which demanded numerous offices and office-
holders as the condition of its existence.

It is pleasing to think that the present civil service rules have in some degree restrained the excesses which Giles predicted, but the excesses exist
more widely ( 1895 ), than at any previous period of
the Republic; and the remark of Polk remains true.
In the single item of pensions, the South has paid
$1500,000,000, all of which has been spent in the
North. The tariff lords have received a much larger
sum, and they and all their beneficiaries are dependents of the present vast, centralized government.
The modern reformers propose to regulate the terms
of office, but the old states-rights presidents, Jefferson and Tyler, did a better work by abolishing and
preventing needless offices.

It is laughable to talk of reform, as the Reform Clubs are doing, when Congress lavishly creates every year so many new places for plunder. Mr. Jefferson was a true civil-service reformer, when he had the entire internal revenue system abolished, and thus at one blow got rid of three-fourths of the office-holders.    Mr. Tyler was a true civil-service reformer when by his vetoes he prevented the creation of numerous places.    I respectfully suggest to Mr. Roosevelt and other reformers to reduce the pension service, wipe out the tariff, cut down the expenditures and bring the government to a proper limit of economy.    This is true reform; for with the disappearance of the office, necessarily disappears the corruption attendant on it.    At the same time, I do not mean to decry the good of the present civil-service system.    It is good.

## APPENDIX A.

*CASES OF THE ENTERPRISE AND CREOLE.*

(See Vol. II, 204.)

Nothing shows better the unjust manner in which Dr. Von Holst writes than the account he gives of these cases. His manner is not only unjust but unworthy of a historian. It is fairly inferable from his "Life of John C. Calhoun," first, that Mr. Calhoun's resolution of March 4, 1840, asserted that slavery was a principle of the law of nations; and second, that nothing was ever obtained from Great Britain but an empty declaration of regret.

But is this the fact? Mr. Calhoun's resolutions in 1840 asserted nothing more than that a ship engaged in lawful voyage is, according to the law of nations, under the exclusive jurisdiction of the State to which its flag belongs. (See the record for his resolutions.)  The Senate in unanimously approving these resolutions affirmed what is good international law to-day  The "unanimous" vote was no proof of the awe in which "almost all northern politicians stood of the slave power."

Again, it is true that the Treaty of Washington did not contain a provision regarding the *Enterprise* or *Creole*, but the principle being conceded in the correspondence the adjudication of the damages was referred to a future day. The convention of February 8, 1853, provided for the adjustment of all claims, and, under it, the owners of the negroes on the *Creole* were awarded $110,333.00. In the claim of the brig *Enterprise* the sum of $49,000.00 was awarded. (See Senate documents, 1st and 2d Session, 34th Congress, Vol. 15).

The correspondence itself fully disposed of the *Caroline* affair, the owners being deemed not entitled to damages, and the only question being the infringement of the sovereignty of soil, for which, in fact, no treaty article was necessary in addition to the apology offered in the correspondence. The owners of the *Caroline* had no true claim to damages and got none, but neither did Alexander McLeod, who was imprisoned by the New York authorities, who demanded damages, and was refused by the arbitrators.

## APPENDIX B.

*REMINISCENSES* [1] *OF MRS. JULIA G. TYLER.*

We were in Italy when we heard of our President General William H. Harrison's death, and the accession to the presidency of the United States of the Vice-President, John Tyler. My parents had taken their two daughters, Julia ( myself ) and Margaret, for their gratification, after leaving school, on a trip to Europe, and the period since our arrival in England, October 24, 1840, had been one continuous round of pleasure in many ways. Starting from Liverpool, we travelled leisurely *via* London, Dover, and Boulogne to Paris, where we lingered several delightful months, and then resumed our journey through France to Italy, meeting many agreeable companions, forming many valuable friendships, and leaving nothing unseen or unenjoyed that foreign countries afforded at that period. The news from America of Harrison's death startled us in the midst of enjoyment, and the black crape with which we young ladies draped our left wrist testified to the sense of grief universally felt by Americans, whether at home or abroad, for the death of the good man and soldier, the " Hero of Tippecanoe."

But it was not until the succeeding fall that we returned once more to the loved shores of our native land. Resuming our travels after a long tarry in Italy, we left Rome by post, the mode of journeying we had adopted on leaving Paris, and far to be preferred to any other, having purchased a travelling carriage there and secured the services of an accomplished courier. We visited the cities and towns of many countries, passing over the Simplon Alps and by the storied Rhine, giving ourselves new leases of enjoyment by sojourns here and there. Ah ! what could be more enchanting than our experience in Brussels, and not alone there; but I dare not stop to call up too many of the memories of the past. We returned at length to London, and after rich enjoyments there, in due time time pursued our course of travel, and with an experienced valet instead of our continental courier, accomplished in many tongues, we went

(1) This paper first appeared in the Cincinnati *Graphic News* of June 25, 1887, and was republished in the Richmond *Dispatch*, July, 21, 1889. Mrs. Tyler died July 10, 1889.

MRS. JULIA G. TYLER,
Widow of President Tyler

again by post on a minute and extended tour through England, Ireland, Scotland and Wales, but of the incidents of this tour I may not now speak.

It was in the month of September, 1841, that, after undergoing the trials of an equinoctial storm—the severest, the captain of the steamer said, that he had ever encountered—we landed at Boston.

My father was of an old family of New York, and possessing means and leisure, placed his time at his daughters' disposal, and there was no wish personal to ourselves which he did not attempt by every available means to gratify. Having become acquainted in former days, while a member of the New York State Senate, with nearly all the prominent politicians of the State, he conceived the idea of a visit to Washington during the session of Congress, thinking that our education would be singularly imperfect if, after seeing the capitals of nearly all the governments of the old world, we should neglect to see our own. Impressions of our public men began with our trip from New York to Washington. A handsome, portly gentleman came several times into the car in which we were seated and excited the interest of myself and sister by the self-conscious manner in which he looked into the mirror at the head of the car and adjusted his cravat, while he cast several furtive glances in our direction. These glances were, doubtless, accidental, though soon after our arrival in Washington the gentleman alluded to called upon our parents, in company with an old friend of my father, the Hon. Silas Wright of New York. Then we found that the handsome stranger was no less a personage than Millard Filmore, the then chairman of the Committee on Ways and Means of the House of Representatives, and alas! also married. By this latter discovery mine and my sister's little romance was dissolved, for, though perhaps a little vain, we always thought him an accomplished gentleman. He afterwards followed in the footsteps of General Taylor as President of the United States.

Our boarding house in Washington was Miss Peyton's, on the corner of Pensylvania Avenue and Four-and-a half Street. It had been selected by our friend, Mr. Arthur Middleton of South Carolina, late Minister to Madrid, and a most agreeable one it proved. It was quite a rendezvous, at the time, for congressmen. Mr. Van Buren's Secretary of the Treasury, Senator Woodbury and family from New Hampshire, boarded there with his family, and we met almost daily a *coterie* of young statesmen, whose types were well represented by the chivalrous Sumter and Pickens, members from South Carolina; Hubard and Mallory from Virginia; McKeon and Davis of New York; Cushing of Massachusetts; Butler King, of Georgia. Often with these as our escorts, whose politeness never lessened, we visited the chief places of interest and triflled away the moments in conversation on the several topics of the day. I recall our visits to the halls of Congress. In the House our attention could not fail to be attracted by the distinguished individuals whose names daily filled the newspapers upon the exciting subjects which made Mr. Tyler's administration so unique in history.

I remember the appearance of Mr. Adams as he sat day after day watching his opportunity to present his mammoth petition on the subject of slavery. Mr. Adams was excessively bald, and as he sat in the middle of the House, with his immense petititiou rolled around a kind of windlass to sustain it, his excitment was manifest in the flaming redness of his bald head, which acted as a chronometer to his audience.

There, too, was Henry A. Wise of Virginia, fearless in his support of the President, and in the vehemence of his defense spreading terror among his enemies, his eyes beaming with the intensity of his emotions, and his lips aglow with the fires of his eloquence. I cannot describe them all—Gilmer, Filmore, Cushing, Pickens, Ingersoll, and a long host of others. Their names are the favorites of history, and beyond the compass of what I design to be a very, very cursory notion of men and things that crowd upon my memory.

I remember my first visit to the White House, where we went a few evenings after our arrival in Washington with a congressional party. I was introduced to the President by the Hon. Fernando Wood of New York, who years afterwards liked to revert to the occasion. I own that it was with a great deal of interest I, with the rest of our party, had anticipated the interview. The President's break with the Whigs had been the occasion of unprecedented political excitement, and his name was on all lips. When I look back at this day and see him as he stood in the "Green Room," the room between the "East" and the "Blue," at the moment of our introduction, it appears to me no marvel, acquainted as I am with his high-toned nature, that the wild phrenzy of po-

litical misrepresentation left no impression of bitterness either upon his countenance or his voice or demeanor. He welcomed us with an urbanity which made the deepest impression upon my father, and we could not help commenting,
after we left the room, upon the silvery sweetness of his voice,
that seemed in just attune with the incomparable grace of
his bearing, and the elegant ease of his conversation. I am
here reminded how, in after days, meeting the novelist James
at a dinner party, he remarked to me that he had not met in
all his American experiences one who so completely rounded
his sentences in conversation as did President Tyler; that he
left nothing more to be said.

I was married to President Tyler on the 26th of June,
1844, and immediately became interested in the great political topic of the day—the annexation of Texas. Mr. Clay I
had met at Saratoga the summer preceding my visit to
Europe, and had appreciated, though still a school girl, his
attentions and the charm of his manner, which every one
conceded. He was now the leader of those bitterly opposed
to the crowning glory of Mr. Tyler's administration, which
had even roused the muses. I have not forgotten the amuse-
ment I felt to see my name connected with it in a madrigal
in a morning paper by Mrs. Cutts, the aunt of Mrs. Stephen
A. Douglass:

" Texas was the captain's bride,
    Till a lovelier one he took;
With Miss Gardiner by his side,
    He, with scorn, on kings may look."

But this measure was too serious for gay verses, a measure which so greatly extended the confines of the Union by
leading to the acquisition of the great West. I know that no
ignoble motive animated the President in this measure. Endorsing the views of the old Virginia school, of the gradual
abolition of slavery, he looked upon the annexation of Texas
with the breadth of a patriot's view as a matter of vital interest to the whole Union. The bitterness of Mr. Clay and
the unscrupulous misrepresentation of those times appear to
me at this date as incomprehensible. Mr. Tyler's Secretary
of State, during the time I occupied the White House with
him, was Mr. Calhoun. Mr. Webster had filled the office until the summer of 1843, and was always spoken of by Mr. Tyler as the model of a Cabinet officer. Mr. Upshur followed
Mr. Webster, and the melancholy issue of his life, in company

with my revered father on board of the Princeton, has stamped his massive appearance indelibly upon my memory. His portrait, in oil, remarkably well and correctly painted by Ringgold, was presented to us by his family. We valued it greatly, but it went the way, with a great deal else, during the late war and was burned up in Richmond, where we had stored it. Mr. Upshur, though not so well known in public life as Mr. Tyler, by reason of his quiet duties of his office as Circuit Judge of Virginia, until called into the national Cabinet, was truly an extraordinary man. He was physically a much larger man than Mr. Webster, though there was a striking sameness about the the brow of each, as if the brain forced it forward. He usually wore upon his shoulders a handsome cloak with tassels which lent dignity to his appearance. His piquancy in conversation rendered him a favorite with all, and his death on the Princeton was a heavy blow to the nation. He had brought the navy, while Secretary of that Department, to a high state of perfection. Mr. Calhoun took Mr. Upshur's place in the Cabinet, occupying it at the time of my marriage. I think of him now, with his glistening eye, his gray hair brushed back, and the lines in his face marked with the precision of a Grecian statue. Of one whose reputation as a statesman is so universal, I may justly pause to say a few words.

Mr. Calhoun's mind was generally occupied with some matter of State, even in the midst of gayety, and the times in which he figured were times of pre-eminent interest. But when he chose to relax, few could be more interesting or attentive. We were always excellent friends. At my wedding reception at the Executive Mansion, he led me to the table on his arm and helped me to cut the great cake that adorned it. I placed the knife in the middle and he cut the first slices. In all my many conversations with him, he made himself particularly engaging. It was at the first large dinner at the White House that the following incident occurred: Mr. Calhoun sat at my right hand and our conversation had fallen upon the Texas question, when a query was made as to the views of Judge John McLean, who was present, and who was one of my warmest friends. I said that I should make it a matter of honor with him that he should vote for Texas. Mr. Calhoun startled me by replying, "There is no honor in politics." I said, "We will see," and writing on a slip of paper, "Texas and John Tyler," sent it to the Judge, who was on the opposite side of the table, with the request that he should drink the toast with me. The Judge turned with much gallantry toward my direction, raised his glass, bowed, and said, "For your sake."

I afterward mentioned this circumstance to the President and quoted the remark of Mr. Calhoun. Mr. Tyler, whose sense of political honor was rigid, recoiled, and asked, surprised and almost sternly: " Did Calhoun say that?" Alas! Mr. Calhoun's sentiment may not have appeared a very poetic one, but experience has taught me that politics is not the best school for the propagation of the purest code of morals! General Mirabeau B. Lamar was present at the dinner I allude to, and gave, requiring all the gentlemen to rise with filled glasses, a very elegant toast, but as it was personal to myself, I will refrain from repeating it. I remember on another occasion of a dinner given by one of the members of the Cabinet in November, 1844. Mr. Pakenham, the British Minister, was there—the only gentleman not of the Cabinet. We talked across and all around the table, and it was very witty and merry. Mr. Calhoun sat on one side of me. Attorney-General John Nelson on the other. Both were so exceedingly agreeable it was difficult to say which was most so. Mr. Calhoun was never so sociable before, for none of his admirers ever heard of his repeating poetry, which he did in my ear with infinite sweetness and taste. When I narrated this incident to the President he could scarcely have been more astonished if an explosion had occurred beneath his feet. "Well," said he, "upon my word, I must look out for a new Secretary of State if Calhoun is to stop writing dispatches and go to repeating verses."

After the election of 1844, which resulted in the victory of Mr. Polk, Washington raged with the excitement of the Texas question. The President looked confidently to the passage of the measure, and his thoughts were greatly occupied with devising means to ensue its success. His last annual message created a prodigious sensation throughout the country. I well remember Mr. McDuffie, former colleague of Mr. Calhoun in the Senate, enthusiastically telling me that he regarded the measure as the finest that had ever at any time proceeded from the Executive Mansion.

On the 15th of February, we gave our farewell party, " Mrs. Tyler's retiring ball, ' it was termed. Some two thousand persons were present. A *bonmot* of the President went the rounds. When some one congratulated him upon the brilliant gathering of beauty and fashion, he said: ' Yes, they cannot say *now* that I am a President *without a party.*

History tells us how, in defiance of every difficulty, he consummated the great object of his ambition. The joint resolution for annexing Texas passed on the 3d of March, 1845. A special gold pen had been provided for the President's signature, which he afterward presented to me, but it vanished one day, I am sorry to say, from my cabinet of curiosities. The day before we left the Executive Mansion, we gave a dinner party to Mr. and Mrs. Polk. I wore a black blonde over white satin. Mrs. Polk was present and wore black velvet and a head dress with plumes. She impressed all who saw her with her vivacity and information. Mr. Polk, I think, was absent, but I well remember Vice-President Dallas, with his bright black eyes, and thick, gray, almost white, hair.

Then came the hour of departure. At 5 in the afternoon of the 3d of March, 1845, a crowd of friends, ladies and gentlemen, assembled in the East Room to shake hands with us and escort us from the White House. As the President and myself entered they divided into two lines, and when we passed to the head of the room, surrounded and saluted us. General Van Ness, a distinguished citizen of Washington, requested them to stand back and himself stepped forward and delivered " on behalf and at the request of many ladies and gentlemen, citizens of Washington," a farewell address. I saw, before he concluded, a response of some kind would be necessary from the President, and I felt a good deal concerned, for I knew he had prepared none and did not expect to deliver any. But I might have spared myself all and every fear, for as soon as General Van Ness had concluded his remarks by saying that he deeply regretted that his awkwardness in public speaking prevented him from making his farewell offering "a more polished stone," the President raised his hand, his form expanded, and the deep admiration and respect his words elicited was told truly in the sobs and exclamations all around. "Sir," said he, as his silvery voice quivered with beautiful and poetic eloquence, "you do yourself injustice. Say you that this offering is an unpolished stone? It is a brilliant gem, polished by the hand of friendship, and sparkles rare in my heart."

We did not attend the inauguration ball. The next morning we determined to depart from Washington, adopting "French leave," but when we reached the wharf at 9 o'clock in the morning, the boat had gone and we had to return, almost to our regret. At the hotel our visitors did not fall off, for all that day our parlor was thronged. We left again that night, an immense fire raging in the city, the theatre and many houses burning, reaching Richmond next day; then, the day after, we took the steamer down the James river and reached the President's home in Charles City County, "Sherwood Forest," at 12 o'clock M., on the 7th of March, 1845. (1)

(1).  It is perhaps undignified seriously to notice the effusions of Ben Perly Poore in his " Reminiscences, " but the statement that he makes that Mr. Tyler left Washington on the 4th of March, 1845, "not caring to assist in the inauguration of his successor," is, like most of his history, untrue.  Mr. Tyler did take part in the inauguration of his successor, and did not attempt to leave Washington till the 5th of March. The original letters of Mr. Tyler's from which he quotes were purchased by Dr. J. S. H. Fogg, of Boston, at the sale of Poore's collection of MSS. some years ago.  They were found to be addressed to Henry A. Wise.  In 1882, when I began the Life of Mr. Tyler, I wrote to one of the sons of Henry A. Wise for material, but his reply was, that the Federal authorities had during the war seized his father's letters, and he said that though, after the peace, "a pretense had been made of their return, it was found on examination that all the letters of any value had been abstracted. " Poore's connection with the government in Washington rendered his piracy upon the government archives an easy matter.  As a collector, his ways were immensely different from the high toned Dr. Fogg.

## APPENDIX C.

———

### *CONFESSION OF HON. RICHARD W THOMPSON.*

———

There is no lack of evidence that the conduct of the Whig leaders to President Tyler was saturated with deceit. But, perhaps, the latest confession of the fact comes from Hon. Richard W. Thompson, who was a member of congress in 1841. This gentleman in his "Personal Recollections" (1895) retails the old hearsay charges, but refutes them by the following personal testimony. He was one of a committee to wait upon Mr. Tyler about the Bank bill. During the course of the conversation Tyler "was entirely uncommittal." But says he: "Our anxiety however, was so great, that we put such construction upon the interview as our hopes and desires dictated—the wish being father to the thought, *and so reported to those in whose behalf we acted!*" In the light of this declaration we can readily understand the weight of the President's refusal to have any further conversations with members of Congress who so misrepresented him. See Bell's *Statement* Vol. II., p. 8f, Note 2.

## APPENDIX D.

———

*ANECDOTE OF HON. WILLOUGHBY NEWTON.*

———

In March, 1844, the Whigs decided upon a convention of the party to be held in Richmond, and a committee was appointed, at the head of which was the Editor of the Richmond *Whig*, to invite the presence of distinguished Whig statesmen. An invitation was extended to Hon. Willoughby Newton, member of Congress from the Westmoreland District. Mr. Newton replied in a long letter, which without reading, it seems, the Editor of the Whig published in his paper with introductory remarks of a nature highly flattering to Mr. Newton. Mr. Newton's letter, however, was not such as to commend itself to the strict party Whig. In fact, it was a long arraignment of the Whig party for treachery to the President and to the people, spoken by one in the confidence of the party, as Whig congressman and Whig Presidential elector; and its conclusion was an admonition to the Whig party to avoid the errors of the past by taking an open and straightforward attitude in the future.

The letter, of course, afforded Mr. Ritchie an excellent opportunity to attack the Whigs in the next issue of his paper, the Richmond *Enquirer*; and the Whig leaders were greatly mortified. The editor of the *Whig*, thrown on the defensive, tried to get out of the difficulty by saying that he had not read Mr. Newton's letter; and was provoked into an attack on Mr. Newton so lately the object of his eulogy. This conduct compelled Mr. Newton to fall back upon the columns of the *Enquirer*, to which he addressed a letter complaining of the Editor of the *Whig* for inviting the free expression of his sentiments, and yet ungenerously assaulting him after he had submitted his letter to his consideration. He indignantly vowed that he had done with the *Whig* newspaper forever! During all this time old Mr. Ritchie was in ecstasy over the discomfiture of his enemies. (See newspapers of that day.)

## APPENDIX E.

---

## *NOMINATION OF MR. TYLER FOR VICE PRES-IDENT.*

---

It is well known that Mr. Clay's nomination at Harrisburg was defeated by the Anti-Masons, whose real leader was William H. Seward, of New York. The opposition to Clay came from the North, and his support from the South, which was only natural, as in his public specches and private letters he had come out against tariff, Bank, internal improvements, abolition, and anti-masonry. Something of the same kind of intriguery was attempted against Mr. Tyler, and by the same parties, who tried to make Tallmadge, Leigh, Bell, Preston and others the instruments of their purposes. But so contemptible were these movements to Tyler's injury, that, according to the statements of the conspirators themselves, the effort failed in the case of Preston "since not a single Southern delegate approved the suggestion of his nomination for Vice-President." (Niles 61, p. 232). After Mr. Tyler's succession to the presidency, the importance ascribed to these movements was immensely magnified, and it was represented that the Vice-Presidency was tendered to Mr. Tyler because all the rest had declined it. In reply to this, Benjamin Watkins Leigh, in a letter highly honorable to his own character, indignantly denied the application, and said that he was assured that he was not the wish of the convention, and that Mr. Tyler was. (Niles 61, p. 232). These detractors ignored the fact that Mr. Tyler had already receive a nomination for Vice-President in 1835. They made the great mistake also of supposing that their whispering in dark corners was the express voice of the convention. The defeat of Clay strengthened Mr. Tyler's chances, but Mr. Tyler was undoubtedly the most distinguished Southern Whig; and had Clay been nominated the convention would nevertheless have decided in his favor.

## APPENDIX F.

——

## *MR. TYLER AND THE ASHBURTON TREATY.*

——

Mr. J. Q. Adams, when President, agreed to a reference of the dispute in relation to the North-eastern boundary to the award of the King of the Netherland. There were, in fact, no really defined lines, and the King in proceeding to make a conventional line did what any sensible man would have done. He divided the disputed territory up in an equitable manner, and Jackson, who was then President, was strongly in favor of accepting the award. The Senate, influenced by the violent opposition of the New England Senators, repudiated the decision of the arbitrator on the ground that he had no right to decide except in favor of the American contention or the English contention. Littleton Waller Tazewell, the senior Senator from Virginia, was the chairman of the committee of foreign relations, and both he and his colleague John Tyler were in favor of the award; and thus early as 1831 pronounced in favor of a conventional line. According to Mr. Benton (Vol. II., 441) Webster fiercely opposed the compromise principle of the award, and his recorded votes seem to affirm the truth of the statement (Niles 42, p. 460). Mr Curtis himself states that when in 1837 the movement was made in Congress for the appointment of a special minister to England, to negotiate a settlement, and the Massachusetts and Maine delegations united in recommending Mr. Webster, President Van Buren doubted whether Mr. Webster's views "would be sufficiently pacific" (Curtis' Webster II. 37). There was, however, no question as to the position of President Tyler in favor of a conventional line and a peaceful policy. And Webster subsequently came over to the same view. In the negotiations with Lord Ashburton the part taken by the President was all important. Mr. Webster himself says that "the negotiations proceeded from step to step and from day to day under the President's own immediate supervision and direction," and that the President "took upon himself the responsibilty for what the treaty contained and what it omitted" (Niles 64, p. 79). The Secretary of War, John C. Spencer, declared: that it was "bare justice to President Tyler to say that his suggestions and advice were frequently of the most important character." (Niles 63, p. 143.) The President wrote the letters to Gov. Seward, setting forth the positions of the government in relation to the trial of McLeod (Vol. II., page. 208), and it was entirely due to his influence with Lord Ashburton that he did not break up the negotiation and go home. (Vol. II., p. 217.) The President himself relates that everything was agreed upon by informal conferences between the negotiators and himself, and that after an agreement was thus reached the correspondence in each case was submitted to him and received his correction. (Vol. II., p. 242). Some of the President's notes to Webster are preserved in the collection of Mr. C. P. Greenough, of Boston, according to which, the case of Creole was clearly covered by his suggestions. (See vol. II., 212, 251). The question of impressment was brought to the attention of the negotiators by the President (See Note to Webster II., 224,) and he it was who originated the idea of keeping a fleet on the coast of Africa to execute our own laws against the slave trade. (Vol. II., 219, 23$^x$, 240). Finally, Webster was anxious to submit the separate articles of the treaty in separate treaties to the decision of the Senate but the President overruled him in this: and there can be no doubt that the large vote given to the treaty was due to this union of questions which appealed with different force to different sections of the Union. (See vol, II,, p, 225). This sagacious policy was followed by the President in his note upon the tripartite treaty for the settlement of the war with Mexico and the acquisition of the West. The three interests of Texas, Oregon and California were to be united so as to satisfy all sections of the country." (Vol. II., 261).

In respect to the *Creole*, Mr. Tyler settled the principle by which full damages were accorded by Great Britain to the owners in 1853, by the award of an arbitrator, (See Appendix A). And in respect to the North-eastern Boundary the principle of Mr. Tyler's vote in 1831, was entirely vindicated by the treaty of 1842, which was one of compromise, though an improvement upon the decision of the award of the King of the Netherlands, in the matter of territory gained for the United States.

## APPENDIX G.

---

### I.  OPINIONS REGARDING JOHN TYLER, SR.

---

" A veteran patriot, who from the first dawn of the Revolution to this day has pursued unchangeably the same honest course "—*Thomas Jefferson.* Vol. I. p. 35.

" Mr. Henry was very fond of John Tyler as a warm-hearted patriot, and an honest, sensible man."—*Judge Roane* to William Wirt.  Henry's *Henry* II., 517

" As for the understanding of Judge Tyler it was of the highest order  *  *  He was plain in his address and appearance, for his great soul disdained the tinsel of pomp and parade and was intent only on virtue."—*Judge Spencer Roane,* of the Supreme Court of Virginia.

" I knew the father of the President, Judge Tyler of the General Court of Virginia and a purer patriot or more honest man never breathed the breath of life, and I am one of those who hold to the safety which flows from honest ancestors and the purity of blood"—*Henry Clay,* Cong. Globe, 1841. Appendix p. 345.

" A venerable patriot of the Revolution, a faithful and able legislator, Judge and Chief Magistrate of this Commonwealth, a man of fixed and undeviating integrity, yet endeared to his friends by every softer virtue."—*Resolutions of the General Assembly.*  Vol. I, p. 268.

### II.  OPINIONS REGARDING JOHN TYLER.

---

" The most felicitous among the orators I have known,"—*Jefferson Davis.*

"Without a particle of hauteur or assumption in his aspect or demeanor, eminently frank and unconstrained in his conversation, he evinced as much of good nature and high-bred politeness, as of intellectual resources "—*Henry S. Foote's Casket of Reminiscences.*

"He became his station as President singularly well,"— *Charles Dickens*, American Notes.

"His own State papers compare 'favorably in point of ability with those of any of his predecessors."—*Alexander H. Stephens*, Stephens' Pictorial Hist. U. S,

"His personal appearance was very attractive, six feet in height, spare and active, his movements displayed a natural grace. He was one of the most facinating man I had ever known—brilliant, eloquent, even more charming than Mr. Calhoun in conversation."--*Henry W. Hilliard*, Member of Congress, &c. See p. 57.

"I shall not cease to remember his steady and really able co-operation in, as well as well as his official sanction, of my own poor *labors* in the treaty of Washington--*Daniel Webster*, Vol. II., p. 191.

"His tact and talent for a suggestive policy were remarkble."—*Henry A. Wise*, Seven Decades of the Union.

"Mr. Tyler was a man of far more than the average ability of our statesmen."--*George Tickner Curtis*. Curtis' Webster II , p. 211.

"With John Tyler a great man has fallen in Israel, and in that fall a grand career has been closed."—*R. M. T. Hunter.* Vol. II., 191.

"He was so frank and generous, so social and cordial, so genial and kind, and withal so manly and high toned and so familiar with the duties of his station, that you were ready to give him your hand and head in return for his which he was ever ready to proffer."—*George Wythe Munford*, Secretary of the Commonwealth of Va. Vol. I., p. 356.

On the strength of Mr. Tyler's maiden speech in Congress against the tariff, Judge Baldwin, of the Supreme Court of the United States, predicted for him the highest political promotion. See Vol. I., p. 334.

# TYLER FAMILY SIGNATURES

( Died 1729 High Sheriff of York Co.)

( Chancellor. Died, 1812, )

( Grandfather of President Tyler. )

(Died, 1773, Marshal Vice-Admiralty Court,)

( Governor, &c    Died 1813.)

(President of the U. S., 1841-45.)

# APPENDIX H.

————

*PEDIGREES OF TYLER AND RELATED FAMILIES.*

## I. TYLERS OF YORK, JAMES CITY AND CHARLES CITY COUNTIES.

1, HENRY[1] TYLER, born (according to his deposition about 1604, is mentioned first in the York Co. records in 1645. He patented 254 acres at Middle Plantation Jan. 7, 1652-3 granted him for importing six persons into the colony—himself, his wife Mary, and four other persons. He subsequently in 1666 received a certificate from York Court for 1800 acres for importing 36 persons. In 1653 "Mr. Henry Tyler" was Justice of the Peace for York County. One John Orchard died in 1655, and soon after his widow Ann married Mr. Henry Tyler, who in the meantime had lost his first wife Mary. Henry Tyler was a man of some standing. When Mr. Francis Wheeler said at Robert Harrison's house that "he would pay a debt to Capt. Warner for Mr. Tyler," the latter said "noe, hee had tobaccoe in his owne houses to pay his debts."

Lt. Thomas Dobbs signed an apology in Court: "I have very much iniured Mr. Tyler who hath always been a very helpful friend to me; in the negligent carriage of his business and in selling his tobaccoe I have very much predjudiced him but I hope hee will out of his charitable nature remit it."

On April 13, 1672, administration on his estate *cume testamento annexo* was granted to his wife, Ann Tyler. He left a nuncupative will. At June Court, 1672, " Ann Tyler, relict of Henry[1] Tyler, of Middletown parish, in Yorke County," recorded a deed of gift to her " well beloved sons " 2, Henry[2]; 3. John[2]; and 4, Daniel[2], "sons of her deceased husband Henry[1] Tyler." As 2, Henry Tyler was the "heir" of his father, there could have been no children by the first wife, Mary. Soon after her husband's death Mrs. Ann Tyler married Martin Gardner, "grocer of London," who emigrated to York County, and became Justice and high sheriff of York Co. He was one of those who subscribed Bacon's oath at Middle

Plantation in 1676. He died without issue May 19, 1693. His wife, Ann, died April 2, 1679.

3, JOHN[2] TYLER ( Henry[1]) gave a receipt to Martin Gardner, his guardian, for the share given him by his mother's deed, on Jan. 23, 1685. It was witnessed by Samuel Bainton, Robert King, and Ann Marrienburg. He may have been the ancestor of the Hanover Tylers.

4, DANIEL[2] TYLER (Henry[1]) was carried off by the Turks, and I have not met with his name after bill filed by his brothers for his property.

2, HENRY[2] TYLER (Henry[1]) on Jan. 5, 1681–82 gave a receipt to Martin Gardiner for the share given him by his mother's deed. In 1690, he and his brother John filed a petition in York Court to require Martin Gardner, called father-in-law, but who "married their mother Ann Tyler" to divide between them the property left by their mother's deed to their Brother Daniel, who had been carried into Algiers by the Turks, and had not been heard of for seven years. This was done. On Oct. 24, 1681, Henry Tyler "of York Co. in Virginia, gentleman," leased the land at Middle Plantation, patented by his father, to Martin Gardner, in return for "one man servant and a house to be builded thereon of 30 feet with one chimney at each end, covered with sawn plank." He was Constable in 1689-90 for the lower precinct of Bruton Parish; and on Nov. 25, 1694, he was sworn Justice for York Co. April 10, 1700, he qualified as Sheriff, and was Sheriff again in 1702. Coroner in 1703, Sheriff in 1705, and continued Justice until his death in 1729. In 1699, he was appointed one of the directors for building Williamsburg, and the General Assembly purchased 74 acres of his father's original tract for the site of the Governor's Palace (Hening's Statutes.) His will was proved Dec. 15, 1729. (See Vol. I., p. 48.) He was for a long time Churchwarden and Vestryman of Bruton church, and headed the petition of the Vestry in 1710 to the Legislature for the new brick church, which finished in 1715, is still standing, a venerable relic of the past. (See William and Mary Quarterly Mag., III., 169.)

Henry[2] Tyler's first wife was Elizabeth Chiles, of whose family the following account, taken from the contemporary records, may be given.

Walter Chiles, merchant, patented lands in Virginia as early as 1638. Among his headrights were his son Walter, and wife Elizabeth. He represented Charles City Co. in

1642–43 in the House of Burgesses, and James City Co. in 1645, 1645–46, 1649, and in 1652. In the last year he was elected Speaker, and had the title of Lieutenant Colonel. (Hening's Stats.) In a deed in the Charles City Co. records he is entitled " Esq.," a term at this time applied to but few besides the councillors. He engaged largely in the shipping business. (See W. and M. C. Quarterly, I., p. 75.) He was probably dead before 1658, as the Walter Chiles, who represented James City that year and in 1663, was designated as "Mr. Walter Chiles," and not "Lieutenant Colonel." He was certainly dead before 1670, as Walter Chiles, the son, received a patent for 70 acres in James City Island called " Black Point, " formerly granted to "Walter Chiles, father of the said Walter Chiles, and by right descending unto him as sonne and heyre of his said father deceased." In April 1671, "Mr. Walter Chiles in behalf of his sons John and Henry" obtained from the General Court an order for 1500 acres in Westmoreland Co. He was dead before May 15, 1672, when his widow Susanna received from Gov. Berkeley a lease for 99 years of 200 acres in Passbehayes, James City Co., for improvements made on the Governor's land there by her late husband, Walter Chiles, deceased. It was provided in this deed, that after the death of the said Susanna, John Chiles, eldest son of the said Walter Chiles, (in the Deed the name is spelt "Giles" should enjoy the balance of the term. (See Deed in the Ludwell MSS.) In 1690, John Chiles and Mary his wife deeded to Sir Edmund Andros the land for 77 years, being the unexpired period. From the land patents John Chiles appears to have settled in King William Co., and Henry Chiles in New Kent Co., where their descendants spread into Louisa, Caroline, and Spotsylvania (W. and M. C. Quarterly, I., 75 ) Col. John Page, who died in 1692, aged 65, calls Elizabeth Tyler, wife of Henry Tyler, grand daughter, and John, Chiles his grandson. An order in York Court, June 25, 1683. mentions Henry Tyler as "having married Elizabeth Chiles." So that there can be no doubt that Elizabeth Chiles was a daughter of "Mr. Walter Chiles, " and granddaughter of Lt. Col. Walter Chiles. Assuming that she was at the time 16 years old (generally the marriageable age) she was born about 1666, her mother may have been either the daughter of John Page, or the daughter of nis wife by a former marriage, of which however there is no record. Dr. Page suggests that the word " granddaughter " is too general to infer any certain relation-

ship; that " nephew meant grandson, niece meant anything in-
general, especially aunt, and cousin meant any relations more
distant than sister or brother." The latter part of this statement is certainly true; "cousin" was especially used to desig-
n'ate a nephew, but the records do not bear out the assertion
that "niece means aunt." Nor have I seen in the early records of Virginia " nephew " used to designate a "grandson,"
and certainly "grandson" is never used to designate "nephew,"
or any other relationship but " grandson " or " grandson-in-
law. " Grandchildren and great-grandchildren were both described by grandchildren. And so Col. Page in leaving a legacy and land to John Tyler, son of Henry and Elizabeth Tyler, calls him grandson; and John Tyler, sometime after attaining 18 years of age, gave Col. Page's administrator a receipt
for the legacy styling himself in the same way " grandson of
Col. John Page." (See Page *Family.* )

Issue of Henry[2] Tyler and Elizabeth Chiles, his wife: 5,
Henry[3] who died Sept. 27, 1684; 6, John[3] born before 1686,
the date of Col. John Page's will in which he is mentioned; 7,
Elizabeth[3], who died July 30, 1695; 8, Francis[3]; 9, Henry[3]; 10
Anne[3] who died in 1712. (Bruton Register and will of Henry
Tyler.). Henry Tyler's wife Elizabeth died January 19, 1702-
3 (Bruton Register.) He married, 2dly., Sarah —— who died
in 1710, and 3dly., Edith (whose "brother" was Thomas Harda-
way), who survived him and married Mathew Pierce. Edith's
will was proved in 1739 No issue by last wives.

8. FRANCIS[3] (Henry[2], Henry[1]) was a student at William
and Mary in 1702, marshal of the vice-admiralty Court in
1714, subsheriff of James City in 1723. He married Rebecca
——., and had issue: 11, Henry[4]; 12, Francis[4]; 13, John[4]. As
Francis Tyler lived in James City in his latter days
his will was perhaps lost with the destruction of the papers and books in the Clerk's office. His sons are not mentioned in the York records, except in the will of Henry[2] Tyler,
and appear to have left this part of the country.

9. HENRY[3](Henry[2], Henry[1]) received by the will of his father the ancestral homestead. He was Vestryman of Bruton
Parish, but in 1752 went to Sussex County to live. Before
doing so, he sold to Dr. John Amson all that tract (except the
Palace land) granted in 1653 to his grandfather, Mr. Henry
Tyler, which " *descended* to his son Henry, who *devised*" the
same by his will to the grantor (See Vol. I., p. 51.) In Sussex he was distinguished for raising a hog weighing 1200

pounds (Va. Gazette.) He married Sarah——, and had one
daughter Mrs. Jones, who died before him. He died Jan. 2,
1774, aged 73 (Albemarle Parish Register, Sussex Co.) His
will was dated in 1772. and proved March 17, 1774. An ab-
stract is as follows: To his godson John Tyler of Charles
City, Attorney at law, he gave the place (500 acres) he then
lived on in Sussex, r4 slaves and various articles of furniture;
to Edward Champion Travis 40 shillings for a ring; to his
nephew William Tyler a tract of land on south side of Poplar
swamp, to said nephews William and John his mill; to William
Tyler 15 Negroes; that a debt of 176 pounds current money
due by him to Peter Jones' estate be paid out of a sum due to
him from William Preston in England, the balance of said
debt to be divided between Ann Tyler, sister to my godson
John, Ann McKenzie, and the eldest daughter of Francis Tyler; to godson John Tyler that tract of land on the south side
of the Poplar Swamp called the Pine Log Quarter of 275 acres.
Residue of the estate to be equally divided between his two
nephews beforementioned, who are appointed executors; witness: John Judkins, Charles Judkins, and Gray Judkins.

14, William Tyler mentioned in the will must have been either
the son of 11, Henry[4], 12, Francis[4], or 13. John[4], sons of Francis[3]
Tyler. He lived and died in Sussex, and his will dated March
1, 1792, was recorded in Sussex May 3, 1792. In it he gives
Nancy Tyler, daughter of John Tyler, 100 pds. current money,
Peggy Tyler, daughter of his brother Frank, 400 pounds current money; to nephews William Tyler and Frank all the residue, appointing said William and John Massenberg executors.

7. John[3] (Henry[2], Henry[1]) was a student at William and
Mary College in 1704. Under the will of John Page he was
given a tract of land in the forks of Powhatan swamp, James
City, and a legacy of 50£. There was standing there a few
years past a house pointed out as his residence. John Tyler's
receipt for his legacy is dated 19 Aug., 1706. In 1721 he received from the State Council 16 pounds sterling in consideration of the maiming of his Negro man, Priamus, "in firing the
great guns on the anniversary of his Majesty's coronation."
On May 2, 1727, "Henry Cary and John Tyler, gent." were appointed to view the Governor's house and report what repara-
tions are necessary therein. He died soon after, as he is
mentioned in his father's will in 1729 as deceased. He married Elizabeth——, (perhaps Elizabeth Low, as she had a
daughter of that name) and had issue: 15, John died Oct. 2,

1714, (Bruton Register.) 16, John, 17, Joanna, 18, Elizabeth Low, 19, Mary, 20, Edith, 21, Anne, died in 1728.

17, JOANNA[4], (John[3], Henry[2], Henry[1]) married in 1736 Dr. Kenneth McKenzie, a distinguished physician (*Va Gazette*). His will was proved March 7, 1755, and her will on Jan. 19, 1767; and they had issue 22, Anne born Apr. 10, 1739. 23, (Dr.) William McKenzie, born April 10, 1746, whose daughter Anne was second wife of Judge James Semple, father of Dr. George William Semple of Hampton and Major Henry Churchill Semple, of Alabama, 24, Mary was born April 14, 1748 (Bruton Register.)

18, ELIZABETH LOW[4] (John[3], Henry[2], Henry[1],) married 1st Bowcock, by whom she had at least one child Mary, and 2dly John Palmer, attorney-at-law, Bursar of William and Mary College, who died in 1760.

19, MARY[4], (John[3], Henry[2], Henry[1],) mar. Rev. William Preston, Professor of Moral Philosophy in William and Mary College. In 1758, he returned to England and was Minister of *Warcop*. The present Minister of Warcop, Rev. Charles Mayes Preston, is the great-grandson of Mary Tyler (See William and Mary College Quarterly History Magazine, for pedigree of Preston Family, Vol. III., p. 139.)

20, EDITH[4], married Rev. Thomas Robinson, Professor of Humanity in William and Mary College. The marriage of the two sisters, Mary and Edith, with the two Professors created disturbances which led to the temporary eviction of the two incumbents, it being contrary to the rules of colleges at the time for any but the President to have a family (See Perry's *Va. Historical Collections.*) Issue of Thomas Robinson and Edith Tyler 25, John[5], born Oct. 30, 1746; 26, Mary[5], born Feb. 5, 1748-9, married Thomas Jameson, a nephew of Hon. David Jameson, Lt. Governor of Virginia, and had issue: 25, Thomas Robinson Jameson, and 26, Dorothy Jameson (born July 27, 1768,) who married Dr. Samuel Ayres. Hon. David J. Ayres, of Keokuk, Iowa, is Dr. Ayres' grandson. (See William and Mary College Quarterly for Jameson Pedigree.)

16, JOHN[4] TYLER (John[3], Henry[2], Henry[1]) born circa 1715, will dated July 24, 1773, proved Sept. 20, 1773. He was educated at William and Mary College, and was marshal of the Colonial Vice-admiralty Court. He married Anne, only child of Dr. Louis Contesse, a French Huguenot physician, and Mary Morris his wife. Dr. Contesse died in Williamsburg Sept. 11, 1729. (Bruton Register.) His wife who is said to

have been a celebrated beauty was married four times.  Issue
of John[4] Tyler and Anne Contesse: 27, Mary[5].  28, Elizabeth[5].
29, Rachel[5]. 30, Anne[5]. 31, Louis[5]. 32, John[5]. 33, Joanna[5].

27, MARY[5] married William Irby, of Charles City Co.
Issue Mrs. Faulkner, Mrs. Nesbit, and Mrs. Morgan, mother
of Senator John T. Morgan, of Alabama

28, ELIZABETH[5] married John Greenhow, a wealthy merchant of Williamsburg.  Her tomb in Bruton church yard
states that she was born Jan. 30, 1744, and died July 23, 1781.
(See "Greenhow Family" in William and Mary Quarterly
Hist. Magazine.)

29, RACHEL[5] TYLER married, 1st, William Drummond, of
James City, whose will was proved in York Co. June 21, 1773.
He was, I think, a great-grandson of Gov. William Drummond,
hanged in Bacon's Rebellion; married, 2dly., Col. Stith Hardyman, of Charles City Co. and had issue Tyler Hardyman, who
married Miss Catharine Christian, and moved South, where his
descendants still live.

30, ANNE[5] married Dr. Anthony Tucker Dixon, a sur-
geon of the Revolution.  No issue.

31, LOUIS[5] was a lawyer, who moved to Charlotte County, at the outbreak of the Revolution.  His will dated June
30, 1775, and proved in Charlotte Co. Sept. 1st, 1777, mentions his wife Mary Barradill Tyler.  He resided at "Red
Hill," on Staunton River, which place was afterwards the
home of Patrick Henry.  His only son is buried with him at
"Red Hill."

32, JOHN TYLER[5], Governor of Virginia etc. (born Feb. 28
1847, died Jan. 6, 1813.) married Mary Marot Armistead, only
daughter of Robert Booth Armistead and Anne Shields.  Issue
34, Anne[6]. 35, Elizabeth[6]. 36, Martha Jefferson[6]. 37, Maria Henry[6]. 38, Wat Henry[6]. 39, John[6]. 40, William[6]. 41, Christiana[6].

33, JOANNA[5] came to Charlotte to live with her brother
Louis at "Red Hill."  After her brother's death, she lived
alternately with Mrs. Clement Reade and Parson Johnson,
until her marriage with Major Wood Bouldin.  Some account
of her is given in the "Old Trunk," by Powhatan Bouldin
(For her descendants See Bouldin Family in W. and M. C.
Quarterly.)

34, ANNE[6] married Judge James Semple.

35, ELIZABETH[6] married John Clayton Pryor of Glouces
ter and had Anne Contesse[7], Maria Emily[7] married Alfred.
B. Davies, William[7] died young, Christiana[7] married Dr. Geo.

William Semple, of Hampton.

36, MARTHA JEFFERSON[6] married Thomas Ennalls Waggaman (See for "Ennalls and Waggaman Families" William and Mary College Quarterly Hist. Mag.)

37, MARIA HENRY[6] married John B. Seawell (See William and Mary College Quarterly Hist. Mag. for Seawell family)

38, WAT HENRY[6], physician, educated at William and Mary College, etc., married 1st. Eliza Walker, and had John[7] *d. s. p.*, William Wyat[7], Mary Elizabeth[7], Wat Henry[7]; married 2dly. Margaret Govan and had James[7], *d. s. p.*, and Betty* married 1st Rev. John Points, 2, Dr. John Drew. *William*

40, WILLIAM[6], member of House of Delegates &c., married Susan Harrison Walker. Issue John Harrison[7], Thomas Walker[7], Anne Contesse[7], Maria, * Patty.[7], * William[7], Lewis[7] and Benjamin Harrison[7].*

41, CHRISTIANA BOOTH[6] mar'd Dr. Henry Curtis, of Hanover. Issue : William Henry[7], John Foushee[7] died a student at the University, Anne Elizabeth[7] married Dr. Robert Mumford ( Issue : John[8] died in the war 1861–65, Robert[8]* Revenue Comm'ssioner of Richmond, and Christiana[8] * married George F. Merrill, *) Maria[7]* unmarried, Benjamin[7], Bartlett Anderson[7], Armistead[7], and Mary Christiana[7] *, who married Lieutenant Williams of the Army, and lastly Tyler[7]

39, JOHN TYLER[6] (born March 29, 1790—died Jan. 18, 1862,) President of the United States, married, 1st, Letitia Christian, and had 42, Mary[7]. 43, Robert[7]. 44, John[7]. * 45, Letitia[7]. * 46, Elizabeth[7]. 47, Tazewell[7]. 48, Alice[7]; married, 2dly, Julia Gardiner, and had 49, David Gardiner[7],* 50, John Alexander[7], 51, Julia[7], 52, Lachlan[7],* 53, Lyon Gardiner[7],* 54, R. Fitzwalter[7],* 55, Pearl[7] *.

42, MARY[7] TYLER married L. Jones. Issue: John, Hnery, Henry, and Robert.

43, ROBERT[7](born Sept.9,1816,) married Priscilla Cooper. Issue : Letitia,* Grace* married John Scott, of Alabama, Lizzie m'd Thomas G. Foster, Priscilla (" Toozie ") married Mr. Albert G. Goodwin of Alabama, Julia married Mr. Henry H. Tyson and Robert *

44, JOHN[7] ( born April 27, 1819,) mar. Martha Rochelle Issue : Letitia married Gen. William B. Shands, of Southampton, Martha* unmarried, and James Rochelle.*

45, Letitia[7]* married James Semple, U.S.N. and C.S.N. No issue.

46, ELIZABETH married William Waller. Issue: Mary* married Gen. Young, William, John, and Robert.*

47, TAZEWELL married Nannie Bridges. * Issue : Mar-

LYON G. TYLER, LL. D.
(President of William and Mary College.)

tha* and James. *

48, ALICE[7] married Rev. Henry M. Denison. Issue: Bessie* mar. 1st Mr. Allen, 2d Rev. Mr. Williamson. *

49, DAVID GARDINER[7]* Member of Congress (born July 12, 1846, ) married Mary Morris Jones.* Issue : Mary Lyon.*

50. JOHN ALEXANDER[7] TYLER married Sarah Gardiner. * Issue ; Samuel Gardiner, and Lillian Horsford. *

51, JULIA[7] : born Dec. 25, 1850 married William H. Spencer. Issue : Julia * who married George Fleurot. *

52, LACHLAN[7],* M. D. married Georgia Powell. * No issue

53, LYON GARDINER[7]* (born Aug., 1853) married Annie Baker Tucker, * daughter of Col. St. George Tucker, C. S. A. Issue : Julia Gardiner,* born Dec. 7, 1881. Elizabeth Gilmer* born March 13, 1885, and John,* born February 1, 1887.

54, ROBERT FITZWALTER[7]* married Fannie Glenn.* No issue.

55, PEARL[7]* married William M. Ellis.* Issue : Pearl Tyler, * John Tyler,* Leila, * Cornelia Horsford, * Gardiner Tyler,* Munford, *

* Those marked with the asterisk are living in 1896.

## II. ARMISTEAD FAMILY.

1, ANTHONY[1] ARMISTEAD, of Kirk-Deighton, Yorkshire, md. Frances Thompson : Issue : 2, *William*[2], the immigrant to Virginia.

2, WILLIAM ARMISTEAD[2] was baptized at Kirk-Deighton August 3, 1610. He married Anne——, and came to Virginia, about 1636 : Issue 3, William[3] Armistead, s. p. 4, John[3]. 5, *Anthony*[3]. 6, Frances,[3] md. 1st. Rev. Justinian Aylmer; 2d. Anthony Elliott, Lt. Colonel; 3d. Christopher Wormeley.

5, ANTHONY[3] resided in Elizabeth City Co., was captain buurgess &c, married Hannah,dau. of Robert Ellyson, of James City Co., burgess, sheriff, &c. Issue 7, William Armistead, captain, burgess &c. 8, Anthony. 9, *Robert*[4]. 10 Judah. 11, Hannah 12, Dunn.

9, ( Capt.) ROBERT[4] (died about 1742) sheriff and justice of York Co., md. 1st.——Booth; mar. 2d. Katharine, dau. of Capt. Thomas Nutting, and widow of William Sheldon. Issue by first wife, 13, *Ellyson*[5]. 14, Booth, who received a legacy from Thomas Booth, and died 1727 : by 2d wife, 15, Robert. 16, Booth. 17, Angelica,

13, ( CAPT. ) ELLYSON ARMISTEAD (will proved Dec. 19, 1757,) sheriff, justice &c., of York Co., married Jane, one of the daus. of Rev. Charles Anderson, minister of Westover. Issue: 18, *Robert Booth*[6] *Armistead,* 19, Ellyson Armistead. 20, James Bray. 21, Frances Anderson. 22, Jane. 23, Elizabeth.

18. ROBERT BOOTH[6] ARMISTEAD married Anne, b. July 31, 1742, dau. of James Shields of York Co., by his 2d. wife, Anne, dau. of Jean Marot. Issue an only child 24, MARY MAROT ARMISTEAD (1760-1797), who married Judge John Tyler.

In the York Co. books is a bond dated 1777 from John Tyler, of the County of Charles City, to Nathaniel Burwell, of "Carter's Grove," in the County of James City binding himself to sell 400 acres in Yorkhampton Parish adjoining the lands of Nathaniel Burwell on Queen's Creek, "to which the said John is entitled in right of his wife Mary, the only child and heiress of Robert Armistead decd., and which descended to her on the death of the said Robert." I have not found any authority for the tradition that Robert Booth Armistead lived at Buck-roe in Elizabeth City Co., or indeed that Buck-roe was ever owned by the Armistead Family.

The book-plate of William Armistead of the Revolution bore: Or a chev. between three points of spears sable, tasseled in the middle. Crest: a dexter arm in armor embowed, ppr., holding the but end of a broken spear. Motto : *suivez raison.*

### III. SHIELDS FAMILY.

1, JAMES[1] SHIELDS (died June 2, 1727) was an early resident of Williamsburg, where he kept an ordinary. He married Hannah——, and his will shows that he had issue 2, James[2]. 3, Matthew[2]. 4, William[2]. 5, Elizabeth[2], married—— Vaughan. 6, Mary[2], married——Cobbs.

3, MATTHEW[2] SHIELDS (James[1]) married Lucretia, daughter of Jean Pasteur, "barber and perukemaker." Issue: Mary Magdalene, that married William Pearson, who kept the tan yard at Williamsburg.

2, JAMES[2] (James[1]) was appointed surveyor for York Co. in 1744, married 1st. Elizabeth, daughter of Robert Cobbs and Rebecca Pinkethman (dau. of William Pinkethman) his wife. (Robert Cobbs married 2dly. Elizabeth——, who married after his death in 1725 Samuel Weldon of James City Co.) James Shields married 2dly. Anne Marot, widow of James Inglis (died before 1737). Issue by first wife: 7, Elizabeth[3]. 8, Frances[3]. 9, Hannah[3]. Issue by second wife: 10, James[3], born

Oct. 27, 1739. 11, Anne[3] born July 31, 1742. 12, Christiana, born Dec. 23, 1745. (Bruton Parish Register.)

After the death of James[2] Shields in 1750, Anne, the widow, married Henry Wetherburn, who continued the business of ordinary keeper carried on by his predecessor. Of the ordinary keepers, Smythe in his "Travels" (1773) says, in connection with his stay at the inn kept by Jethroe Sumner, who attained the rank of General in the Revolution: "more than ⅓ of the general officers of the American army were innkeepers and have been chiefly indebted to that circumstance for their rank, because by that public but inferior station their principles and persons became more generally known; and by the mixture and variety of the company they conversed with in the way of their business, their ideas and their ambitious views were more excited and extended than the generality of the honest and respectable planters, who remained in peace at their homes."

3 COL. JAMES[3] SHIELDS (James[2] James[1]) married Susannah (born Dec. 26, 1745,) daughter of John and Mary Page. His will dated Sept. 11, 1794, and proved in James City Co., July 13, 1795, mentions children 13, James[4] Shields. 14, Mary[4] Coleman, 15, Susannah[4] Allen (she, Susannah Allen, widow, afterwards married Hamlin Willcox of Charles City Co.—See inscription on her tombstone, Va. Hist. Society Collections, Vol. XI.) 16, John Page[4] Shields. 17, Page[4] Shields. 18, Anne[4] Taylor. 19, Christiana Brown[4] Shields. 20, David Minge[4] Shields. 21, Henry[4] Shields. 22, Judith Bray English[4] Shields, born Oct. 11, 1785, (afterwards married Thomas Walker), 23, Matthew Wyatt[4] Shields, and 24, Thomas Lawson[4] Shields. The last was by his 2d. wife, Rebecca Lawson.

23 MATTHEW WYAT[4] SHIELDS married Mary Royster Bell, daughter of Capt. John Bell of Charles City; and his son James W[4]. Shields resided, till lately, on Church Hill, in Richmond. Son of the last is Dr. Chas. M. Shields.

12, CHRISTIANA[2] SHIELDS (James[2], James[1]) married 1st. David Minge of Charles City, and had 25, Rebecca Jones[4] Minge, 26, Anne Shields[4] Minge (both born before 1777), 27, Judith Bray[4] Minge (born between 1777 and 1781, the dates of the will and the codicil of David Minge in which last she is provided for.) Judith Bray[4] Minge married Edmund Christian, clerk of Charles City Court, ancestor of Judge E. C. Minor of Richmond.

ANNE[3] SHIELDS (James[2], James[1]) married 1st. Robert Booth Armistead, of York Co. Her husband died about 1766, as the following order of Court at Yorktown shows :

"At a Court &c. held for York Co. 21 July, 1766. Anne Armistead is appointed guardian to her daughter, Mary Marot Armistead, an infant orphan of Robert Booth Armistead decd., and she with James Southall as her security entered into and acknowledged bond as the law directs. "

Anne Armistead married 2dly, Frederick Bryan Jr., as is shown by the record :

"On motion of Frederick Bryan, Jr. and Anne his wife, dower is assigned to said Bryan and Anne his wife in the lands of her former husband, Robert Booth Armistead," Dec[r]. 19, 1767.

By the second marriage, Anne had Anne Shields Bryan, born Feb. 28., 1768. Until 1770, Mr. Bryan was guardian of Mary Armistead, then her uncle James Shields was guardian. At the time of her marriage to Gov. John Tyler, Mary Armistead was living with her aunt, Mrs. Christiana Shields Minge, at Weyanoke, in Charles City Co.

### IV. THE MAROT FAMILY.

1, JEAN MAROT came to Virginia in the Huguenot emigration in 1700 (Va. Hist. Soc. Coll. Vol. V., p. 24 ). He was in 1704 secretary of Col. William Byrd at Westover, and was then 27 years old. The next year he obtained a license to keep ordinary at Williamsburg. He married Anne——, and his will was proved in York Co. Court in 1718, his inventory showing a large estate. His will shows that he had issue 2, Edith[2]. 3, Anne[2]. 4, Rachel[2]. His widow, Anne, married Timothy Sullivant.

2, EDITH[2] MAROT (Jean[1]) married Samuel Cobbs, first of York Co , and then of Amelia. 4, RACHEL[2] died *sine prole.*

3, ANNE[2] married, 1st, James Inglis, and had issue: Judith Bray Inglis, who married William Armistead, and was mother of Henry Armistead, of Charles City, born Jan. 8, 1753. James Inglis was the son of Mungo Inglis ( 45 in 1702. ), first Master of the Grammar school in William and Mary College. His mother was Anne (daughter of James Bray, Esq., and Angelica, his wife) who married, 1st. Robert Booth, ( died in 1692 ), son of Robert Booth (died in 1651) Clerk of York Co.; 2d., Capt. Peter Temple, ( died in 1695 ), 3d. Mungo Inglis.

ANNE[2] MAROT married 2dly. James Shields, son of James

Shields of York Co., innkeeper. Issue: 5, James[3], born Oct. 27, 1737. 6, Anne[3]. 7, Chistiana[3].

6, ANNE[3] SHIELDS married. 1st. Robert Booth Armistead, of York Co., and, 2d. Frederick Bryan, Jr. Issue by first marriage : Mary Marot, who married Gov. John Tyler.   Issue by second marriage : Anne Shields Bryan.

### V. WESTMORELAND AND PRINCE WILLIAM TYLERS.

CHARLES TYLER[1] was living in Westmoreland Co. as early as 1690. He died about 1723. He married Jane——. His issue was 1, Charles[2]. 2, Benjamin[2]. 3, Joseph[2]. 4, William[2]. 5, Christian[2] Monroe, 6, John[2] ( ? ),    The will of 3, Joseph[2], dated Dec. 23, 1737—proved Jan. 31, 1737-8, mentions brothers Benjamin and William Tyler, sister Christian Monroe, cousins Elinor Monroe, Sarah Monroe, Spence Monroe, Andrew Monroe ; other persons mentioned, Anne Harrison, James Lovell, Christopher Edrington, and John Edrington.

4, WILLIAM[2] TYLER had in 1725 a wife, Margaret Pratt, daughter of John Pratt.   As the records of King George show that he was living until 1770, he was probably the William Tyler who about 1755 marr.ed Esther, the widow of James Jones, brother of Hon. Joseph Jones, uncle of James Monroe.   The will of Esther Tyler proved in King George in 1770 shows that she had issue 1, William[3] 2, James[3] and 3, Blanche[3]. William3, the first of these married Sarah——, and died in King George without issue, in 1784, (will). Charles[2] Tyler witnessed in 1766 several deeds in King. George of William[2] Tyler; and 1784 John Tyler and Joseph Tyler, of Prince William Co., deeded 226 acres, a tract left to them by their father, John Tyler, in King George Co., lying south-east of the land of "the late William Tyler." The deeds were witnessed by Blanche Tyler.   Before this time (in 1777 ) a part of Westmoreland was added to King George.

In Prince William there is a deed dated Oct. 1. 1764 from William Tyler of Westmoreland Co. to his daughter Elizabeth Tyler of Prince William, single woman, for a negro in posesssion of her brother Charles.   These are suggestions of an identity in origin between the Tylers of Prince William and the Tylers of Westmoreland. (See Hayden's *Va. Genealogies* for descendants of John Tyler, of Prince William.)

### VI. ESSEX AND CAROLINE TYLERS.

RICHARD[1] TYLER was living in Essex Co in 1691. He married Susannah——, who had 1, Richard[2]. 2, John[2]. 3, William 4, Mary married Capt. James Boughan, justice and sheriff of Essex Co. 5, Susannah[2]. (The will of Richard[1] Tyler was proved in 1734,). Richard[2] (Richard[1]) married, 1st, Catharine Montague, 2d, Anne——, who survived him. He rose to the rank of justice of the Peace, major of the militia, &c. His will dated Oct. 21, 1761, proved Nov. 16, 1761, mentions wife Anne, dau- Franky, wife of Robert Cole, grandsons William Gatewood and his brother Philemon, Anne, dau. to Abraham Montague; directs that his negroes be equally divided among the surviving children of Richard Gatewood, and leaves a legacy to Elizabeth, daughter of John and Catharine Corrie.

2, JOHN[2] (Richard[1]) dated his will Dec. 20, 1757, and it was proved March 21, 1758. It mentions daughters Catty, Mary Ann, Hannah, Betty, Susannah and Frances; brother Richard Tyler & Archibald McCall made executors. According to the Family account of Robert Anderson, Esq. of Williamsburg (born in 1781) living in 1860, the children of John Tyler of Essex were 1, Sukey who m. Mr. Winter of Georgia, 2, Frances who married Mr. George Whitefield, of Georgia. 3, Hannah, born in Essex Co. Dec. 25, 1740, married to James Anderson, father of said Robert Anderson of Williamsburg Feb. 8, 1766. James Anderson died in Williamsburg in Sept. 1798, and his wife was buried near him in Bruton Parish church yard in 1803.

3, WILLIAM TYLER[2] (Richard[1]) was perhaps William Tyler, clerk of Caroline, which was taken from Essex and King William. In 1767, Willam Tyler, gentleman, was a justice of Caroline and moved to settle the accounts of William Tyler, decd. The will of Catharine Tyler, of Caroline, dated June 30, 1815, proved in 1816, mentions as legatees, kinsman Richard Keeling Tyler, George Tyler, Nancy Hewlett, Kemp Gatewood, Kemp Evans, nieces Kitty Mickleborough, Dorothy and Mary Evans, sisters *Jane* and *Lucy Cole*, sister Frances Smith, brother *Philemon Gatewood*, kinsmen George and Charles Terrell. Richard Keeling Tyler and Philip Redd executors. This will bears internal evidence of relationship between the Caroline and Essex people.

Judge C. W. Tyler, of Clarksville, Tennessee, gives his line as follows : William[1] Tyler of Caroline Co. Va., living before the Revolution, was father of Richard Keeling[2] Tyler (born about 1759), who married Mary Cluverius Duke, parents of John Duke[3] Tyler, father of Judge C. W.[4] Tyler (1895)

Another prominent representative of the Caroline Family

is Lt. Gov. J. Hoge Tyler of Va. His father, Mr. George Tyler, was in the State Legislature, and wrote that his grandfather, Capt. George Tyler, was an officer in the Revolution, and one of three brothers. This officer was doubtless a brother of Richard Keeling Tyler, and a son of William Tyler, of Caroline.

In the General Court records John Smith, of "Purton" in Gloucester Co., Va., was agent in 1674 for Mr. Richard Tyler, of London, who owned lands in Gloucester Co., Va., by the courtesy of England.

### VII. NORFOLK TYLERS.

Mrs. D. Tyler Earle, of Linden Ave., Baltimore, daughter of William Tyler of Norfolk, gives this account of her ancestors. In an old English prayer book is recorded : William Tyler, born in King William 1750, died May 3, 1788 at Norfolk

Eliza Bolling Tyler, born at Warwick in 1754, died at Norfolk Jan. 22d, 1772. [ The above are great-grand parents of Mrs. Earle. ]

Charles F. Tyler, born in Norfolk Jan. 22, 1772, died Dec 21, 1821.

Sally H. Tyler, born in Henrico County, March 9, 1774 died at Norfolk April 26, 1826. [ The above are the grandparents of Mrs. Earle, and their tombstones are in the churchyard of St. Paul's, Norfolk. ]

Mrs. Earle writes that she has some old silver with the Family coat-of-arms, and the seal her father wore bears a crest.

### VIII. TYLER FAMILIES OF NEW KENT AND HANOVER.

The following entries appear in the St. Peter's Parish Register :

Sara, daughter to John Tyler, bapt. the 18th day of May 1690.

Ann, daughter to John Tyler, bapt. the 17 March 1699.

John, son of John Tyler, bapt. the 4 July, 1703.

Susannah, daughter of Thomas Tiler, bapt. 23 Jan. 168⅞.

Hanover Co. was cut out of St. Peter's Parish, and in 1728, John Tyler Jr. was living in Hanover. A family of the name still lives in Hanover Co. The John Tyler, first above mentioned, may have been John[2] Tyler, son of Henry[1] Tyler, the emigrant to York Co. (See *Tylers of York* &c.)

### IX. TYLERS OF STAFFORD AND KING GEORGE.

The following entries appear in the Overwharton Parish Register, Stafford County.

Margaret Tyler married William Waugh Sept. 10, 1738.
John, son of Henry and Elsie Tyler, born April 17th, 1743.
Francis Tyler married Anne Strother May 17, 1844.

Anne, daughter of Henry and Elsie Tyler, baptized January 30th, 1747.

Mary, daughter of Henry and Alice Tyler, bapt. March 20, 1751.

Henry Tyler, so mentioned, was clerk of Stafford Co., until after 1770, when he was succeeded by his son, Thomas Gowry Strother Tyler (Journal House of Delegates, 1783,) In King George Co. is the record of the will (proved June 2, 1757) of John Tyler who directs his body to be buried in "Falmouth churchyard." He mentions his daughter Margaret, and his grandsons Tyler, Thomas, and William Waugh, and granddaughters, Million and Priscilla Waugh. To Tyler Waugh he leaves his plantation in Stafford and King George, and makes his "friend and benefactor", Charles Carter, Esq., of Stafford, Harry Tyler, and John Fitzhugh of Stafford, his executors. These names in the records suggest some connection with 11, Henry[4], 12, Francis[4] 13, John[4], sons of 8, *Francis Tyler*[3] in the pedigree of Tylers of York &c.

In 1775, one Charles Tyler gives notice of his intention to, leave Stafford Co., for Fairfax Co. (Va. Gazette.)

### X. TYLERS OF RICHMOND, CITY.

John Tyler was in Wallingford, Conn., previous to 1670. This John Tyler was grandfather of John Tyler, the preacher, who was born in 1742, educated at Yale, taking there the degree of A. M. in 1765. In 1768 he went to London and was ordained by Richard Fennick, Bishop of London. The same year he returned to Norwhich, Conn., and was rector of Christ (Episcopal) church. His grandson, John H. Tyler, settled in Richmond, Va., some years before the war. His sons, John Tyler, James Tyler, and Henry Tyler are now residents of Richmond, Va.

### XI. CHRISTIAN FAMILY.

1. WILLIAM CHRISTIAN, of New Kent married 1. Susannah Atkinson, Elizabeth Collier. By second marriage he had among other children: 2, *Robert* born May 5, 1760, married, Mary Browne, daughter of William Browne and Alice Eaton of James City Co. (See W. & M. Coll. Hist. Mag., Vol iv., p. 204, 279.)

2. ROBERT CHRISTIAN and Mary Browne had issue: 3,
William A., of the U. S. Navy; 4, John Beverley Christian,
judge of the General Court, who married Martha, daughter
of Judge James Semple and Anne Contesse Tyler, (dau. of
Gov. John Tyler Sr.,) his wife; 5, Dr. Oliver Christian, who
married Christiana, daughter of Major Edmund Christian, U.
S. marshall, and youngest brother of 2. Robert Christian; 6,
Elizabeth who, mar. William Douglas, father of William R. C.
Douglas, and Beverley Douglas, member of Congress; 7, Alice
who mar. Patrick Hendren, a distinguished lawyer of Charles
City Co.; 8, Letitia, born Nov. 12, 1790, married March 29,
1813 John Tyler, President U. S.; died Sept. 10, 1843; 9,
Jeannetta, who married John G. Miller and moved with him
to Columbus, Ohio, leaving a son and daughter; 10, Mary
who mar Dr. Nathaniel Miller; 11, Minerva, who mar. Heath
Jones Miller.

### XII. GARDINER FAMILY.

Lion Gardiner was "engineer and master of works of
fortifications in the legers of the Prince of Orange in the Low
Countries." He came to New England in 1635 under contract of 100£ per annum to serve the company " in the drawing, ordering and making of a city, towns, and forts of defense. " He commanded at Fort Saybrook, but finally settled
at Gardiner's Island, New York, which he purchased from the
Indians. The Island has remained in the possession of his
descendants ever since, the present proprietor being John
Lyon Gardiner. Lion Gardiner wrote an interesting history
of the "Pequot Wars," in which he took an active part. The
second wife of President John Tyler, Julia Gardiner, was descended from him as follows : Lion[1], David[2], John[3], David[4],
Abraham[5], Abraham[6], David[7], Julia[8]. (See "Lion Gardiner
and his Descendants," by Curtiss C. Gardiner, St. Louis, Mo.)
Mrs. Tyler's mother was Juliana McLachlan, daughter of
Michael McLachlan, a rich merchant of New York, whose
father was killed at the battle of Culloden.

# LETTERS AND TIMES OF THE TYLERS.
## General Index to Vol. II.

## I. SUBJECT INDEX.

## II. INDEX OF PERSONS.